International Research on Poverty Reduction

Series Editors
Xiaolin Wang, Fudan University, Shanghai, China
Qianqian Liu, Finance Center for South-South Cooperation, Hong Kong, China

AF779974

This book series covers poverty reduction practices and experience, knowledge mobilization, poverty reduction strategy analysis, and comparative research of different poverty reduction models. By analyzing China's poverty reduction approaches and experiences, and comparing them with those of other countries, this book series provides policy makers, researchers and practitioners in poverty reduction with theoretical and technical support, as well asproviding a new channel for sharing experiences as well as facilitating collaboration and communication in poverty reduction development fields between China and the rest of the world. Poverty remains a crucial development issue for the world, and China has become an important player in the global endeavor in poverty reduction and development. China has made a substantial contribution to the achievement of the Millennium Development Goals (MDGs) by reducing half of its poverty population.

More information about this series at https://link.springer.com/bookseries/11685

Xiaolin Wang

Multidimensional Poverty Measurement

Theory and Methodology

SSAP

Springer

Xiaolin Wang
Institute for Six-sector Economy
Fudan University
Shanghai, China

ISSN 2195-9781 ISSN 2195-979X (electronic)
International Research on Poverty Reduction
ISBN 978-981-19-1191-0 ISBN 978-981-19-1189-7 (eBook)
https://doi.org/10.1007/978-981-19-1189-7

Jointly published with Social Sciences Academic Press
The print edition is not for sale in China (Mainland). Customers from China (Mainland) please order the print book from: Social Sciences Academic Press.

© Social Sciences Academic Press 2022
This work is subject to copyright. All rights are reserved by the Publishers, whether the whole or part of the material is concerned, specifically the rights of reprinting, reuse of illustrations, recitation, broadcasting, reproduction on microfilms or in any other physical way, and transmission or information storage and retrieval, electronic adaptation, computer software, or by similar or dissimilar methodology now known or hereafter developed.
The use of general descriptive names, registered names, trademarks, service marks, etc. in this publication does not imply, even in the absence of a specific statement, that such names are exempt from the relevant protective laws and regulations and therefore free for general use.
The publishers, the authors, and the editors are safe to assume that the advice and information in this book are believed to be true and accurate at the date of publication. Neither the publishers nor the authors or the editors give a warranty, express or implied, with respect to the material contained herein or for any errors or omissions that may have been made. The publishers remain neutral with regard to jurisdictional claims in published maps and institutional affiliations.

This Springer imprint is published by the registered company Springer Nature Singapore Pte Ltd.
The registered company address is: 152 Beach Road, #21-01/04 Gateway East, Singapore 189721, Singapore

Preface I

The elimination of poverty and the realization of common prosperity are essential requirements of the socialist system. Since the reform and opening up of China, the Chinese government has liberated and developed productivity through a series of institutional arrangements, such as economic reform, development-oriented poverty alleviation, minimum living standards, continuous technological progress and innovation, and human resources development, through which it has achieved world-renowned economic growth and poverty reduction. Moreover, it has made significant contributions to the global cause of poverty reduction.

Development-oriented poverty alleviation for China's rural areas has now entered a new historical stage. Its main task has shifted from affording food and clothing to consolidating the gains of food and clothing, accelerating poverty alleviation, improving the ecological environment, increasing development capability, and narrowing the development gap. A clear task proposed in the *Outline for Development-Oriented Poverty Alleviation for China's Rural Areas (2011–2020)* is to strengthen research on theories and policies of poverty alleviation. Compared to the tremendous achievements in development-oriented poverty alleviation in China, past efforts were insufficient. China needs to intensify its efforts in the summing up of its experience in this aspect; the impact assessment of the principles, measurement, and monitoring of poverty levels; anti-poverty policies and projects; and the research on specific poor groups such as the elderly, children, women, the disabled, and ethnic minorities.

Dr. Wang's book, *The Measurement of Poverty: Theories and Methods*, fills a gap in the research on poverty measurement in China. The book has the following distinctive features:

First, the methods are comprehensive. The main methods of poverty measurement widely used by the international community are covered. The author has compiled a large number of calculation programs and used household data to measure poverty in China by urban and rural areas, multiple dimensions, across years, and multiple groups. The measurement methods include both traditional methods of measuring poverty and inequality by income and consumption and the dynamic analysis of poverty, as well as analyses of multidimensional poverty, subjective well-being, and relative poverty. The pro-poor and inclusive nature of economic growth is also assessed.

Second, the methods are forward looking. The analysis methods of multidimensional poverty and subjective well-being as well as the measurement methods of the pro-poor and inclusive nature of economic growth are forward looking in the current poverty research. The author not only uses these theories and methods to analyze the poverty situation in China but also innovates and expands on them. In particular, the multidimensional poverty analysis incorporates the asset dimension and indicators into the analytical framework, expanding on the MPI released by the United Nations Development Programme in 2010.

Third, the research subjects are diverse. The book analyzes both rural and urban poverty in China. In the past, analysis in China has focused on rural poverty, but this book uses a large amount of household data to analyze urban poverty, thus enabling a comprehensive comparison between the two types. For the first time, various methods are used to analyze urban poverty in China, providing academic research support for a complete understanding of urban and rural poverty. The groups investigated include ethnic minorities, the elderly, and children. A quantitative analysis of subjective well-being and relative poverty was also conducted. These analyses are of great value for an objective understanding of poverty in China.

The book uses a large number of models and extensive data to thoroughly examine poverty in China, and some conclusions can be used as references to the implementation of the *Outline for Development-Oriented Poverty Alleviation for China's Rural Areas (2011–2020)*. The study on the dynamic changes of poverty clearly demonstrates the relative rural poverty that existed in China in 1989–2009, which increased in 1989–2006 and then decreased in 2006–2009. This objectively describes the process of the widening income gap in China and clearly shows the importance and suitability of the many policies adopted by the Chinese government since 2006 to narrow the development gap through strengthening agriculture (benefiting farmers and enriching rural areas), special development-oriented poverty alleviation policies, and the minimum living security system. The measurement of multidimensional poverty clearly indicates that Chinese farmers are poorer in five areas: sanitation, health insurance, consumer durables, productive assets, and modern fuels. A clear-cut direction for policy intervention is suggested to improve the overall quality of life of farmers. Such measurement methods have important policy implications when applied to development-oriented poverty alleviation in a certain area. In addition, the analysis of poverty among ethnic minorities, the elderly, and children can be used as a reference for development-oriented poverty alleviation for special groups in the new stage.

It is with great pleasure that I preface this book owing to its academic value in promoting theoretical and methodological research on poverty in China and the policy implications of its conclusions. I believe that its content will be useful to poverty theorists and policymakers, and I hope that the author will continue to make achievements in the study of poverty theory.

The State Council Leading Group for Poverty Alleviation and Development
Deputy Leader
The State Council Leading Group Office for Poverty Alleviation and Development
Director

Beijing, China
September 2012

Xiaojian Fan

Preface II

I have long wanted to write a book on the theories and methods of poverty measurement. The first reason is that theories and methods of poverty measurement seriously lag behind the practice of poverty alleviation. While teaching at Inner Mongolia Agricultural University in 1997, I was fortunate to participate in a feasibility study of the World Bank loan project for poverty alleviation in western China (Phase III Poverty Reduction Project under the World Bank), to assist World Bank experts in investment estimation and cost-benefit analysis. As this was my first exposure to poverty research, I was eager to acquire reading material on poverty measurement to supplement my knowledge; however, very few general references to poverty and discussion around anti-poverty policies could be found. In 2009, I was transferred to the International Poverty Reduction Center in China (IPRCC) and noted with interest that although India and Bangladesh, two countries with enormous numbers of poor populations, gave birth to two Nobel laureates in anti-poverty (Amartya Sen and Muhammad Yunus, respectively), they have not yet achieved large-scale poverty reduction. While China has made internationally acclaimed poverty reduction achievements, to date there is no accurate poverty measurement method or world-renowned poverty research expert. As measured by the World Bank's poverty line of less than USD1.25 a day consumption (PPP dollars in 2005), the poor population in developing countries decreased from 1.938 billion in 1981 to 1.289 billion in 2008, that is, by 649 million globally. During the same period, the poor population in China decreased from 835 million to 173 million (i.e., 662 million). As a result, with the exception of the section of China's population that was lifted out of poverty, the poor population worldwide did not decrease but increased slightly. Incongruent with China's tremendous poverty reduction achievements is the fact that the country is lagging behind in poverty theory research, especially poverty measurement. This is the first reason I wanted to write such a book.

Poverty reduction in China has entered a phase where it is necessary to target the poor and measure poverty levels. As a country moves from a low- to a middle-income stage, the main driver of poverty reduction is the "trickle-down effect" of economic growth, that is, growth drives poverty reduction. At this stage, since the majority of the population is poor and income distribution is relatively equitable, there is little need for precise targeting and measurement of the poor population. However, when a country enters the upper middle-income stage, it generally experiences a widening income gap; here, the impact of income distribution on poverty reduction is important. Poverty reduction depends not only on the "trickle-down effect" of economic growth but also on the effect of income distribution. When the poor population decreases, poverty reduction can be achieved through the combined effect of economic growth and income distribution, which requires accurate measurement and targeting of the poor population. Clearly, China has been at such a stage since we entered the new century. This is the second reason I wanted to write about the theories and methods of poverty measurement. However, during the period 2001–2005, with the implementation of the national rural tax reform and the collapse of the system which financed rural public services in the collective economy, there was an extreme mismatch between the supply and demand for rural public services and an urgent need to promote the equalization of urban and rural public services. With this development I felt that there was something more important than this book; therefore, in the 3 years I worked at the Research Institute for Fiscal Science, Ministry of Finance, I concentrated on writing *Rural Public Services and Public Finance Policy in Structural Transformation*. In 2006, I worked at UNICEF's Social Development Division as a researcher on children's budgets and spent 6 months writing *China's Budget System and the Financing of Children's Education and Health Services* with Mei Hong. In the second half of 2006, I was transferred to the Chinese Academy of Science and Technology for Development, Ministry of Science and Technology. At the time of China's major medical and health system reform, I focused my efforts on the medical reform plan, the maternal and child healthcare service package and financing system, and the orphan subsidy system. In the years 2001–2008, despite the support of the World Bank, the Asian Development Bank, the United Nations Development Programme, and UNICEF, I was only able to work intermittently on poverty research. Due to time constraints and difficulties in obtaining data from farmers, although the book *The Measurement of Poverty: Theories and Methods* has been on top of my mind, its substantive writing has not been forthcoming.

In the first half of 2009, I was fortunate enough to visit the Oxford Poverty and Human Development Initiative, which was founded by the distinguished poverty researcher and Nobel laureate Amartya Sen, to conduct research on human development and multidimensional poverty measurement with Dr. Sabina Alkire. I had the opportunity to systematically read a large body of theoretical work on human development and poverty measurement at the University of Oxford, which provided the theoretical basis for writing this book. Immediately after my return from the visit, I participated in the "Survey of Thousands of Households in Contiguous Destitute Areas in Aba Prefecture" organized by a friend Dr. Cao Hongmin. The survey covered 1,351 villages in 13 counties in the prefecture and provided first-hand data on poverty measurement. If the theories and methods of poverty measurement are the first element for carrying out the measurement, then the availability of data is the second element. In the second half of 2009, Dr. Wu Zhong, the then director of IPRCC, invited me to join them as a full-time poverty researcher, which undoubtedly afforded the best platform for writing this book. After joining this professional poverty reduction organization with the mindset of dedicating myself to the global cause, I accepted the first research assignment, a study on poverty thresholds in various countries worldwide, as endorsed by Fan Xiaojian, Director of the Office of the State Council for Development-oriented Poverty Relief. While conducting this study, I learned from the literature review that China was not only weak in poverty *measurement* research but also lagged behind in poverty *threshold* research; I devoted myself to researching the latter. During this research, another major problem emerged: we lacked a professional research team. One or two people alone could not support the important task of summarizing and disseminating China's experience in poverty reduction as well as drawing on the experience of other countries. Consequently, we spent almost 3 years training and building a small research team. This team is now all set, and its academic papers have been published in eminent international and domestic academic journals, narrowing the gap between China and the international community in this field. In the process, I moved toward my original goal: writing this book. Data were collected from various sources, models were developed, programs written, and computational analysis performed.

The year 2011 was a major turning point in the history of development-oriented poverty alleviation in China. The Chinese government promulgated the *Outline for Development-oriented Poverty Alleviation for China's Rural Areas (2011–2020)*, of which one goal was to narrow the development gap. During the preparation of the new Outline and the regional development and poverty alleviation plan for contiguous destitute areas, Director Fan Xiaojian and Deputy Director Zheng Wenkai repeatedly instructed that poverty theory research should be strengthened because China's poverty theory research could not keep pace with the requirements of the work. This meant both pressure and motivation for me. In response to the implementation of the new Outline and considering the current poverty research in China, I suggested that two aspects needed development urgently: poverty measurement and the assessment of the impact of poverty alleviation projects. This book initially fills the gap in poverty measurement. With the new round of development-oriented poverty alleviation, more financial and social resources will be invested in poor areas and poor people, and whether it is important for government or the public to understand the impact of poverty alleviation projects on poor areas and poor people will be determined. This is the frontier of international poverty reduction research as well as an area that needs development in a domestic setting.

In the first half of 2012, according to the arrangement of the Leading Group of the State Council for Development-oriented Poverty Relief and IPRCC, I had the honor to participate in a division-level cadre training course at the State Organ Branch of Central Party School. During these 3 months, I had the opportunity to systematically study Party theory and also read, program, and analyze data at ease. Such complex and extensive calculations were time-consuming and labor-intensive. Now that this book is finally in print, it is a relief to have fulfilled this long-cherished dream. Just prior to the book's completion, I was informed that it was officially listed as the *12th Five-Year National Key Book Publishing Planning Project* by the National Press and Publication Administration, which is, without doubt, a considerable encouragement for me.

The book consists of ten chapters. Chapters 1–8 are organized according to the logic of the evolution of the poverty concept, identification of the poverty threshold, and measurement of poverty. Chapters 1 and 2 describe the evolution of poverty concept and the identification of its threshold, while Chapters 3–8 provide an objective and systematic measurement of poverty in China from different perspectives. The measurement methods include poverty and inequality measurements from the aspects of income and consumption, as well as the measurements of dynamic poverty, multidimensional poverty, relative poverty, and subjective well-being poverty. The measurement subjects include both rural and urban dwellers, and the measurement groups cover ethnic minorities, the elderly, and children. Chapters 9 and 10, rather than measuring the poor population, specifically measure the pro-poor and inclusive nature of economic growth. The pro-poor nature highlights the benefits of growth to the poor (i.e., outcomes), whereas inclusiveness highlights equitable access to development opportunities for the poor (i.e., beginnings). In a society where the poor benefit more from growth and have equitable access to development opportunities, economic growth is considered inclusive and pro-poor.

Chapter 1, "The Evolution of Thinking About the Concept of Poverty," examines the evolution of poverty concept from the viewpoints of economics, sociology, development studies, and political science. Mankind's understanding of poverty is a process of continuous evolution along with human development. From an economic perspective, poverty is the deprivation of well-being, that is, an individual or family has insufficient income to meet its basic needs. Thus, income support policies are the primary anti-poverty policies. From a sociological perspective, poverty is regarded as a phenomenon of social exclusion. Individuals are separated from groups, and vulnerable groups in particular, such as the elderly, and the weak, sick, and disabled, do not have adequate citizenship rights to participate in economic and social activities. Thus, social inclusion policies are crucial anti-poverty policies. From a development perspective, poverty is defined by income. The instrumental role of income is underlined, while the real purpose of promoting human development is ignored. Development is the expansion of the real freedoms cherished by mankind. Poverty is caused by the lack of basic viable capabilities of an individual or family. These include equitable access to employment, education, health, social security, safe drinking water, sanitation, and other basic needs for a decent human life, and even subjective perceptions. Thus, the promotion of human capabilities from a multidimensional perspective is at the core of anti-poverty policies. From a political science perspective, there are two typical views: one is Marxist stage theory, which suggests that poverty is the deprivation of the proletariat by the bourgeoisie and that the kernel of poverty eradication is proletarian revolution. The other is Sen's theory of rights, which holds that poverty is caused by a lack of basic rights such as production, trade, and mobility and that the kernel of anti-poverty policies should be the empowerment of citizens.

Chapter 2, "The Poverty Principle and World Poverty," outlines the three mainstream methods for identifying poverty threshold, namely, the income/consumption principle, the Human Development Index (HDI), and the Multidimensional Poverty Index (MPI), and presents global poverty as measured by these three methods.

Poverty criterion is a crucial tool for measuring and identifying the poor people. Income poverty has been the most widely used poverty criterion globally. The poverty line, as defined by the income principle, generally includes monetary expenditure on food and non-food items to meet the basic needs of households. The World Bank defines the world poverty line using the income poverty criterion for the world's least developed countries. Income is a major tool for achieving poverty eradication as well as a significant proxy variable for poverty measurement, but it does not fully reflect true poverty. The Human Development Index is designed to compensate for the inadequacy of the income principle but remains insufficient to capture the deprivation of basic human viable capabilities. For this reason, based on Amartya Sen's capability approach, Alkire and Foster constructed the MPI, offering a full picture of the multidimensional deprivation of the poor. The 2010 *Human Development Report (HDR)* released the multidimensional poverty of 104 countries and regions worldwide for the first time. The three methods of the income/consumption principle, the HDI, and the MPI are significant for strengthening the monitoring of poverty in China and implementing the *Outline for Development-Oriented Poverty Alleviation for China's Rural Areas (2011–2020).*

Chapter 3, "Poverty Measurement: A Case of the Aba Tibetan Autonomous Prefecture," introduces the measurement methods of poverty and inequality as well as poverty identification models. The measurement findings show that the Northwest Animal Husbandry Economic Zone (NWLEZ), mainly inhabited by Tibetans, has the highest poverty incidence and the deepest poverty. Among the four ethnic groups, the poverty incidence in descending order is Tibetan, Qiang, Han, and Hui, demonstrating the significant ethnic characteristics of poverty. Incidence is higher in the pastoral than the agricultural zone, significantly higher among households headed by females than by males, and significantly higher among children than among adults, in particular, the poverty incidence among girls is much higher than among other groups. Among the four ethnic groups, the highest inequality was found for the Han ethnic group while the Qiang was the lowest. The inequality analysis results imply that inter-ethnic inequality contributes little to overall inequality, and that inequality emanates principally from within ethnic groups. Similarly, inequality between pastoral and agricultural zones contributes little to overall inequality, and the latter derives mainly from within these zones. Poverty identification models show that ethnic minorities have a 2.5 percent higher probability of falling into poverty compared to the Han group. For each additional person in the labor force, the probability of falling into poverty decreases by 1.6 percent for farm households; for each additional year of schooling, the probability of falling into poverty decreases by 0.5 percent for farmers. Meanwhile, farmers with agricultural vehicles have a 10.1 percent higher probability of falling into poverty than those without.

Chapter 4, "Dynamic Change Measurement of Poverty in China," investigates the changes in relative and absolute poverty of urban and rural residents during the period 1989–2009, based on household survey data in nine Chinese provinces. The results show that the relative poverty of rural residents increased steadily in 1989–2006 but then declined in 2006–2009. A similar pattern was observed in urban areas, where the incidence of relative poverty increased before 2004 and declined thereafter. The measurement results of absolute poverty exhibit a significant decline in the incidence of absolute poverty in both urban and rural areas, indicating that China has made significant gains in eliminating absolute poverty. Analyses from two demographic characteristics, education and age, reveal that a higher education level leads to a lower incidence of absolute poverty. The analysis of data on adults over the age of 16 in this book shows a U-shaped relationship between age and poverty incidence: the poverty incidence decreased with age but then increased after reaching middle age. The Gini coefficient shows that in 1989–2009, urban and rural income inequality peaked in 2006 at 44.35 and 53.69, respectively, but slightly declined in 2009. The decomposition of Theil's *L* demonstrates that unequal income distribution in rural areas contributes the most to urban-rural income gap, while unequal urban-rural income distribution contributes less. The elasticity of the Gini coefficient on poverty incidence shows that if it increased by 1 percentage point in 2009, the poverty incidence for urban and rural residents increased by 4.24 and 5.01 percentage points, respectively. Thus, in the future, improving income distribution should be a major policy tool for poverty reduction. From the analysis of the growth rate curve, it can be seen that the income growth rate of the poor in 1989–2006 was lower than the average and the growth was not pro-poor, resulting in an increase in the Gini coefficient and a widening of the income gap. In 2006–2009, the growth rate of the poor was higher than the average and the growth was pro-poor, contributing to a decline in the Gini coefficient and a narrowing of the income gap. This shows that supporting rural areas and benefiting farmers via the development-oriented poverty alleviation policy for rural areas and the rural minimum living security system after 2006 have played a positive role.

Chapter 5 is titled "Multidimensional Poverty Measurement of China." Poverty is the phenomenon of the deprivation of human viable capabilities in multiple dimensions. The MPI measures and reflects the incidence of multidimensional poverty and the intensity of deprivation suffered by poor people or households. This chapter expands the dimensions of MPI by incorporating the asset dimension into the multidimensional poverty analysis framework. The data on nine provinces in the *2009 China Health and Nutrition Survey* were measured using the AF method. The findings indicate that among the ten indicators in four dimensions, the poverty incidence (H) was 9.1 percent, deprivation intensity 37.0 percent, and the MPI (M_0) 0.034 for three indicators simultaneously. With an urban contribution of 22.8 percent and a rural contribution of 77.2 percent, it can be seen that multidimensional poverty is dominant in rural areas. The five indicators with the highest contribution to multidimensional poverty in China are, in descending order, sanitation, health insurance, consumer durables, productive assets, and modern fuels. The results provide a clear priority for public anti-poverty policies.

Chapter 6 is titled "Subjective Well-being and Relative Poverty of Urban and Rural Residents in China." The main task of development-oriented poverty alleviation in China has shifted from solving the problem of subsistence to narrowing the development gap, and relative poverty has become a prominent issue for poverty reduction. Subjective well-being is the self-evaluation of life satisfaction and happiness, which demonstrates quality of life. This chapter quantitatively analyzes the subjective well-being and relative poverty of urban and rural residents in China, revealing that although income poverty is prominent in China, the evaluation of subjective well-being evaluation has fared better. The incidence of income poverty is significantly higher for rural than for urban residents. As the urban residents age, the incidence of income poverty decreases, and with it, the chance of poor or very poor subjective well-being evaluation. Conversely, the incidence of income poverty increases for aging rural residents, along with the likelihood of poor or very poor subjective well-being evaluation. Marital status had a significant impact on subjective well-being, with residents with a spouse more likely to have a higher subjective well-being evaluation than single residents. Healthcare coverage and the Internet have positive effects on the subjective well-being evaluation for both urban and rural residents, with a higher education level indicating a greater chance for a positive evaluation of subjective well-being.

Chapter 7 is titled "Subjective Well-being and Poverty of the Elderly in China." From the perspective of income poverty, incidence among the elderly in rural China was 9.7 percent in 2006. However, from a subjective well-being poverty perspective, the incidence was much higher. Overall, 16.2 percent of the elderly in rural areas and 11.5 percent in urban areas rated their life satisfaction as poor or very poor. Income is positively correlated with subjective well-being, that is, a higher income leads to a higher subjective well-being value among the elderly, but the coefficient of the effect of income on subjective well-being was not significant. In terms of the income poverty criterion, the presence or absence of poverty has an effect on subjective well-being. Income is more sensitive to subjective well-being for seniors below the poverty line than for those above, indicating that the poverty line is equivalent to an approximate threshold of the curve between income and subjective well-being, beyond which the probability of increasing income to improve subjective well-being is low. Using data from China, this also validates the hypothesis that income and subjective well-being are positively correlated but not linearly related. Subjective well-being is lower for older women than older men, lower in rural than in urban areas, and lower for older people living alone than for those with a spouse. Health is highly sensitive to subjective well-being poverty. Personal attitudes have a significant impact on the subjective well-being of the elderly and enhancing positive attitudes among the elderly greatly increases their life satisfaction. The elderly will be a special group among the poor in China. Within this group, poverty reduction strategies and social assistance policies need to focus on the elderly, rural elderly, female elderly, and those with a low education level. With regard to public policies, there is a need for not only old-age insurance but also the provision of appropriate care services. Current poverty reduction efforts will reduce income and subjective well-being poverty among the elderly.

Chapter 8 is titled "Analysis of Multidimensional Child Poverty in China." Child poverty manifests itself in many ways, such as a high rate of malnutrition, child mortality, social discrimination, and exclusion due to poverty, and a severe sense of inferiority. Poverty in childhood undermines individual development opportunities and leads to the intergenerational transfer of poverty, creating a "poverty trap" that can turn temporary poverty into a long-term issue. The eradication of child poverty is the key to breaking the chain of intergenerational transfer of poverty as well as a vital component of achieving equity and justice in social development. Based on Amartya Sen's capability approach, this chapter conducts a multidimensional child poverty assessment from the standpoint of the basic child rights of survival, health, protection, development, and participation, as defined by the *Convention on the Rights of the Child (CRC)* and the *Law of the People's Republic of China on the Protection of Minors*. The data used are the 2010 baseline survey data from the five provinces (regions) of China that are demonstration areas for child well-being services. In these provinces, 28 percent of children live in poor households, 2.42 percent do not have enough food, 50 percent do not have access to running water, 19.16 percent are physically or verbally abused by teachers, and 2.49 percent are subjected to violence in society.

Chapter 9, titled "Pro-poor Measurement of China's Economic Growth," examines the extent to which the poor benefit from economic growth influenced by both growth and distribution. This chapter measures the pro-poor nature of China's economic growth in 1989–2009 using three different measurement methods, from which the conclusion was drawn that growth in 2006–2009 was more pro-poor, consistent with the relative poverty measurement in Chapter 4. Government policies to support rural areas and benefit farmers, as well as special poverty alleviation policies introduced after 2006, have played a positive role in promoting the pro-poor nature of economic growth.

Chapter 10 is titled "Inclusive Measurement of China's Economic Growth." This chapter first provides an overview of the basic connotations of inclusive growth, on the basis of which a set of indices was constructed consisting of 4 dimensions, 7 domains, and 13 indicators; then, weights were assigned to the evaluation indicators to form a comprehensive evaluation index system for inclusive growth; and finally, the index system was applied to measure the inclusiveness of China's economic growth from 1990 to 2009 and recommendations made based on the measurement results. The results found that China's economic growth has generally shown a trend toward inclusiveness, with rapid economic growth leading to employment growth and improvements in basic human capabilities and basic social security. However, the overall level of inclusive growth in China is relatively low and slow, and income inequality is becoming increasingly pronounced, constituting a huge obstacle to the achievement of inclusive economic growth in China. Therefore, policies should be designed to pursue inclusive economic growth from the perspective of achieving equality of opportunity.

Stata software was used in Chapters 3–10 to program most of the calculations. Each chapter has been analyzed in a relatively independent context and is self-contained; thus, each is a complete academic paper. The book is organized in such a way that the reader can easily read any of the chapters as needed.

The book is based on a large amount of household survey data and a considerable amount of programming and arithmetic. Despite the author's painstaking efforts, errors and shortcomings are inevitable, and it is hoped that readers will provide critical assessments. The book is targeted at professional poverty reduction researchers and can be used as reference reading for theoretical practitioners, master's and doctoral students, as well as policymakers and poverty reduction practitioners.

My warm thanks to colleagues at the China International Poverty Alleviation Center (CIPAC) who actively supported this body of research and provided the greatest motivation for me to persist in writing this book. Once again, I sincerely thank you for your support and encouragement!

Shanghai, China Xiaolin Wang

Author's Note

By the year 2020, China will have built a moderately prosperous society in all respects, thus achieving its first centenary goal. In 2013, the Central Committee of the Communist Party of China ("the CPC Central Committee") and the State Council of the People's Republic of China ("the State Council") proposed a basic strategy of targeted poverty reduction and alleviation. On November 29, 2015, *the CPC Central Committee and the State Council's Decision on Winning the Battle Against Poverty* (*the Decision*) was issued, launching a 5-year (2016–2020) battle against poverty. *The Decision* targeted poverty reduction and alleviation as a basic strategy. The overall goal was that "By the year 2020, rural poor populations will have no concerns about food and clothing and will be guaranteed compulsory education, basic medical services, and housing. The per capita disposable income of farmers in impoverished areas will grow at a rate higher than the national average, and the indicators in major areas of basic public services will be close to the national average. We must ensure that all rural residents living below the current poverty line have been lifted out of poverty, and poverty is eliminated in all poor counties and regions." Accurate identification and evaluation of poor populations are the basis for winning the battle against poverty. Against the backdrop of this new round of poverty alleviation campaign, the number of researchers engaged in targeted poverty reduction has increased rapidly, and the demand for the book, *The Measurement of Poverty: Theories and Methods*, has grown accordingly among diverse readerships. To meet that demand, I have now revised the book at the request of the Social Sciences Academic Press. The result of a theorist and practitioner in poverty reduction, this book is dedicated to all fighters in the battle against poverty!

This revision has 12 chapters, of which Chaps. 5, 8, and 10 have been newly added. Chapter 5, "On Relationship Between Income Poverty and Multidimensional Poverty in China," has been added. Before 2010, global poverty measurement was based on the income/consumption poverty criterion; since then, however, the emergence of the Multidimensional Poverty Index (MPI) has attracted close attention from countries worldwide, and more than 40 countries have either developed or are developing multidimensional poverty indexes. Academic and policy circles focus on the debate and discussion about the relationship between income poverty and multidimensional poverty, which is the question this chapter aims to answer. The contribution of this chapter is to suggest, from the definition of the Chinese term *pinkun* (literally "poverty"), that *pin* (literally "insufficiency") means that income is insufficient to meet basic needs and *kun* (literally "hardship") means that individuals and families, due to a lack of basic capabilities, are trapped in natural, environmental, and social hardships that are difficult to eliminate without intervention. The income poverty criterion reflects "insufficiency," while the global MPI captures "hardship." Traditional Chinese culture advocates "helping the poor and needy." China's goal of building a moderately prosperous society in all respects is multidimensional, and the goal of poverty reduction in China by the year 2020 intends to ensure that "the basic living needs of rural poor populations are met and that such people have access to compulsory education, basic medical services, and housing." China's future poverty criterion should be a multidimensional principle that measures both "insufficiency" and "hardship." Poverty cannot be measured by income alone, because income is only a means of satisfying basic needs; rather, meeting basic needs such as compulsory education, basic medical services, and housing is the real goal of development-oriented poverty reduction.

The second newly added chapter is "The Multidimensional Poverty of Migrant Women in China: A Case Study of Domestic Services in Beijing" (Chap. 8). China has a migrant population of 250 million. Population mobility has opened up employment opportunities for rural poor populations in cities, specifically in industry and service sectors; however, this has made targeted poverty reduction more complicated. Addressing how to measure the poverty of migrant women, this chapter, in line with the Chinese notion of "poverty," establishes an expanded multidimensional poverty framework that includes both objective well-being and subjective feelings. Following this logic, an analysis of the poverty of migrant women in Beijing's home services industry reveals that, measured from an income perspective, migrant women have been lifted out of poverty, whether using the national rural poverty reduction standard of an annual income of RMB 2,300 per capita (constant prices in 2010) or the minimum living standard of local urban residents (Beijing) as the poverty line. However, using the multidimensional poverty approach to measure the poverty of migrant women suggests that income poverty alleviation masks the true poverty of migrant women. The measurement of objective "insufficiency" and subjective "hardship" via the aspects of income, education, health, standard of living, and social integration suggests that social integration of migrant women in the home services industry is the most deprived, followed by the standard of living, education, health, and income. The subjective well-being indicator most in need of improvement is social relations, followed by urban belonging and job satisfaction. The urban-rural analysis results show that the MPI, reflecting the incidence and degree of multidimensional poverty in migrant women, is significantly higher in rural registered households than in the urban ones. The analysis results by years of schooling also show that the incidence and degree of multidimensional poverty is higher for mobile women with fewer years of schooling.

The third new chapter is "Child Poverty in Rural China: Multidimensional Perspective" (Chap. 10). Eliminating child poverty is the key to blocking the intergenerational transfer of poverty, and child poverty cannot be measured by income standards. Based on the basic human rights of children as stipulated in the *Convention on the Rights of the Child* (CRC) and *the China National Program for Child Development (2011–2020)*, this chapter constructs a multidimensional child poverty index in China, consisting of child survival, health, protection, development, and participation, which is measured using AF analysis. The results indicate that the multidimensional poverty of children with disabilities, from AIDS-affected families, and from ethnic minorities is particularly prominent.

In addition, errors in the first edition have been revised. Appropriate adjustments have been made to the arrangement of the chapters of the book for logical purposes. Despite my strenuous efforts, errors and shortcomings are inevitable. I sincerely hope that readers will bring these to my attention so that they can be corrected. It is hoped that this book will assist both theorists and practitioners in targeted poverty reduction and alleviation. Finally, I would like to express my sincere gratitude to Ms. Zhou Li, Deputy Editor-in-Chief of the Social Sciences Academic Press, and Ms. Yun Wei, the Editor of the Social Sciences Academic Press, for their full support in the revision and publication of this book.

September 2016 Xiaolin Wang
Pudong, Shanghai

Contents

About the Author

Xiaolin Wang is Deputy Dean and Professor of the Institute for Six-Sector Economy, Fudan University, former member of the Expert Advisory Committee of the Leading Group on Poverty Alleviation and Development of the State Council, P. R. China. His main research areas including: innovation and international development, poverty governance and measurement, public service, industry convergence and the digital economy. He has served as Deputy Director-General of the Information Center of the State Council Leading Group Office of Poverty Alleviation and Development, China. He has also served as a consultant to international organizations such as the World Bank, the Asian Development Bank, WFP, UNOSSC, UNESCAP and UNICEF, and the coordinator of the China-OECD/DAC Study Group, Steering Committee member of Multidimensional Poverty Peer Network (MPPN).

Chapter 1
The Evolution of Thinking about the Concept of Poverty

1.1 Introduction

Poverty elimination or reduction is a basic requisite for the development of human society. In traditional Chinese culture, development is defined as where "the old are cared for until death, the adults are gainfully employed, and the children are nurtured. Widowers, widows, orphans, childless seniors, the disabled and diseased are all taken care of." (*The Book of Rites*). In Western development theory, development is for the benefit of all members of society, and the poor need special attention.[1] In essence, the human quest for development is a journey against poverty.

Encyclopedia Britannica defines "poverty" as a state where one lacks a socially acceptable amount of money or material possessions. This concept is essentially twofold: the first is "socially acceptable," indicating that poverty is a concept with temporal and spatial variation; the measure of a socially acceptable amount of money or material possessions changes over time as human society develops. The second is the ability to purchase a certain amount of goods and services, as reflected by a certain amount of money or material possessions. In the Chinese language, *Analytical Dictionary of Chinese Characters* defines "*pin*" (literally "insufficiency") as "having little wealth"; the *Xinhua Dictionary* defines "*kun*" (literally "hardship") as "having little income and living in hardship." "Hardship" is defined as "trapped in a difficult or painful circumstance from which there is no escape," which is a plight. "*pinkun*" (literally "poverty"), then, means that inadequate income or possessions trap a person in a difficult and painful plight from which he/she is unable to escape.

As human understanding of poverty evolves with the development of human society, the issue of development and the relevant policy tools to promote human development and poverty reduction are improving. At present, China's per capita GDP exceeds US$8,000, reaching the average level of middle- and high-income countries; however, the income gap and social contradictions are prominent. A

[1] Kanbur and Squire (1999).

© Social Sciences Academic Press 2022

X. Wang, *Multidimensional Poverty Measurement*,
International Research on Poverty Reduction,
https://doi.org/10.1007/978-981-19-1189-7_1

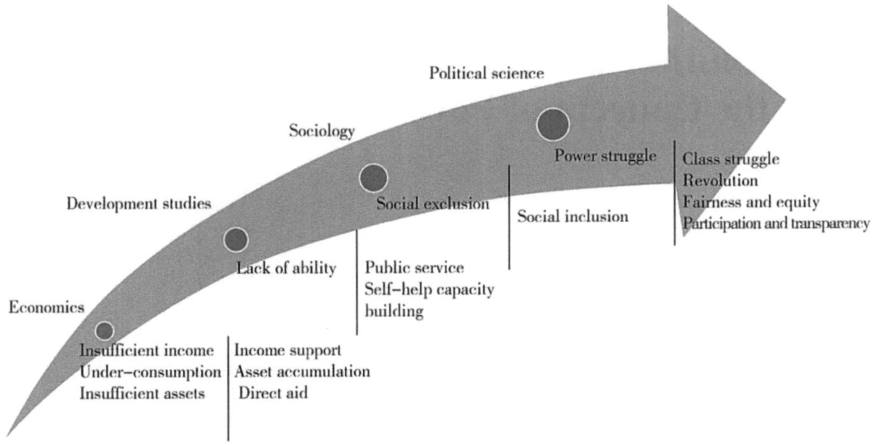

Fig. 1.1 Evolution of the poverty concept

theoretical review of the human understanding of poverty is of strategic significance in examining China's current development issues and building a harmonious society. The following discusses the poverty concept from four disciplinary perspectives: economics, development studies, sociology, and political science. Figure 1.1 summarizes the defining characteristics of poverty in different disciplines and the corresponding anti-poverty measures.

1.2 Basic Needs Theory from an Economic Perspective

1.2.1 Basic Needs

Poverty occurs when people lack the means to meet their basic needs (too few possessions). To determine whether a person is in a state of poverty using this definition, one must determine what constitutes "basic needs." Amartya Sen, in *Development as Freedom*, tells a classic Sanskrit story (*The Upanishads*): In the eighth century BC, Matriy asked her husband if she could achieve immortality through the wealth of the world if it belonged to her alone. Her husband said, "No! Your life will be like the lives of other rich people, but don't expect to achieve immortality through wealth." Matriy said, "Then what do I want with wealth that won't make me immortal?"[2] This story tells us that the growth of personal wealth and economic growth are not the real purpose of human development. The real purpose is the pursuit of improved quality of life and happiness, not the growth of income or wealth alone, which is only a means to improve the quality of life.

---

[2] Sen (1999).

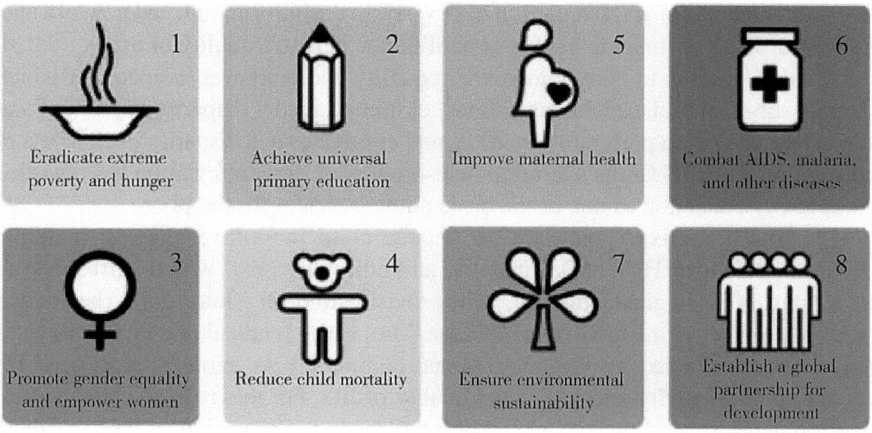

Fig. 1.2 The United Nations Millennium Development Goals (MDGs). *Source* Official website of the United Nations Development Programme (http://www.undp.org)

Britain was an early adopter of a sophisticated social welfare system. William Beveridge, who published *Social Insurance and Allied Services* in 1942, summed up the "five giants" that stood in the way of post-war reconstruction: want, disease, ignorance, squalor, and idleness, providing an understanding of "basic needs." The United Nations Millennium Development Goals (MDGs) set out eight goals for human development (Fig. 1.2). The first seven are the basic goals of human development, which are a list of "basic needs" accepted by all countries worldwide, while the eighth goal, "global partnership for development," is a means of international governance for achieving the first seven goals. We will discuss what "basic needs" are by combining the "five giants" proposed by Beveridge and the first seven basic goals of MDGs.[3]

The first goal is to "eradicate extreme poverty and hunger," which corresponds to Beveridge's first giant, "want." Here, "want" fundamentally means a lack of food; this can be extended to being able to walk down the street with a piece of cloth covering the body. Therefore, food and clothing are the primary basic needs. The goal of poverty alleviation set out in the *Outline for Development-Oriented Poverty Alleviation for China's Rural Areas (2011–2020)* is that, "rural poor populations will have no concerns about food and clothing and will be guaranteed compulsory education, basic medical services, and housing." Thus, food and clothing are the most basic needs.

The second goal is to "achieve universal primary education," which corresponds to Beveridge's third giant, "ignorance." Education is the best response to ignorance. A basic level of literacy is widely recognized as the basis for economic productivity and individual quality of life, as well as the formation of human capital and interruption

[3] Beveridge (2004).

of the intergenerational transmission of poverty. In this information and network age, it is not difficult to imagine how poor an illiterate person's quality of life is.

The third goal is to "promote gender equality and empower women," of which the first sub-goal is also about education: "eliminate gender disparity in primary and secondary education preferably by 2005, and eliminate such disparity in all levels of education by 2015." China's development-oriented poverty alleviation has regarded compulsory education as one of the basic public services for the poor.

The fourth to sixth goals are to "reduce child mortality; improve maternal health; and combat HIV/AIDS, malaria, and other diseases," which correspond to Beveridge's second giant, "disease." The provision of professional public health and medical services is the answer to "disease." Improved medical and health services have been recognized by the international community as another basic need for economic productivity and individual quality of life. For this reason, China's rural development-oriented poverty alleviation has made the provision of basic medical services for the poor one of the "three guarantees."

The seventh goal is to "ensure environmental sustainability," which corresponds to Beveridge's fourth giant, "squalor." It calls for satisfying two needs: shelter and a habitable environment. The United Nations proposed that, "By 2020, we will achieve a significant improvement in the lives of at least 100 million slum dwellers." A global issue is the growing number of urban slums as a result of rapid industrialization and urbanization. It is estimated that there are one billion slum dwellers worldwide, and this number will double by 2030. In developing countries, over 40% of the urban population lives in officially defined slums.[4] China aims to relocate 10 million poor people and upgrade more than six million poor households living in dilapidated housing by 2020.

The sub-goal of the first goal, "eradicate extreme poverty and hunger," contains the key message of promoting employment, namely, "full and productive employment and decent work for all, including women and young people." Employment, therefore, deals with Beveridge's "idleness."

Comparing the MDGs with the "five giants," we can first identify a list of basic needs: food, clothing, housing, health, and education, among which the most difficult to address is the need for housing. According to Beveridge, "This is because housing requires land, which is often associated with power. Moreover, in capitalist societies, land becomes a valuable and therefore expensive commodity."[5]

In document *No. 10 of 2011*, the CPC Central Committee promulgated the *Outline for Development-Oriented Poverty Alleviation for China's Rural Areas (2011–2020)*. The overall goal of *the Outline* was that "By the year 2020, rural poor populations will have no concerns about food and clothing and will be guaranteed compulsory education, basic medical services, and housing." This can be identified as the list of "basic needs" defined by the Chinese government as poverty, which is time-bound and measures the basic needs of China's rural residents from 2011 to 2020. In November 2015, the CPC Central Committee and the State Council's *Decision on Winning the*

[4] Dean (2009).

[5] Beveridge (2004).

Battle Against Poverty further clarified the basic needs of China's rural population. The overall goal of development-oriented poverty alleviation for China's rural areas was that "By the year 2020, rural poor populations will have no worries about food and clothing, and will be guaranteed compulsory education, basic medical services, and housing. The per capita disposable income of farmers in impoverished areas will grow at a rate higher than the national average, and the indicators in major areas of basic public services will be close to the national average. We must ensure that all rural residents living below the current poverty line have been lifted out of poverty, and poverty is eliminated in all poor counties and regions."

1.2.2 Income/Consumption Poverty

The first step of translating the definition of poverty into a policy tool for its reduction is to translate it into a measure of poverty, namely, the poverty line.

Benjamin Seebohm Rowntree, in his 1901 book *Poverty: A Study of Town Life*, estimated the poverty line in York, England, on the basis of the monetary budget needed for a "shopping basket" of "minimum needs for physical subsistence." The minimum food budget for a family of 6 was 15 shillings/week, with certain housing, clothing, fuel, and other sundries, a poverty line of 26 shillings/week was measured for such a family. At that time, an estimated 10% incidence of poverty was found in York.[6] This was the earliest method of quantifying poverty monetarily, according to both food and non-food components. Since then, it has been applied to a greater or lesser extent in most countries and regions worldwide. After 1950, the modern welfare state was established in the UK, by 1979, the "shopping basket" was abolished, and poverty was defined as "a household earning less than 60% of the median income." The median income refers to the after-tax income earned by households in the median income distribution class. The UK poverty line was calculated separately according to family structure. In 2007, the poverty line was £270/week for a couple with two children under the age of 14 and £193/week for a couple with no dependent children. By this measure, the incidence of poverty in the UK was 13.2% in 2007 (International Poverty Reduction Center in China (IPRCC) Research Team, 2009). In 2014, the number of people in absolute poverty in the UK was 10.9 million, about 16% of the total population.

In 1963, the American economist Mollie Orshansky measured the poverty line in the United States, based on the food and non-food components of the minimum basic needs. The food poverty line was the monetary expenditure on each type of food to meet the minimum caloric needs of different household sizes; non-food expenditures were estimated at two-thirds of household consumption expenditures. Orshansky's method was used to determine the national poverty line in 1964, when President Johnson adopted the political slogan "War on Poverty." As of 2015, the US has continued to use this method to adjust and publish its national poverty line.

[6] Kanbur and Squire (2007).

In 2015, the poverty line for a family of four in the US was an annual household income of less than USD24,250, equivalent to USD17/person/day. In 2014, there were 47 million people in absolute poverty in the US, with a poverty incidence of approximately 15%. In *Principles of Economics*, the economist N. Gregory Mankiw criticized, "While data on income distribution and poverty rates help us understand the extent of inequality in our society, interpreting the data is not as simple as it seems. They are based on annual household income, but people are not interested in their income, but in their ability to maintain a good standard of living."[7]

The World Bank defines "poverty" as "the deprivation of well-being."[8] The definition of poverty therefore depends on how well-being deprivation is measured. According to the World Bank's approach, well-being deprivation occurs when people lack the means to meet their basic needs, which is usually measured by income. Thus, the World Bank defines and measures poverty in accordance with the cost of basic needs approach. Basic needs consist of two components: food essentials to satisfy adequate nutrition, mostly calculated as 2,100 cal/person/day, and non-food needs such as clothing and housing (World Bank, 2010). This approach is inherited from that of Langtry's proposed in 1901.

In the 1990s, World Bank economist Martin Ravallion et al. collected consumption data from 86 countries (including developed and developing countries) in the period 1980–1990 and found that the minimum per capita consumption was USD22/month (PPP per USD in 1985), which was close to the then-poverty line of USD23/month in India. Of these, eight low-income countries (Indonesia, Bangladesh, Nepal, Kenya, Tanzania, Morocco, the Philippines, and Pakistan) were more representative of the absolute poverty line at USD31/month.[9] The World Bank accordingly established the first absolute poverty line of USD1/day.

The USD1/day poverty line was revised by Ravallion and Chen et al. in 2008. Of the 75 developing countries (including countries in transition) selected, the average poverty line for the 15 poorest countries was USD37.98/month (USD1.25/day), with a median of USD38.51/month. The median poverty line for these 75 countries was USD60.81/month (PPP per USD in 2005), that is, USD2/day.[10] These are the sources of the current poverty lines of USD1.25/day and USD2/day widely used in the World Bank's World Development Report.

Following the release of the 2011 International Purchasing Power Parity by the International Comparison Program, the World Bank updated the poverty lines of USD1.25/day and USD2/day. The update of the poverty line of USD1.25/day was conducted among the same 15 poorest countries by adjusting national poverty lines to consumer prices in 2011 and using the international PPP in 2011 to convert national poverty lines expressed in national currencies to those expressed in PPP dollars. The final average calculated was USD1.88/day; thus, the poverty line of USD1.25/day was updated to USD1.9/day, while that of USD2/day was updated to USD3.10/day.

---

[7] Mankiw (2009).

[8] World Bank (2010).

[9] Ravallion et al. (1991).

[10] Ravallion et al. (2008).

As the quality requirements of the "shopping basket" that meets "basic needs" vary in different periods in different societies, in general, the standard of income or consumer poverty increases with per capita consumption. Ravallion et al. (1991) conducted a study using sample data from 36 countries, revealing that a 10% increase in per capita consumption led to a 7.1% increase in the official poverty line. Based on income and consumption poverty, anti-poverty policies worldwide have focused on income support and income distribution. Thus, from the perspective of income/consumption poverty, anti-poverty strategies are chiefly about increasing income and improving distribution. The author used the data of 64 countries in 2007 to examine the relationship among the incidence of poverty, GDP per capita, and the Gini coefficient. The results showed that, all else being equal, for every 1% point increase in GDP per capita, the incidence of poverty decreased by 0.3% points, and for every 1% point decrease in the Gini coefficient, the incidence of poverty decreased by 1% point. Therefore, increasing growth and improving distribution are important for poverty reduction.[11]

1.2.3 Asset Poverty

In an attempt to remedy the deficiencies of defining and measuring poverty from a consumption/income perspective, some scholars have developed the concept and measurement of "asset poverty." In 1995, American social policy experts Melvin Oliver and Thomas Shapiro published the book *Black Wealth/White Wealth: A New Perspective on Racial Inequality*, which had a tremendous impact on American society; a tenth anniversary edition was published in 2006. The book reveals an important fact: according to the traditional measures of income poverty, the income gap between black and white Americans has narrowed, but the situation is entirely different when viewed from the perspective of assets. On average, if a white person has USD1 in assets, a black person has only 10 cents. This reveals the enormous wealth gap between whites and blacks in American society. In 1995, American scholars Robert Haveman and Edward N. Wolff defined and measured asset poverty in the US in the period 1983–2001.

According to Haveman and Wolff, poverty depends on the "economic resources" a household can control and the minimum socially acceptable "basic needs." The measurement of income poverty captures the significant aspect of "basic needs" but ignores another significant aspect of "economic resources."[12] In fact, income poverty demonstrates the economic gains of a household in the current year, rather than the accumulation or stock of past wealth. The accumulation or stock of wealth is a major economic resource for a household to cope with the shock of risk to avoid falling into poverty. A household's "safety cushion" against poverty comprises labor and business income, government transfers, and assets. If the household's "safety

[11] IPRCC Research Team (2009).

[12] Haveman and Wolff (2004).

cushion" comprises either a low proportion of assets or none at all, it will be in a vulnerable economic situation, which is because only assets can keep households from falling into poverty when alternative income support resources such as labor and business income and government transfers are in jeopardy.

A household is considered to be in asset poverty when it does not have sufficient assets to meet its "basic needs" in a certain period. This concept does not make allowance for the annual income stream of the household and can therefore be used as a complementary concept for poverty measurement. If income and assets are measured together, poverty can be defined as not having enough assets and income to meet "basic needs." To measure asset poverty, we need to identify three concepts: a certain period, assets, and "basic needs." In the following, we discuss how to define asset poverty using Haveman and Wolff's approach (Haveman & Wolff, 2004).

First, defining asset poverty goes back to the original problem of defining poverty: "basic needs." In 2001, basic needs were defined in the US as food, clothing, housing, and daily needs such as household amenities, personal care, and non-work-related transportation expenditure. On this basis, the poverty line in 2001 was determined to be approximately USD17,960 in annual family income. The poverty line for a family of one couple with two children was USD17,653.

Second, the issue that needs to be determined is the period during which assets are used to meet "basic needs." Haveman and Wolff suggested that, in the absence of other resources, assets should be sufficient to meet a family's basic needs for 3 months (i.e., 25% of the poverty line for 1 year). Based on this, they determined that the asset poverty line in the US in 2001 was approximately USD4,413 (= USD17,653 × 25%), that is, a family of four was in asset poverty when their net worth was less than USD4,414.

Finally, there is a need to define assets (i.e., net worth). As we know that there are fixed and liquid assets in the household, it is more appropriate to use liquid assets to meet 3 months of basic needs, for the reason that liquid assets can be converted to cash more easily. From a moral point of view, a family cannot be expected to sell a durable asset such as a property just because of temporary poverty in a specific year; therefore, Haveman and Wolff suggested that it would be more reasonable to define asset poverty by net liquid assets. Using this approach, they measured asset poverty in the US in the period 1983–2001.

Measuring poverty by assets rather than by income has several advantages. First, assets reflect a household's wealth status after years of income accumulation and consumption smoothing, which more accurately demonstrates a household's chronic poverty. Conversely, income/consumption poverty exhibits a family's poverty status in that particular year. Second, assets can be acquired through inheritance, transfer, and movement, which are more reflective of the social status of a family or individual. Third, measuring asset inequality more accurately displays the real inequality of a family or individual. There are always differences among people in terms of economic wealth. Poverty has many causes: some people are poor because they lack resources and opportunities; others are poor because they are discriminated against by institutions, policies, and customs. Dinitto (2011) argues that public policy is concerned with poverty resulting from inequality.

To examine how the concept of asset poverty is applied to welfare policy, American scholar Michael Sherraden (2007) proposed the concept and policy design of an "individual development account" (IDA), which is used to promote future orientation, long-term planning, savings and investment, individual innovation, personal choice, and the achievement of life goals. These IDAs, which are held in an individual's name and limited to a specific purpose, facilitate asset accumulation by the poor and enhance their development capabilities. Governments can facilitate the accumulation of IDAs through policy instruments such as quota savings, grants, and tax incentives. Sherraden argued that a fairer and more effective policy can create a universal system of asset accumulation for all Americans, but only the poor are given special incentives. In summary, welfare policies are designed in such a way so as to encourage and promote savings and investment by the poor.[13]

China's rural residents' sources of disposable income include net income from household operations and income from property, transfers, and wages. Property income demonstrates a family's ability to turn its assets into income. In 2015, China's rural residents' per capita disposable income was RMB 11,422, of which property income was RMB 252, accounting for only 2.2%.[14] Property income is a major economic resource for tackling poverty, but the proportion of rural residents' property income in China is very low. In the future, asset construction of rural residents should be strengthened.

In 2007, the Office of the State Council for Development-Oriented Poverty Relief launched a pilot project in Yilong County, Sichuan Province, to "improve development-oriented poverty alleviation and build a harmonious socialist society," of which one component was "pilot mutual aid funds for poor villages." In accordance with the principle of "government grants of shares to poor households, allocation of shares to ordinary poor households, and purchase of shares by wealthy households," farmer-oriented mutual aid cooperatives were established to carry out pilot projects on mutual funds for poverty alleviation. The farmers themselves selected the poor households and elected their own management committee to manage the funds; they also adopted a "lump sum loan and separate payments" approach to solve the financial difficulties of the many in production. Mutual aid funds are equivalent to shares in the form of IDAs set up for members. If individuals need funds, they can use them in the form of loans. In addition, at the end of the year, they can receive dividends based on the income earned by the funds.[15] The key to the design of this system is that, for the absolute poor households, financial capital grants are used as individual development funds to determine the form of shares, leading to a one-time increase in individual assets. For relatively poor households, through the government grant of RMB 500 per share, the farmers invest RMB 500 in their own shares, resulting in

[13] Sherraden (2007).

[14] Household Survey Office of the National Bureau of Statistics, Key data from the China Household Survey 2016, China Statistics Press, 2016.

[15] Wu Zhong, Cao Hongmin, Lin Wanlong et al., The Yilong Model of Mutual Aid Funds for Poverty Alleviation and Rural Anti-Poverty in the New Era. China Agriculture Press, 2008.

the accumulation of assets. For wealthy households, voluntary shareholding realizes asset reserves and provides a source of funds for poor household development.

A multidimensional measurement of asset poverty was conducted by this author for "*Research on Impacts of Economic Growth and Pro-agriculture Fiscal Policies in Shanxi Province*," a sub-project under the World Bank's *TCC5* ("*China Economic Reform Implementation Project*") program. For this project, asset poverty was measured on four dimensions: housing, durable goods, productive fixed assets, and arable land. The housing-deprived were those living in caves or mud houses; the durable goods-deprived were those who owned none of the following—a color TV, refrigerator, telephone, or motorcycle; households were deprived of fixed production assets if they did not own an automobile, a tractor trailer of any size, a rubber-tired vehicle, and a draft animal; and, depending on the local conditions, a household with less than two *mu* (approx. 0.1334 hectares) of cultivated land per capita was considered to be land-deprived. Households deprived of at least two of these dimensions met the criteria for asset poverty.[16] In China, the lack of household asset survey data as accurate as that found in the US makes it difficult to calculate household net worth and to measure asset poverty in line with Haveman and Wolff's approach. The asset count approach is essentially an alternative to the measurement of asset poverty. While inconsistent with Haveman and Wolff's definition of asset poverty, it is still a valid measure.

1.3 Social Exclusion Theory of the Sociological Perspective

An economic definition of poverty emphasizes the importance of income but ignores the social context in which individuals or families live and the social disadvantages. To understand poverty more fully, sociologists distinguish between deprivation ("missing out") and social exclusion ("left out") while analyzing the social disadvantages in which individuals or families find themselves. The concept of deprivation is used to identify exactly who is poor and to help set poverty lines, such as measuring income poverty. Accordingly, social exclusion is used to identify those who are excluded from the welfare system and those who are unable to participate in social and economic activities.[17] Social exclusion affords a broader perspective on the analysis of poverty, which is more closely linked to institutional structures.

The concept of deprivation underlines poverty caused by a lack of resources. It helps identify who is poor and how much income is needed to eliminate their deprivation. Thus, defining poverty involves three steps: identify which goods and services are necessary (i.e., the basic needs discussed earlier), identify who lacks these goods and services, and distinguish between those who cannot afford these necessary goods and services and those who can but do not want them. Those who

[16] Shanxi Academy of Social Sciences (2011).

[17] Saunders et al. (2007).

cannot afford the necessary goods and services are those who are eventually identified as poor.

The concept of social exclusion, which emerged earlier in France, stresses the disconnection between the individual and society as a whole (Lenoir, 1974). These individuals are those who are not covered by the traditional social security system, such as single parents, the disabled, the unemployed, and other vulnerable groups. In 1997, British Prime Minister Tony Blair paid great attention to social exclusion and set up a "Social Exclusion Department" under the Prime Minister's Office. The department defined social exclusion as "the phenomenon that occurs when certain people or areas are affected by a combination of problems such as unemployment, lack of skills, low income, housing difficulties, a crime-prone environment, loss of health, and family breakdown." (Saunders, 2003). The UK government investigated social exclusion on many dimensions, including exclusion to resources, the labor market, services, and social relations. By the late 1980s and early 1990s, the concept of social exclusion was gradually adopted by other countries in and outside the EU. According to the EU, social exclusion is the process by which some individuals are marginalized from full social participation either because of poverty, lack of basic skills and lifelong learning opportunities, or discrimination. This process leaves individuals with few opportunities for work, income, education, and training, as they are unable to participate in social and community networks and activities. The United Nations Development Programme (UNDP) defines "social exclusion" as the lack of recognition of basic civil and social rights (such as access to adequate medical services, education, and other non-material benefits) and, where these are present, lack of access to the political and legal institutions necessary to realize these rights.[18]

The dimensions and causes of social exclusion are manifold. Considering Western scholars' definitions of social exclusion, this study summarizes it as the phenomenon whereby individuals or groups are excluded from equal access to public resources and basic public services as well as participation in the labor market and social activities and affairs. Its essence lies in the lack of equal citizenship rights. When considered in this light, it is clear that there remain many excluded groups in China. In some remote rural communities, banks are reducing credit because of high lending costs and management difficulties, resulting in the exclusion of these groups from the credit market. Moreover, informal credit is illegal, resulting in these groups being excluded from the credit market at an institutional level. The lack of formal employment leads to the inability to participate in social security, thus excluding some groups from the system. Children of migrant workers are excluded from the system as "left-behind children" because of the household registration system and the urban-rural disparity with education and medical services.

Most scholars attribute the phenomenon of social exclusion to institutional causes including systems such as (1) democracy and legal systems, (2) the labor market, (3) social welfare, and (4) family and community systems. Therefore, an institutional

[18] Ding (2009).

approach to social exclusion should aim at eliminating social exclusion from a "top-level design" of the political, economic, cultural, and social systems of a country or region.

While the concepts of poverty and deprivation emphasize the phenomenon itself, the concept of social exclusion stresses the nature or causes of the phenomenon. Thus, the development and widespread application of the concept of social exclusion is a theoretical sublimation of human society's understanding of the phenomenon of poverty. Poverty and deprivation are more associated with insufficient economic resources, whereas social exclusion is more associated with political, economic, cultural, and social systems.

1.4 Capability Approach and Multidimensional Poverty Theory from a Development Studies Perspective

According to the traditional definition, "poverty is a deprivation of well-being," and deprivation of well-being is usually defined by the monetary amount needed to meet certain "basic needs." It is undeniable that inadequate income is a strong requisite for living in poverty and that income can be used to purchase "basic needs" to improve well-being or eliminate poverty. In reality, income is merely a tool to achieve a certain level of well-being, while the real goal is to improve the quality of life. Thus, too much focus on income poverty tends to divert public policy from the real purpose of improving people's quality of life, and poverty needs to be examined from a new perspective. Amartya Sen's book *Development as Freedom* (1983) with its profound discussion on the "capability approach to poverty" has, at its core, made a revolutionary leap in the history of human understanding of poverty.

1.4.1 Capability Approach

Sen's capability approach or concept of capability poverty was influenced by Adam Smith. Smith viewed a person's capability to appear in public without shame as a basic need, the inability of which was regarded as poverty. He believed that owning a linen shirt was a necessity to attend meetings. Sen discussed Smith's views and argued that the ability to be unashamedly present in public was an absolute capability, while the need for a linen shirt to achieve this was a relative need dictated by social interaction (Sen, 1983).[19] Sen suggested that there is good reason to think of poverty as a deprivation of basic capabilities, not merely low income. Deprivation of basic capabilities can lead to premature mortality, pronounced malnutrition (especially in

[19] Amartya Sen, "Poor, Relatively Speaking," Oxford Economic Papers, New Series, 35(2), 1983, pp. 153–169.

children), persistent morbidity, widespread illiteracy, and other deficiencies (Sen, 1999).

Sen's contribution is essentially an extension of the logic of defining poverty, namely, "poverty—deprivation of well-being—basic needs—capabilities." According to Sen, it makes more sense, in terms of policy, to recognize poverty from the angle of capability deprivation. First, poverty can be easily identified by capability deprivation, which highlights the essence of deprivation, while income is only a means or instrument to identify poverty itself. Second, income is not the only tool for generating capability, and there are other factors that influence capability deprivation in the case of poverty. Third, the instrumental connection between low income and low capability varies across communities, families, and individuals. The relationship between income and capability is influenced by age (the elderly and children have specific needs), gender and social role (e.g., specific responsibilities of motherhood or customary family obligations), location (e.g., susceptibility to floods or droughts, insecurity or violence in some cities), epidemic-prone environments, and a variety of other factors over which individuals have no or limited control (Sen, 1999). This suggests that the translation from income to capability is influenced by many factors. Children, the elderly, the disabled, and the sick need more income to function in the same way as others. Based on Sen's views, Wang et al. (2010) argue that the elderly, due to their dysfunction, need additional living costs to achieve the same quality of life as others. Such additional costs need to be taken into consideration when measuring poverty in the elderly and formulating income support policies. Accordingly, additional living costs for the elderly are measured (Wang et al., 2010). Similarly, barriers to translating income into capabilities need to be considered when defining child poverty, especially for disabled children and orphans.[20]

The important contribution of analyzing poverty from a capability perspective is shifting attention from the means (income) to the real purpose (quality of life), thus deepening our understanding of the nature and causes of poverty and deprivation. A proper understanding of poverty naturally broadens our understanding of inequality. In the study of inequality, many economists and social policy experts have focused excessively on the narrow area of income inequality, which has prevented the examination of inequality and inequity from other perspectives; this has a far-reaching negative impact on the formulation of economic policies. Currently, many public policies to address inequality highlight the "Gini coefficient," a measure of inequality in income distribution. According to Sen, who criticizes the use of income as a measure of poverty, the Gini coefficient only stresses the "means" and leaves out the "purposes." Thus, Sen suggested that "the distinction between income inequality and economic inequality is vital" (Sen, 1999). Dean (2009) summarized Sen's views and stated that "our need for goods is relative and depends entirely on the social and economic environments we live in. However, our need for capabilities—the need for the freedom to play an appropriate role as a member of a human society—is absolute."

[20] Wang et al. (2010).

Utilitarian theory claims that the aim of sound social policy is the maximization of well-being. In his 1971 book, *A Theory of Justice*, Rawls explicitly criticized the erroneous idea that utilitarian theory focused only on the overall level of well-being and disregarded its distribution form.[21] According to Rawls, "all the basic values (or basic good) of society—freedom and opportunity, the basis of income, wealth, and self-esteem—are to be distributed equally." These are the socioeconomic rights of citizens.[22] Sen builds on Rawls' theories of "equity" and "justice" and further argues that emphasis should be placed on the state of the individual (such as his/her nutritional levels), that is, what a person is being rather than what he/she is doing. Thus, income equality should emphasize the equality of what a person can achieve. Sen's understanding of poverty and inequality is the rationale behind our current promotion of inclusiveness in social policies or inclusive growth, that is, more equal access to social services and more equal participation in growth.

1.4.2 Multidimensional Poverty

Based on the basic needs approach, the measurement of food and non-food monetary needs required to meet the basic needs captures only one aspect of "poverty," that is, "poor," and ignores "hardship." Sen's basic capability approach has since broadened the understanding of poverty; it is not only a shortage of income but also, more importantly, the inability to access basic services such as education, health, and drinking water. Poverty is a phenomenon of multidimensional deprivation suffered by people. Understanding poverty from the capability approach is a qualitative leap forward at a philosophical level, but many scholars have criticized Sen's theory as too abstract. Public policymaking requires operability and poverty measurement, which is difficult to conduct with Sen's poverty theory.

Since Sen's proposed theory of multidimensional poverty, many scholars have explored multidimensional poverty measurement. Atkinson (year) summarized multidimensional poverty measurement into two categories: the social welfare approach and the counting approach. The social welfare approach assesses the situation of an individual or family by taking the different dimensions of poverty as parameters of a social welfare function.[23] The AF approach, proposed by Sabina Alkire and James Foster in 2007, is one of the counting approaches to multidimensional poverty measurement. The approach sets a dual cutoff for poverty measurement: poverty cutoffs are first set for each dimension and then are set again across dimensions. According to the dual cutoff approach, there are two major steps to complete multidimensional poverty identification: identification of the poor population and aggregation of the poor population.[24]

---

[21] Cohen (2008).

[22] Rawls (1988).

[23] For more on the social welfare approach, see Bourguignon and Chakravarty (1998a, b).

[24] Wang and Alkire (2009).

In the Human Development Report 2010, the UNDP published the global Multidimensional Poverty Index (MPI) using the AF approach, including ten indicators on three dimensions: education, health, and standard of living.[25] Since its development, the MPI AF concept and approach has received widespread attention worldwide. Latin American countries such as Brazil, Mexico, and Colombia have turned to the use of MPI to measure poverty and develop national anti-poverty strategies and policies. Wang and Alkire (2009) adopted the AF approach to measure multidimensional poverty in China. Recently, China has seen a growing literature on the use of the AF approach to measure multidimensional poverty.

In 2013, the Oxford Poverty & Human Initiative (OPHI) established the global Multidimensional Poverty Peer Network (MPPN), which aims to facilitate the sharing of multidimensional poverty measurement methods across the world and explore the development of an MPI that can measure the elimination of all forms of poverty as proposed in the Sustainable Development Goals (SDGs).[26]

1.5 Poverty Theory from a Politics-Based Perspective

From a political science perspective, poverty is viewed as a political issue and its implications extend far beyond the perspectives of economics, sociology, and development studies. Typical representatives of this perspective are Marxist class theory, Amartya Sen's rights theory, and China's common prosperity theory.

1.5.1 Class Theory

The emancipation of man and the free, all-round development of man are the fundamental ideas and consistent goals that run through the entire theory of Marxism. Marx first criticized the idea of using religion to rule people at a philosophical level. He stated clearly that man created religion, not the other way around. Religion uses the illusory world of "the other side" to numb the suffering of people in this world. To abolish religion as the illusory happiness of people is to focus on the real happiness of people. The root of man is man himself. The proletariat uses philosophy as its spiritual weapon to liberate the people.[27]

According to Marx, labor produces wondrous goods for the rich but abject poverty for the workers. Labor produces palaces for those who own the means of production,

---

[25] For the algorithm of the multidimensional poverty index, see the resources section of the Oxford Poverty & Human Initiative (OPHI) website (http://www.ophi.org.uk) and the chapters Multidimensional Poverty Measurement in China and Income Poverty and Multidimensional Poverty in China in this book.

[26] For more on the Global Multidimensional Poverty Peer Network (MPPN), see http://www.mppn.org.

[27] Marx (2011a).

but only shacks for the workers who actually do the work. Labor produces beauty, but it deforms the workers. Labor replaces manual labor with machines, but it returns some workers to barbaric labor conditions while turning others into machines. Labor produces wisdom, but it produces stupidity and dementia for the workers.[28]

According to Marx, the history of all societies to date is the history of the class struggle. Freemen and slaves, nobles and commoners, lords and serfs, guild masters and helpers, in short, oppressors and the oppressed are always in opposition to each other, engaged in constant, sometimes covert and sometimes overt, struggle. Every struggle has ended either with the revolutionary transformation of the whole society or the collapse of the struggling classes. Society, as a whole, is increasingly split into two hostile camps, into two classes directly opposed to each other: the bourgeoisie and the proletariat.[29] According to Marx, poverty arises from class exploitation, and the means to eliminate poverty is a proletarian revolution, which revolutionizes the bourgeoisie.

Marx's theory examined the exploitation of the proletariat by the bourgeoisie to the fullest. The proletariat is an impoverished, exploited, and oppressed class. For this reason, the personal freedom and emancipation of the proletariat can only be achieved by taking up arms for revolution.

1.5.2 Rights Theory

Amartya Sen, the Nobel laureate in economics, conducted an in-depth analysis of the relationship between famine and rights. He revealed that countries which had suffered from famine in world history were not because they had insufficient food but because the food could not be distributed to the people in need. Therefore, Sen attributed the cause of famine to inequality of rights. Famine occurs because one part of a country's population has an inexhaustible supply of food while another part of the population suffers from hunger. Both the inequality of rights and of distribution produces famine. Therefore, the eradication of famine will begin when inequality has been eliminated.[30]

According to Sen, for a person to live a decent life, the poor need to be empowered in production, exchange, and mobility. Land is essential to ensure that a family produces enough food to eradicate hunger, but in many countries, the poor cannot own land. Exchange ensures that the working population exchanges the output of land for other goods and services to improve its quality of life. However, some countries and regions do not allow people to freely exchange their goods and services, resulting in household poverty. Mobility ensures that people move in search of development opportunities. In the UNDP studies, both domestic and international migration in

[28] Marx (2011b).

[29] Marx (2011c).

[30] Sen (2001).

countries worldwide have shown that greater development opportunities were found in mobility and that this contributed to poverty eradication.[31]

According to Sen's theory, empowering the poor is the fundamental way to solve the problem of poverty. Wang et al. suggested that China's history of poverty reduction fully upheld the validity of this theory. During 1981–2008, 600 million poor people in China were lifted out of poverty, making China the first country worldwide to achieve the United Nations Millennium Development Goal of halving the number of poor people by 2015. The fundamental experience of China's successful poverty reduction has been the empowerment of the poor. First, land reform has brought about the empowerment of production rights. Through a system of family contracting for rural land, China has given each family an equal share of land and each farmer the right to farm freely on their contracted land and the right to claim the surplus value of the land. Second, the orderly mobility of labor has allowed surplus rural labor to move to the urban and industrial sectors to take up employment in non-agricultural sectors. Last but not the least, farmers who have become rich first are permitted to start their own businesses, both township and private. Such reforms have fully empowered farmers to produce, trade, and move. These rights are the same basic rights that Sen emphasized for poverty eradication.[32]

In the early stage of reform and opening up, China eliminated most of the absolute poverty through reforms centered on land empowerment. Today, various forms of inadequate compensation for and forced expropriation of farmers' land in some places are the fundamental causes of the return of some landless farmers to poverty, despite the fact that the deprivation of land rights to farmers has many apparently sound reasons, such as urbanization and industrialization.

1.5.3 Common Prosperity Theory

The Communist Party of China has always stressed that the elimination of poverty, improvement of people's livelihoods, and realization of a common prosperity are the essential requirements of socialism. On July 31, 1955, in his report on the Question of Agricultural Cooperation, Mao Zedong put forward the concept of "common prosperity" and specific ideas on how to achieve it. "In the gradual realization of socialist industrialization and the gradual realization of the socialist transformation of handicrafts as well as capitalist industry and commerce, i.e., the implementation of cooperation, we should eliminate the rich farmer economic system and the individual economic system in the countryside, so that the entire rural population will become rich together."[33] In October 1955, in a speech entitled "A Debate on Agricultural Cooperation and the Present Class Struggle," Mao stressed, "To consolidate the alliance of workers and farmers, we have to lead the farmers on the socialist

[31] United Nations Development Programme (2009).

[32] Wang et al. (2014).

[33] *Selected Works of Mao Zedong* (Vol. 5), People's Publishing House, 1977.

road, so that they will prosper together. The poor will become rich, all farmers will become rich, and they will become rich to a much greater extent than the present rich farmers."[34]

In 1988, in an article entitled "*A More Liberated Thought and Faster Steps of Reform,*" Deng Xiaoping proposed that, "The fundamental task of socialism is to develop the productive forces, gradually get rid of poverty, make the country rich and strong, and improve people's lives. Socialism without poverty is not characterized by poverty but by wealth, which is the common prosperity of the people."[35] In his 1992 speeches in Wuchang, Shenzhen, Zhuhai, and Shanghai, Deng Xiaoping indicated that the essence of socialism was to liberate and develop the productive forces, eliminate exploitation and polarization, and ultimately achieve common prosperity.[36] Deng not only recognized politically that poverty was not socialism but also economically created the historical miracle of eliminating extreme poverty in China through an array of reform and opening-up measures. Other Chinese Communist Party leaders, Jiang Zemin and Hu Jintao, have all adhered to the political philosophy that common prosperity is the essential requirement of the socialist system and have fully embodied this idea in their leadership of China's fight against poverty.

President Xi Jinping attaches great importance to the elimination of poverty, noting that "common prosperity is a fundamental principle of socialism with Chinese characteristics, and therefore, more fruits of development can benefit all people more equitably, and we should progress steadily towards common prosperity." "Eliminating poverty, improving people's livelihood, and realizing common prosperity are the essential requirements of socialism and crucial missions of our Party." "Now, the living standards of the majority in China have improved greatly, with the emergence of middle-income and high-income groups, but there remain a large number of low-income masses. It is these masses who really need help." "We should do a good job in development-oriented poverty alleviation, support the needy masses, and help solve their problems, so that more fruits of development can benefit the people more equitably. This is a major manifestation of our Party's adherence to the fundamental tenet of serving the people wholeheartedly, as well as a major responsibility of the Party and the government."[37]

According to political science theory, the fundamental way to eradicate poverty is to create more inclusive development opportunities that give all vulnerable groups equal access to employment, public resources, public services, and social participation. To this end, a more democratic, transparent, and accountable approach needs to be introduced in the political decision-making process.

---

[34] *Selected Works of Mao Zedong* (Vol. 5), People's Publishing House, 1977.

[35] *Selected Works of Deng Xiaoping* (Vol. 3), People's Publishing House, 1993.

[36] *Selected Works of Deng Xiaoping* (Vol. 3), People's Publishing House, 1993.

[37] Office of the State Council for Development-Oriented Poverty Relief, *Excerpts of Xi Jinping's Statements on Poverty Alleviation*, 2015.

1.6 Conclusion and Discussion

Economists emphasize the importance of income for meeting people's basic needs, thus achieving poverty reduction. The content of basic needs evolves with the development of human society. Previously, the MDGs set global targets for basic needs to be achieved by 2015.

In September 2015, after the end of the 2015 MDGs, the United Nations adopted the *2030 Agenda for Sustainable Development* at the World Summit on Sustainable Development, which set the SDGs by 2030. These goals aim to end poverty in all its forms worldwide by 2030. The phrase "end poverty in all its forms" goes far beyond the definition of poverty by economists from the perspective of basic needs and is the embodiment of the concept of multidimensional poverty in the UN development agenda, reflecting a deepening of the international community's understanding of poverty.

Sociologists focus on excluded social groups, trying to promote fair opportunities and eliminate social exclusion through institutional changes at the national level. In China's current situation, eliminating social exclusion by promoting social inclusion is necessary to build a harmonious society. First, in the economic sphere, efforts should be made to eliminate systematic exclusion and discrimination in employment; second, in the social sphere, efforts should be made to eliminate exclusion and discrimination in disadvantaged groups' access to social services. In particular, ensuring that disadvantaged groups have equitable access to education and health services, eliminating the deepening polarization in education and health services, and blocking the intergenerational transmission of poverty should be prioritized. Efforts should be made to accelerate the upward mobility of the poor so that they can lead a decent life through human capital formation and individual efforts.

Developmentalists are concerned both with the disempowerment of vulnerable groups and that everyone has equal access to education, health, social security, employment, and the market through fair and equitable opportunities. In essence, they emphasize the fairness of development opportunities. Currently, the Chinese government advocates scientific development as the theme and the transformation of development mode as the main thrust, the core of which is to create fair development opportunities. The social harm of unfair opportunities far exceeds the social harm of unfair outcomes. Therefore, first, the systemic differences between state-owned enterprises and private enterprises in the economic field need to be resolved and a fairer development environment for the private economy created. Second, social injustice in the employment field needs to be eliminated and a fair employment environment be provided for new graduates, the new generation of migrant workers, and other new labor groups. Third, "mass entrepreneurship and innovation" should be promoted in poor areas.

Political scientists are concerned with the deprivation of rights. Marxist theory has been the theoretical tool that has guided the building of a socialist market economy in China. Theoretical connection with reality and seeking truth from facts are at the core of the Party's theory. Facing the emerging social contradictions in the process of socialist modernization, the Party's theory and governance structure could be improved to serve the people wholeheartedly, as they are the foundation for consolidating the ruling party's position. First, in terms of a fair distribution of benefits, the relationship between the government, enterprises, and individuals needs to be correctly managed and livelihood issues resolved to allow people to fully enjoy the fruits of reform, opening up, and economic growth. The contradiction in the distribution structure should be completely eliminated. China has one of the heaviest tax burdens in the world, but its spending on basic welfare is among the lowest. Second, socialist democratic politics to combat corruption effectively and efficiently should be built upon to ensure the progressiveness and integrity of the ruling party. Improving the socialist democratic system will build China into a "politically free, economically prosperous, civilized, and advanced China."[38]

The Chinese notion of poverty goes far beyond the English term "poverty." The Chinese notion of poverty includes both "poor" in terms of inadequate income and "hardship" in terms of individuals or families who are in an unfavorable natural environment and who do not have access to education and health services. Overall, the Chinese notion of "poverty" is multidimensional. Due to this cultural background, when the Leading Group Office of the State Council for Development-Oriented Poverty Relief was established in 1986, it was set up as a coordinating and deliberative body comprising various departments, including agriculture, education, health, and finance. By 2015, the membership of the Leading Group included more than 40 departments, financial institutions, and social organizations. The profound and accurate definition of "poverty" in Chinese demonstrates our cultural self-confidence and soft power in poverty reduction worldwide. China's goal for development-oriented poverty alleviation by 2020 was multidimensional, that is, "By 2020, rural poor populations will have no worries about food and clothing, and will be guaranteed compulsory education, basic medical services, and housing." China's poverty alleviation goal exhibits the concepts of "pro-poor" and "inclusiveness." "Pro-poor" means "realizing a higher growth rate of per capita disposable income for farmers in poor areas than the national average," while "inclusiveness" means "indicators in major areas of basic public services are close to the national average."[39] China's approach to poverty alleviation is "development-oriented," which is an overarching policy system for multidimensional poverty eradication. This policy system incorporates

[38] Mao Zedong, "*On New Democracy*" (excerpt), *Selected Works of Mao Zedong*. CPC Central Party School Press, 2002, p. 167.

[39] *The CPC Central Committee and the State Council's Decision on Winning the Battle Against Poverty*, issued in December 2015, set the overall goal that, "By the year 2020, rural poor populations will have no worries about food and clothing, and will be guaranteed compulsory education, basic medical services, and housing. The per capita disposable income of farmers in impoverished areas will grow at a rate higher than the national average, and the indicators in major areas of basic public services will be close to the national average. We must ensure that all rural residents living below the current poverty line have been lifted out of poverty, and poverty is eliminated in all poor counties and regions."

policies to increase the income of the poor as well as to improve their education, health, and ability to transfer employment, such as improving drinking water, roads, communications, and housing.

References

Beveridge, W. (2004). *Beveridge report: Social insurance and allied services.* China Labor and Social Security Publishing House.

Bourguignon, F., & Chakravarty, S. (1998a). *A family of multidimensional poverty measures.* DELTA Document.

Bourguignon, F., & Chakravarty, S. (1998b). *The measurement of multidimensional poverty.* DELTA Document.

Cohen, G. A. (2008). Equality of what? On welfare, goods, and capabilities. In Sen and Nussbaum (Eds.), *The quality of life* (p. 12). Social Sciences Academic Press.

Dean, (2009). *Ten lectures on social policy studies.* Truth and Wisdom Press and Shanghai People's Publishing House.

Ding, K. (2009). Western social exclusion theory: Four basic issues. *Foreign Theoretical Trends,* No. 10.

Dinitto, D. M. (2011). *Social welfare: Politics and public policy* (7th ed.) Pearson.

Haveman, R., & Wolff, E. N. (2004). The concept and measurement of asset poverty: Levels, trends and composition for the U.S., 1983–2001. *Journal of Economic Inequality, 2*(2).

IPRCC Research Team. (2009). *Study on poverty standards in various countries of the world.* (IPRCC Research Report, No. 1).

Kanbur, R., & Squire, L. (1999). The evolution of thinking about poverty: Exploring the interactions.

Kanbur, R., & Squire, L. (2007). The evolution of thinking about poverty: Exploring the interactions. In G. M. Meier, & J. E. Stiglize (Eds.), *Frontiers of development economics: The future in perspective.* World Bank and Oxford.

Lenoir, R., (1974). *Les exclus: Un francais surd ix.* Seuil.

Mankiw, (2009). *Principles of economics* (5th ed.). Peking University Press.

Marx, K. (2011a). *Critique of Hegel's philosophy of law.* CPC Central Party School Press.

Marx, K. (2011c). *The communist manifesto.* CPC Central Party School Press.

Marx, K. (2011b). *Economic and philosophic manuscripts of 1844* (abridged). Selected Writings of Marx and Lenin, CPC Central Party School Press.

Ravallion, M., Datt, G., & Van de Walle, D. (1991). Quantifying absolute poverty in the developing world. *Review of Income and Wealth, 37*(4).

Ravallion, M., Chen, S., & Sangraula, P. (2008). *Dollar a day revisited.* (Policy Research Working Paper, No. 4620). World Bank.

Rawls, (1988). *A theory of justice.* China Social Science Press.

Saunders, P., Naidoo, Y., & Griffiths, M. (2007). *Towards new indicators of disadvantage: Deprivation and social exclusion in Australia.* Social Policy Research Centre.

Saunders, P. (2003). *Can social exclusion provide a new framework for measuring poverty?* (SPRC Discussion Paper, No.127).

Sen, A. (1983). *Development as freedom.* Oxford University Press.

Sen, A. (1999). Poor, relatively speaking. *Oxford Economic Papers, New Series, 35*(2).

Sen, A. (2001). *Poverty and famines.* The Commercial Press.

Shanxi Academy of Social Sciences. (2011). *The status and causes of poverty population and income disparity in Shanxi.* World Bank TCC5 Project Report.

Sherraden, M. (2007). *Assets and the poor: A new American welfare policy.* The Commercial Press.

United Nations Development Programme. (2009). *Human development report 2009: Human mobility and development across barriers.* China Financial and Economic Publishing House.

Wang, X., Wang, L., & Wang, Y. (2014). *The quality of growth and poverty reduction in China*. Springer.
Wang, X., & Alkire, S. (2009). Multidimensional poverty measurement in China: Estimates and policy implications. *China Rural Economy*, No. 12.
Wang, X., & Shang, et al. (2010). *Extra costs for urban older people with disabilities in northern China, social policy & society*. Cambridge University Press.
World Bank. (2010). *World development report 2000/2001: Attacking poverty*. World Bank.

Chapter 2
Poverty Criteria and World Poverty

Human understanding of poverty has evolved with the development of society, and its definition has been expanded and enriched. Initially, the understanding of poverty was largely limited to avoiding hunger and malnutrition, the kernel of poverty. In 1901, British scholar Benjamin Seebohm Rowntree was the first to use the term "income" to define poverty in the UK, while in the US, in 1963, American economist Mollie Orshansky followed. In 1981, the World Bank started to officially measure consumption and income poverty in developing countries. In 2010, for the first time, the Human Development Report of the United Nations Development Programme released the Multidimensional Poverty Index (MPI) based on measurements of Sabina Alkire et al., expanding the measurement of poverty in human development theory. So far, the most widely used global measures of poverty can be divided into two categories: the income/consumption principle and the MPI. This chapter systematically introduces these two standards, examines global poverty as measured by them, and concludes with a discussion of the poverty criterion in context of the targeted poverty reduction and alleviation strategy being implemented in China.

2.1 Income/Consumption Principle

As outlined above, the UK was the first country to formulate the income poverty criterion, followed by the US. By the mid-1990s, more than 30 countries worldwide had established an income poverty criterion providing a data basis on which the World Bank could measure global poverty. This section therefore first reviews the poverty criterion and its changes in the UK and the US as well as changes in the poverty line in China; second, it analyzes the World Bank's poverty criterion and its adjustments; and finally, it presents the observations of world poverty according to the World Bank's USD1.9/day principle.

© Social Sciences Academic Press 2022

X. Wang, *Multidimensional Poverty Measurement*,
International Research on Poverty Reduction,
https://doi.org/10.1007/978-981-19-1189-7_2

Table 2.1 Relative poverty lines for different household types in the UK (2013/2014)

Household type	Poverty line: household income, Pounds/week
Single adult	134
Husband and wife, no child	232
Husband and wife, 1 child	278
Single parent, 1 child	181
Husband and wife, 3 children	371

Source Living Standards, Poverty and Inequality in the UK: 2015. The Institute for Fiscal Studies. Income data are the net of housing costs

2.1.1 Income Poverty Criterion in the UK and the US

2.1.1.1 Poverty Criterion and Its Evolution in the UK

In his 1901 book, *Poverty, A Study of Town Life*, the British scholar Benjamin Seebohm Rowntree estimated the poverty line in the city of York, UK, according to the monetary budget required for a "shopping basket" to "obtain the minimum necessary for the maintenance of physical strength." The minimum food budget for a family of 6 was 15 shillings/week, with housing, clothing, fuel, and some other sundries, he estimated a poverty line of 26 shillings/week for a family of 6. York had a poverty incidence of approximately 10% at that time.[1] This was the earliest monetary quantification of poverty from both food and non-food aspects. Prior to 1950, the "shopping basket" of basic food, clothing, and housing needs was the measure of poverty in the UK.

(1) Relative poverty criterion. After 1950, with the establishment of the modern welfare state, the "shopping basket" method of measuring poverty was abolished. Since 1979, poverty has been defined in the UK as "a household with an income of less than 60% of the median income." Median income is the after-tax earnings received by middle-income households. The UK government calculated the monetary amount of income poverty for different household types based on a poverty line of below 60% of the median income for the year (Table 2.1).

Table 2.2 shows the population of the relative poor and poverty incidence rate in the UK in the period 1979–2013/14. In 1979, 13.7% of the population were below the relative poverty line, which had increased to 23% by 2007/2008. Relative poverty in the UK has slightly reduced following the 2008 financial crisis, with the population below the relative poverty line falling to 21% by 2013/14.

(2) Absolute poverty criterion. The UK government follows a relative approach to establish the absolute poverty criterion, which is currently set at 60% of the median income in 2010/11 for different household types (Table 2.3).

(3) Inequality. Figure 2.1 shows changes in the inequality of income distribution in the UK between 1961 and 2013. One indicator is the Gini coefficient of income

[1] Kanbur and Squire (1999).

Table 2.2 Poverty in the UK (1979–2013/14)

Year	Population (in millions)			Share of total population (%)		
	Below 60% of the median income	Below 50% of the median income	Below 40% of the median income	Below 60% of the median income	Below 50% of the median income	Below 40% of the median income
1979	7.6	3.3	1.3	13.7	5.9	2.4
1989	12.9	8.3	3.9	22.9	14.8	7.0
1998/99	14.0	9.4	4.8	24.4	16.3	8.3
2000/01	13.4	8.8	4.9	23.1	15.3	8.5
2002/03	13.1	8.5	4.9	22.4	14.6	8.3
2004/05	12.1	7.9	4.9	20.5	13.4	8.3
2006/07	13.2	9.0	5.6	22.2	15.2	9.4
2007/08	13.6			23.0		
2008/09	13.5			22.0		
2009/10	13.6			22.0		
2010/11	13.0			21.0		
2011/12	13.1			21.0		
2012/13	13.2			21.0		
2013/14	13.2			21.0		

Sources Data for 1979–2006/2007 (http://www.poverty.org.uk), data for 2008/09–2013/14. *Living Standards, Poverty and Inequality in the UK: 2015.* The Institute for Fiscal Studies. Median income is the net of housing costs. Data for 1998/99 onward include those of Northern Ireland

Table 2.3 Absolute poverty lines for different household types in the UK (2013/2014)

Household type	Poverty line: household income, pounds/week
Single adult	136
Husband and wife, no child	235
Husband and wife, 1 child	282
Single parent, 1 child	183
Husband and wife, 3 children	376

and the other is the 90:10 ratio calculated from income decile data. It is clear that the Gini coefficient and 90:10 ratio were on the rise and the inequality in income distribution increased in the period 1961–1990. Since 1991, the inequality in income distribution has gradually improved.

(4) Social exclusion. Social exclusion has been monitored in the UK since 1998. This monitoring differs from poverty monitoring as follows: first, social exclusion is not limited to the income or consumption of material goods but includes basic services such as bank accounts of people living alone at home and fears of crime; second, it monitors "who" is being socially excluded and "who" is socially excluding

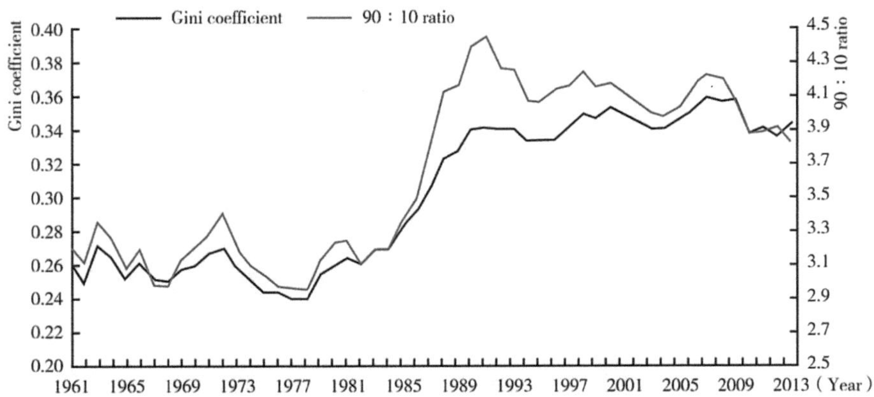

Fig. 2.1 Relative poverty in the UK (1961–2013). *Source Living Standards, Poverty and Inequality in the UK: 2015*. The Institute for Fiscal Studies

others, as well as whether this is caused by the public, private, or voluntary sectors, or employers or service providers. The UK adopts a relative measure to monitor social exclusion. For children aged 6–18, it is measured by whether they are persistently excluded from schooling and vocational training. The results are compared with those in previous years to examine whether school exclusion has worsened or alleviated.

With increasing levels of economic and social development, the UK poverty criterion has undergone the following changes.

First, since 1979, there has been a shift toward relative poverty. With the establishment of the modern welfare state in the UK, absolute poverty was virtually eliminated. In other words, there are very few people in society who are starving. However, to narrow the income gap, the UK government began to identify poor populations through the relative poverty criterion. This is because, in order of income, there will always be a population earning below 60% of the median income. Anti-poverty policies are designed to focus public resources on this low-income group.

Second, social exclusion has been a concern in anti-poverty strategies. When the British Labor Party came to power in 1997, the Blair government focused on the phenomenon of "social exclusion." Social exclusion is present "when an individual or area is temporarily unemployed, with poor labor skills, low income, poor housing, high crime rate, poor health, and high divorce rate." The Social Exclusion Department, established by the Prime Minister's Office, has as its core mission the elimination of social exclusion and, therefore, the promotion of social inclusion at national system and policy levels.

2.1.1.2 Poverty Criterion in the US

There are two versions of the official poverty line in the US: poverty thresholds and poverty guidelines. Data on the former are published by the US Census Bureau and are used to count the poor population. In other words, the official number of poor people in the US is calculated by the Census Bureau using the poverty line. It estimates the poor population each year by type of residence; race; and other social, economic, and demographic characteristics. The poverty guidelines are published by the US Department of Health and Human Services (HHS) and are used primarily for project management. They determine whether a person is eligible for assistance from federal programs.

(1) Poverty thresholds. In 1964, the Johnson Administration declared a "War on Poverty" and established the absolute poverty criterion. The US Council of Economic Advisors (CEA) sets the poverty line at USD3,000/year (in 1962 dollars) for all household types and USD1,500/year for individuals without relatives.

In 1965, Orshansky from the US Social Security Administration expanded the US poverty line to two levels: "economy level" and "low-cost level." First, households were divided into two categories: farm and non-farm. Second, the demographic structure and size of the household were considered, followed by the age of the household head. After considering the above three basic factors, an acceptable minimum standard of living was determined. The consumer goods for basic needs included both food and non-food items, that is, $z^{BN} = z^F + z^{NF}$. Food consumption was set at one-third of the household consumption, making the poverty line equal to three times the food poverty line, that is, $z^{BN} = 3 \times z^F$ (Table 2.4).

The current US poverty line is based on Consumer Expenditure Survey (CES) data, which measures the level of income needed to meet basic needs (food, housing,

Table 2.4 Non-farm poverty line in the US at the economy level and low-cost level (1963) (Unit: dollars/year)

Household size (number of persons)	Poverty line at the economy level	Poverty line at the low-cost level	Poverty line at the low-cost level/poverty line at the economic level
1	1,539		
<65 years	1,580	1,885	1.19
65 ≥ years	1,470	1,745	1.19
2	1,988		
Head of household: <65 years	2,050	2,715	1.32
Head of household: 65 ≥ years	1,850	2,460	1.33
3	2,440	3,160	1.30
4	3,130	4,005	1.28
5	3,685	4,675	1.27
6	4,135	5,250	1.27
7 and above	5,090	6,395	1.26

Source US Census Bureau

clothing, and durable goods) and is adjusted for housing costs in different geographic locations. Beginning in 2011, the US Census Bureau, in accordance with Statistical Policy Directive 14 of the Office of Management and Budget (OMB), established and annually published poverty lines based on various types of monetary income, different household sizes, and the situation of children under the age of 18 in households. The monetary income for measuring the poverty line includes income, unemployment compensation, worker's compensation, social insurance, supplementary security income, public assistance, veteran's allowance, pensions for the family of the deceased, pensions or retirement income, interest, dividends, rent, royalties, income from real estate, income from trusts, educational assistance, alimony, child support, and assistance from outside the family. However, monetary income does not include non-cash allowances for food and housing and is pre-tax income with the exception of capital gains and losses. Furthermore, if a non-relative resides with a family, they are regarded as family. In 2014, the US conducted the Supplemental Poverty Measure (SPM), which added more indicators of economic well-being to provide a deeper understanding of economic conditions and policy implications. The SPM includes additional indicators that capture tax transfers and work expenditures. The US does not specifically set different poverty lines for various regions. Differences between regions are adjusted for the Consumer Price Index for All Urban Consumers (CPI-U). Table 2.5 shows the national poverty line as published by the US Census Bureau in 2014. The 2014 poverty line for a family of four with two children under age 18 was USD24,008.

Poverty line statistics by the Census Bureau show that the 2008 financial crisis had a large impact on the poor population in the US. The poverty incidence increased by 2.3 percentage points from 12.5% in 2007 before the crisis to 14.8% after the crisis. In 2014, the poor population in the US was 46.7 million (Fig. 2.2).

In 2014, the poverty incidence in the US was 13.5% for those aged 18–64, 10% for those aged 65 and older, and 21.1% for children under 18 years. Children under the age of 18 made up 23.3% of the total population, whereas child poverty accounted for 33.3% of the total poor population (Fig. 2.3). Similarly, women are more vulnerable to poverty. In 2014, the poverty incidence among women was 16.1%, 2.7 percentage points higher than that among men.

(2) The poverty guidelines. Because of the complexity of the poverty lines developed by the US Census Bureau, many projects prefer to identify the poor according to the poverty guidelines developed by the HHS as they are simpler and more appropriate for practice. Table 2.6 shows the 2015 poverty guidelines identified by the HHS, which was USD24,250 for a family of four.

(3) Inequality. The median household income in the US was USD53,657 in 2014, 6.5 percentage points lower than that in 2007 before the financial crisis (Fig. 2.4). Blacks had the lowest household income. The wealthiest 20% of Americans had 51.2% of monetary income in 2014. Among them, the most prosperous 5% had 21.9% of monetary income, while the poorest 20% had only 3.1% of monetary income that year. The Gini coefficient of income inequality was up to 0.480. Therefore, tackling inequality remains one of the challenges facing the US.

Table 2.5 Poverty line in the US in 2014 (Unit: dollars/year)

Household size (number of persons)	Children <18 years								
	0	1	2	3	4	5	6	7	≥ 8
1									
<65 years	12,316								
65 $\geq$ years	11,354								
2									
Head of household: < 5 years	15,853	16,317							
Head of household: 65 $\geq$ years	14,309	16,256							
3	18,518	19,055	19,073						
4	24,418	24,817	24,008	24,091					
5	29,447	29,875	28,960	28,252	27,820				
6	33,869	34,004	33,303	32,631	31,633	31,041			
7	38,971	39,214	38,375	37,791	36,701	35,431	34,036		
8	43,586	43,970	43,179	42,485	41,501	40,252	38,953	38,622	
$\geq$9	52,430	52,685	51,984	51,396	50,430	49,101	47,899	47,601	45,768

Source US Census Bureau. *Income and Poverty in the US: 2014*

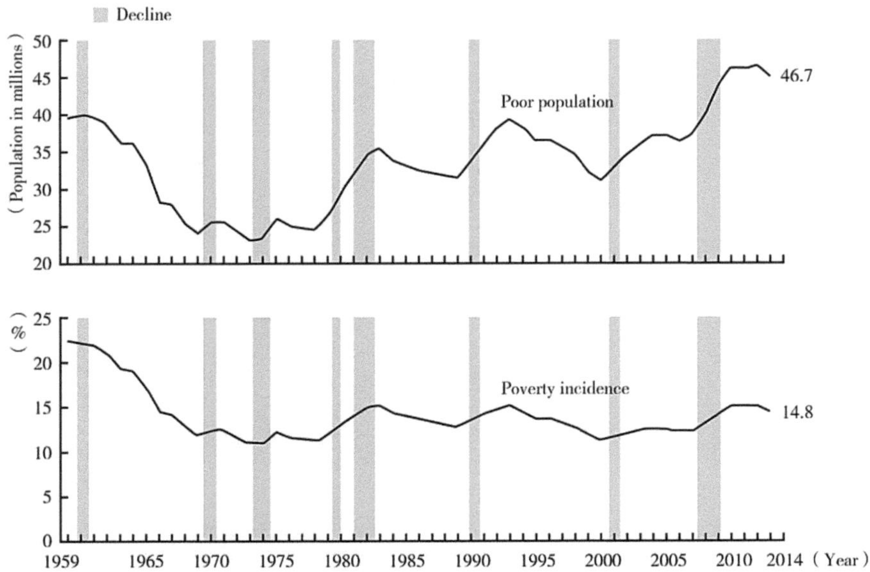

Fig. 2.2 Poor population and poverty incidence in the US (1959–2014). *Source* US Census Bureau. *Income and Poverty in the US: 2014*

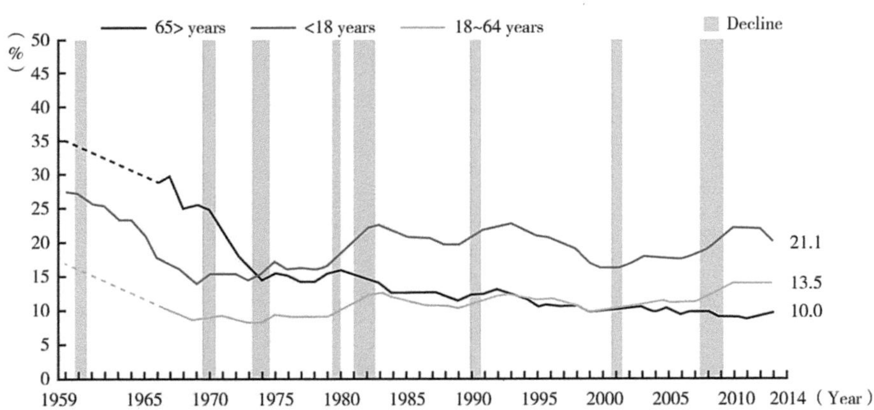

Fig. 2.3 Poor population in the US (by age) (1959–2014). *Source* US Census Bureau. *Income and Poverty in the US: 2014*

Poverty lines in the US take into account differences in household size and structure and vary according to these differences; all people in a household are thus identified as poor as long as their household income is below the poverty line. Relative to the US, China's income poverty line does not factor in household size and structure, which, to some extent, is not conducive to the implementation of the national strategy of targeted poverty reduction and alleviation in the battle against poverty. In China's

Table 2.6 Poverty guidelines for 48 contiguous states and the Columbia region in the US (2015)

Household size (number of persons)	Poverty guidelines (dollars)
1	11,770
2	15,930
3	20,090
4	24,250
5	28,410
6	32,570
7	36,730
8	40,890

Note For households with more than eight persons, the poverty line increases by USD4,160 for each additional person
Source Department of Health and Human Services, Annual Update of the HHS Poverty Guidelines. *Federal Register*, January 22, 2015

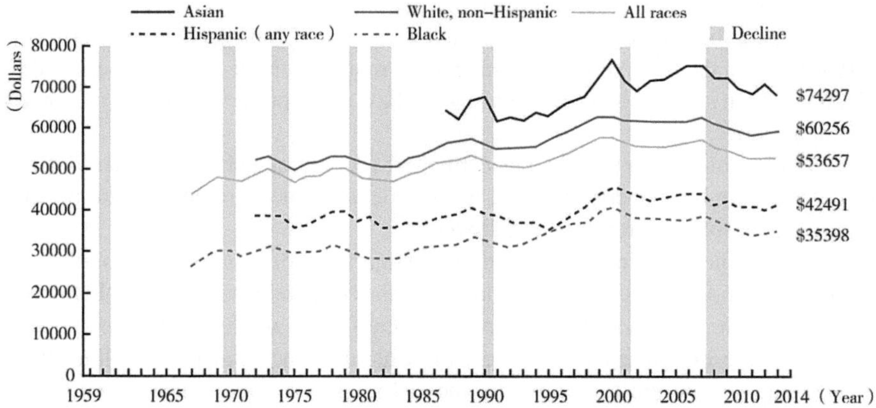

Fig. 2.4 Real median household income in the US (1959–2014). *Source* US Census Bureau. *Income and Poverty in the US: 2014*

practice, when identifying the poor, many families have been artificially "split up" to separate the elderly from their families and identify them as the poor. If varied poverty lines are set for different household sizes and structures, the identification of the poor will be more accurate and the incentive for people to artificially "split up" households will be eliminated.

2.1.2 Poverty Criteria and Their Evolution in China

Regarding the development of China's official poverty line, this book draws on articles by Wang et al. (2006) from the Poverty Monitoring Division of the Rural Department of the National Bureau of Statistics (NBS) and Wang's articles in the *Poverty Monitoring Report of Rural China 2015.*

2.1.2.1 Absolute Rural Poverty

The NBS has published two government poverty criteria: the rural poverty criterion and the rural low-income criterion. From the perspective of academic research, the rural poverty criterion is an extreme poverty criterion, while the low-income criterion is a higher poverty criterion than the former.

China's rural poverty criteria were set in 1985, 1990, 1994, 1997, and 2010 by the General Rural Socio-Economic Survey Team of the NBS, based on household data from the National Rural Household Survey; for other years, the poverty criterion was updated using the rural consumer price index. In 1986, China set a poverty criterion of RMB206 on the basis of a minimum energy requirement of 2,100 cal/person/day, which was then measured in accordance with the consumption structure of the lowest income group.

In 1997, China adopted the basic method recommended by the World Bank for determining the poverty line and made a detailed measurement of the poverty criterion. The specific steps are as follows:

(1) Determine the minimum nutritional requirement of 2,100 cal/person/day. (2) Calculate the food poverty line using data from the National Rural Household Survey. (3) Calculate the non-food poverty line and identify low and high non-food poverty lines using the measurement methods. (4) Calculate the total poverty line. Food poverty line + low non-food poverty line = low poverty line. Farmers who reach the low poverty line can afford only the basic food consumption and the most essential non-food consumption that some farmers are willing to sacrifice for basic food consumption. In the low poverty line measured in 1997, the share of food consumption expenditure of farm households was 85%, indicating that the low poverty line is indeed an extreme poverty line. Food poverty line + high non-food poverty line = high poverty line. (5) Determine the rural poverty criterion.

In the twentieth century, poverty was ubiquitous in rural China, while the national resources for poverty alleviation were limited. Thus, the low poverty line was determined as the principle to measure rural poverty according to the prevailing situation.

2.1.2.2 Rural Low-Income Criterion

To better monitor the movement of the poor who have only achieved basic subsistence and to make international comparisons of poverty, the NBS began to measure the new poverty criterion in 1998, which has been published as the low-income criterion since 2000. The specific method used was as follows: the 1997 food poverty line (adjusted by the price index) and the assumption that food consumption accounted for 60% of the total living consumption under poverty were used to calculate the rural low-income criterion of RMB880 in 1998. China's rural low-income criterion at that time was close to the World Bank's cutoff of USD1/day (Table 2.7).

The NBS has used the dual indicators of per capita income and per capita consumption to measure whether a rural household is poor since 1998, whereas the World Bank uses only per capita consumption to calculate the poor population. The dual income and consumption measure means that a household is considered poor if either its per capita disposable income or per capita consumption expenditure is below the poverty criterion, while the other is below a higher criterion, such as the 1.5-fold poverty criterion. Thus, poor households include three categories of people: the first consists of those whose per capita income and per capita consumption are below the poverty threshold who are undoubtedly poor and should be supported. The second category is those with income below the poverty criterion and consumption above the poverty criterion but below a higher threshold. This is a category of people with relatively low consumption and a very low income. Even if they are not poor from a consumption perspective, their very low incomes may cause consumption to be drastically reduced, placing them in the ranks of the poor, and they should therefore be supported by the government. The third category is those with consumption below the poverty criterion and income above the poverty criterion but below a higher standard. This is a category of people with a low income and very low consumption. Although they occasionally have income slightly above the poverty criterion over a year, their consumption is low and there is no savings to raise the consumption above the poverty criterion. Thus, sustained support should be provided by the government.

For households whose income is below the poverty criterion and whose consumption is above a higher principle, this might be due simply to temporary fluctuations in income; thus, they have the ability to maintain higher consumption. Such households

Table 2.7 Comparison of poverty criteria in China in 2000–2005 (Unit: yuan)

Item	2000	2001	2002	2003	2004	2005
Rural poverty criterion	625	630	627	637	668	683
Rural low-income criterion	865	872	869	882	924	944
World Bank USD1/day[a]	876	882	873	884	918	935

[a] Updated using China's consumer price index after conversion based on the 1993 purchasing power parity (PPP)

Source Wang et al. (2006). A comparison of China's poverty criterion with international poverty criterion. *China's National Conditions and National Power*, 9

should not be targeted by the government's poverty alleviation program. Households with consumption below the poverty criterion and income above a higher criterion have a strong saving capacity and can increase their consumption above the poverty criterion. Consequently, they are not the targets of the government's poverty alleviation program.

In the Third Plenary Session of the Seventeenth Central Committee of the Communist Party of China (CPC), the *Decision on Certain Major Issues Concerning the Advancement of Rural Reform and Development* further clarified the policy measures and priorities for the new stage of development-oriented poverty alleviation. It clearly stated that new poverty alleviation principles would be applied, poverty alleviation policies would be comprehensively implemented for low-income rural populations, and the primary task of the new stage of development-oriented poverty alleviation would be to solve the problem of subsistence for the poor as soon as possible and to lift them out of poverty and into wealth. At the end of 2008, China raised the poverty criterion from an annual per capita income of RMB786 to RMB1,067, that is, China combined the poverty criterion and the low-income principle into one, using RMB1,067 as the uniform poverty criterion. Since then, with changes in the consumer price index and other relevant factors, the criterion was further increased to RMB1,196 and RMB1,274 in 2009 and 2010, respectively.

2.1.2.3 Current Rural Poverty Criterion

From November 30 to December 1, 2011, the Central Poverty Alleviation Work Conference was held in Beijing, and the *Outline for Development-Oriented Poverty Alleviation for China's Rural Areas (2011–2020)* was released. The Outline defined the task of the new stage of development-oriented poverty alleviation as "consolidating the gains of subsistence, accelerating poverty alleviation, improving the ecological environment, enhancing development capacity, and narrowing the development gap." To narrow the development gap and allow more poor people to share the fruits of reform and opening-up, the Central Government has decided to set the poverty alleviation principle at "an annual per capita net income of RMB2,300 for farmers (in constant 2010 prices)." This principle is a 92% increase from USD1,196 in 2009.

After the Central Government's poverty alleviation work conference, Fan Xiaojian, Director of the Office of the State Council for Development-Oriented Poverty Relief, explained the main factors considered when determining the new poverty alleviation criterion.

First, the criterion accords with the goal that "the basic living needs of rural poor populations are met and that such people have access to compulsory education, basic medical services, and housing" by the year 2020. Basic subsistence needs, such as food, clothing, and housing, were not factored in, while the needs of partial development were given consideration.

Second, it should agree with the positioning of "subsistence allowances for survival, poverty alleviation for development." On the basis of subsistence allowances, the need to develop production and increase income was considered to narrow the income gap.

Third, the principle should be consistent with the self-determined poverty alleviation criteria proposed by the provincial governments. These criteria, which were initially set by the provinces, generally range from 25 to 50% of the average per capita net rural income in the previous year, with around RMB2,200 as the provincial average.

Fourth, this principle should be reliable and feasible. As long as we continue to consolidate and improve the progress of poverty alleviation work as well as increase our input and efforts, we can achieve the goal that "the basic living needs of rural poor populations are met and that such people have access to compulsory education, basic medical services, and housing" for poverty alleviation targets under the new principle.[2]

Wang, Director of the Urban and Rural Household Survey Office of the NBS, wrote an article published in *the Poverty Monitoring Report of Rural China 2015* explaining the meaning of the current rural poverty criterion. "In 2014, in the rural poverty criterion of RMB2,800/person/year (RMB2,300 in constant 2010 prices) with basic housing, the proportion of real food expenditure (i.e., Engel's coefficient) was 53.5%, equivalent to RMB4.1/person/day of food consumption expenditure. If 1 catty of rice and noodles (commodity grain), 1 catty of vegetables, and 1 tael of meat or 1 egg/person/day were the basic food consumption needs, an expenditure of RMB3.925 is required based on the composite average price of products sold and purchased by rural residents (Table 2.8). RMB4.10 is around 1.05 times RMB3.925.

Table 2.8 Basic food consumption needs of rural residents in China in 1985 and 2014

Item		Unit	1985	2014
Composite average price[a]	Grain (raw)	*yuan*/kg	0.43	2.48
	Vegetables		0.20	2.96
	Pork		3.44	18.39
	Eggs		2.52	9.53
Expenditure on basic food consumption	A catty of commercial food a day		0.288	1.653
	A catty of vegetables a day		0.098	1.478
	Half a tael of meat a day		0.086	0.460
	Half an egg a day		0.088	0.334
	In total		0.560	3.925

[a] The composite average price is a simple average of the sale and purchase prices of rural households in the rural household survey. A discount factor of 0.75 for raw grain to commodity grain is applied. The consumption expenditure for 1 tael of meat or 1 egg is calculated as half a tael of meat plus half an egg. One egg is calculated as 1.4 taels

Source Poverty Monitoring Report of Rural China 2015, China Statistics Press, 2015

[2] Xiaojian (2011).

Thus, in 2014, food expenditure in the rural poverty criterion can meet the caloric and protein needs for healthy survival."[3]

2.1.2.4 Comparison of China's Rural Poverty Criterion with the World Bank's Poverty Criterion

On October 4, 2015, the World Bank issued an update of the global extreme poverty criterion from USD1.25 (2005 purchasing power parity (PPP)) to USD1.9 (2011 PPP). According to the PPP conversion factor determined by the World Bank, in 2011, China's PPP conversion factor was 3.70, with an urban PPP conversion factor of 3.90, and 3.04 for rural PPP.[4] In the same year, China's rural poverty criterion was RMB2,536, or RMB6.95/day, or 6.95/3.04 = USD2.29/day. Thus, China's rural poverty criterion was 20.5% higher than the World Bank's USD1.9 poverty criterion.

2.1.2.5 Poor Population in Rural China

According to China's current rural poverty criterion of RMB 2,300/person/year (constant 2010 prices), there were 55.75 million poor people in rural China in 2015, indicating a 5.7% poverty incidence. Since 1978, more than 700 million farmers have been lifted out of poverty (Table 2.9).

Table 2.9 Data on rural poverty in China

Year	Poverty standard for the year (yuan/year/person)	Poverty incidence (%)	Size of the poor population (in millions)
1978	366	97.5	77,039
1980	403	96.2	76,542
1985	482	78.3	66,101
1990	807	73.5	65,849
1995	1.511	60.5	55,463
2000	1,528	49.8	46,224
2005	1,742	30.2	28,662
2010	2,300	17.2	16,567
2015	2,855	5.7	5,575

Source Data for 1978–2010 are from the Household Survey Office, NBS: *Poverty Monitoring Report of Rural China 2015*. Data for 2015 are from the NBS: *Statistical Bulletin of the National Economic and Social Development Statistics*, 2015

[3] Wang, Pingping, "The scale of rural poverty reduced by more than 700 million people since the reform and opening up, measured by the current poverty criterion," in *Poverty Monitoring Report of Rural China 2015*, China Statistics Press, 2015.

[4] Ferreira et al. (2015).

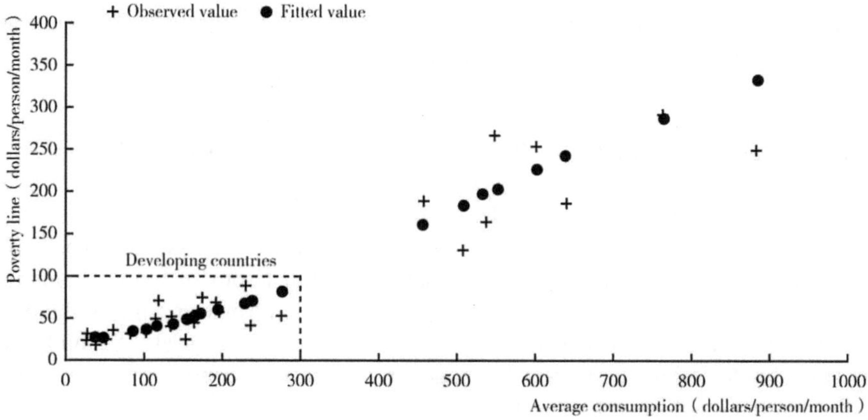

Fig. 2.5 The World Bank's USD1/day poverty line. *Note* At 1985 PPP. *Source* Ravallion et al. (1991)

2.1.3 The World Bank's Poverty Criterion

2.1.3.1 USD1/day Poverty Line

The World Bank defines poverty as a "deprivation of well-being" and therefore uses the basic needs approach to measure whether an individual or household has sufficient resources to meet such needs. Basic needs include both food and non-food items. In the 1990s, the World Bank collected poverty lines for 33 countries, both developing and developed, to determine a poverty line that could be used for global poverty comparisons. First, the poverty lines for these countries in monetary units were adjusted according to the 1985 PPP dollar. Second, scatter plots of poverty lines with average consumption were drawn, which was fitted and projected using semi-logarithmic models (Fig. 2.5). Ravallion et al. examined how the poverty line varied with average consumption levels when both average consumption levels and the poverty line were discounted by common PPP. When the consumption threshold is exceeded, the national poverty line rises sharply with the average consumption level, and the elasticity of rich countries tends to be 1. Thus, it can be argued that absolute poverty (i.e., the real value of the poverty line remains unchanged) is more relevant to poor countries, while rich countries have a higher prevalence of relative poverty (i.e., the poverty line is proportional to the median income). In order to direct limited resources for poverty alleviation to the absolute poor, global poverty should be measured according to the standard of living of the poorest countries.[5] The six poorest countries worldwide (Indonesia, Bangladesh, Nepal, Kenya, Tanzania, and Morocco) all have poverty lines of approximately USD31/person/month, while those of the Philippines and Pakistan are close to this figure. Accordingly, the World

[5] Ravallion et al. (2008).

Bank established a poverty line of USD1/day,[6] which adopted the 1985 PPP and was officially published in the World Development Report 1990.

2.1.3.2 Revision of the USD1.25/Day and USD2.00/Day Poverty Lines

In 2008, the World Bank revised the USD1/day poverty line and the 2005 PPP based on the poverty line data for 75 countries, including countries in transition. The revision followed three principles: first, international comparisons of living standards should be based on recent and reliable relative price information, unless there is sufficient reason to suspect that previous estimates were inaccurate. Second, the revision should follow the minimal changes in real poverty conditions as reflected in the international poverty line to avoid "frequent changes in policies," that is, the adjustment of the poverty line takes into account mainly changes in international purchasing power prices rather than substantive changes in the content of the poverty line. Third, the revision should target the world's poorest people.[7] In line with this estimate, the average poverty line for the 15 least developed countries (LDCs) is USD1.25/day. The median poverty line for 75 countries is USD60.81/month, equivalent to USD2/day. Excluding the 15 LDCs, the remaining 60 countries (including countries in transition) have a median poverty line of USD2.50/day (Fig. 2.6). The World Bank recommends an international poverty line of USD1.25/day for country-by-country comparisons of global extreme poverty. Poverty lines of USD2/day and USD2.5/day are applied to measure poverty in middle-income countries.

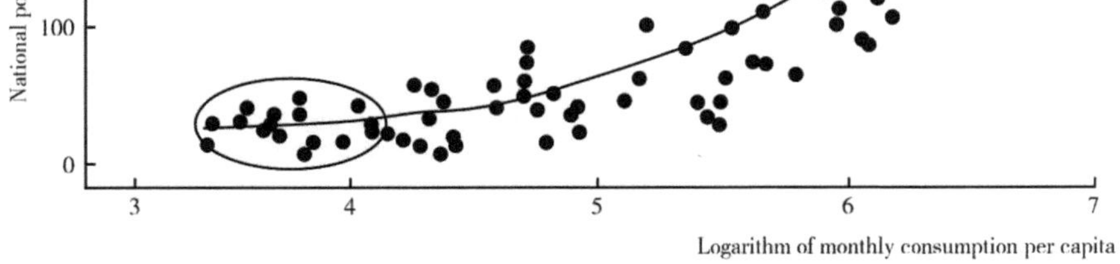

Fig. 2.6 The World Bank's USD1.25 poverty line. *Note* At 2005 PPP. *Source* Ravallion et al. (2008)

[6] Ravallion et al. 1991).

[7] Ferreira et al. (2015).

2.1.3.3 Poverty Line of USD1.9/Day

In October 2015, the World Bank updated the global extreme poverty criterion in its report, *A global count of the extreme poor in 2012: Data issues, methodology and initial results*. The World Bank adjusted the USD1.25 international poverty line to USD1.9 based on the 2011 international PPP. As is customary, when the World Bank's new principle is published, it will be used for a comparative analysis of poverty across countries by the World Bank and the United Nations system and as one of the bases for allocating aid funds. Relying on the World Bank's report released in October 2015 and data from the Bank's website, national poverty lines were collected for the 15 poorest countries worldwide. These 15 countries are those used by the Bank to calculate the USD1.25 and USD1.9 extreme poverty criteria.

Compared to the 2005 International Comparison Project (ICP), the 2011 ICP made a significant adjustment to the relative price level of the purchasing power of currencies between countries. Therefore, the adjustment from the 2005 PPP to the 2011 PPP would be a relatively large change and would accordingly affect the adjustment of the international poverty line. For this reason, the World Bank has set a corresponding conversion factor. Year *t* of the survey period is converted from 2005 PPP-adjusted dollar income ($INC_{\mathrm{PPP05,t}}$) to 2011 PPP-adjusted dollar income ($INC_{\mathrm{PPP11,t}}$) by the following method:

$$INC_{\mathrm{PPP11,t}} = INC_{\mathrm{PPP05,t}} \times \frac{\mathrm{CPI}_{11}}{\mathrm{CPI}_{05}} \times \frac{\mathrm{PPP}_{05}}{\mathrm{PPP}_{11}} \tag{2.1}$$

δ is the conversion factor:

$$\delta = \frac{\mathrm{CPI}_{11}}{\mathrm{CPI}_{05}} \times \frac{\mathrm{PPP}_{05}}{\mathrm{PPP}_{11}} \tag{2.2}$$

The poverty line expressed in the 2011 PPP dollar for each country in the last row of Table 2.10 is calculated according to the formula above. The mean poverty line for the 15 countries is USD1.88, which is the current USD1.9 poverty line.

Table 2.11 shows a summary history of the World Bank's adjustment of the poverty line, and readers who need more detailed information are advised to read the literature listed in the table.

2.1.3.4 Current Global Poverty

According to the World Bank's 2015 poor population with consumption below USD1.90/day (2011 PPP) (Table 2.12), the global poverty incidence in 2012 was 12.73%, with 897 million people living in poverty. Sub-Saharan Africa had the largest poor population, reaching 389 million, and a poverty incidence of 42.65%, followed by South Asia with a poor population of 309 million, an 18.75% poverty incidence.

Table 2.10 The World Bank's re-estimation of the USD1.9 poverty line using the 2011 PPP

	Year of poverty line	2005 PPP	2011 PPP	CPI2011 (2005 = 100)	Poverty line (2005 PPP dollars/day)	Poverty line (2011 PPP dollars/day)
Malawi	2004–2005	56.92	78.02	214.6*	0.86	1.34
Mali	1988–1989	289.68	221.87	119.8	1.38	2.15
Ethiopia	1999–2000	2.75	5.44	297.1	1.35	2.03
Sierra Leone	2003–2004	1,396.21	1,767.19	203.9**	1.69	2.73
Niger	1993	267.33	228.75	116.3	1.1	1.49
Uganda	1993–1998	744.62	946.89	178.0	1.27	1.77
Gambia	1998	10.34	10.83	129.3	1.48	1.82
Rwanda	1999–2001	236.75	246.83	157.8	0.99	1.5
Guinea-Bissau	1991	284.28	248.24	124.8	1.51	2.16
Tanzania	2000–2001	482.45	588.52	169.9	0.63	0.88
Tajikistan	1999	0.93	1.88	334.2*	1.93	3.18
Mozambique	2002–2003	11.63	15.53	173.5	0.97	1.26
Chad	1995–1996	327.57	251.30	112.4	0.87	1.28
Nepal	2003–2004	26.47	25.76	164.8	0.87	1.47
Ghana	1998–1999	0.45	0.79	295.2*	1.83	3.07
Mean					1.25	1.88

Source Ferreira et al. (2015). *A global count of the extreme poor in 2012: Data issues, methodology and initial result* (Policy Research Working Paper 7432). World Bank Group

The poverty reduction targets of the United Nations Millennium Development Goals (MDGs) can be achieved as scheduled in 2015 because of two aspects: the tough poverty reduction measures in China and the global achievements in poverty reduction since 2000. The MDGs have helped lift more than one billion people out of extreme poverty, reduced hunger, allowed more girls than ever before to attend school, and protected our planet. Since the MDGs were set in 2000, concerted global, regional, national, and local efforts have saved millions of lives and improved the situation of many more. The MDGs have fostered a new global partnership for development, galvanized public opinion, and demonstrated the immense value of setting ambitious goals. By considering people as the focal point and prioritizing their immediate needs, the MDGs have transformed policymaking in both developed and developing countries.[8] The unremitting efforts of countries and international organizations worldwide to achieve the goals promised in this declaration have played a vital role in accelerating the reduction of global poverty.

According to the World Bank's poverty criterion of consumption lower than USD1.90/day, China's poor population was 878 million in 1981 and, with a poverty incidence of 88.32%, accounted for 43.95% of the global total. In 2015, China's

[8] United Nations, "*Millennium Development Goals Report 2015,*" United Nations, 2015.

Table 2.11 Summary history of the World Bank's international poverty line

	1979 Indian poverty line	1990 USD1	2001 USD1.08	2008 USD1.25	2015 USD1.90
Source	Ahluwalia et al. (1978)	World Development Report, Ravallion et al. (1991)	Chen and Ravallion (2001)	Ravallion et al. (2008)	Ferreira et al. (2015)
ICP data	1975 PPPs, Kravis et al	1985 PPPs	1993 PPPs	2005 PPPs	2011 PPPs
Poverty line used in countries	1 (India)	8 countries	10 countries	15 countries	15 countries (as in 2008)
Method	Indian poverty line	Mean	Median	Mean	Mean
Poverty line (ICP base period USD)	USD0.56	USD1.01 (1.00)	USD1.08	USD1.25	USD1.88 (1.90)
Poverty line (1985 USD)	USD1.12	USD1.02	USD0.80	USD0.69	USD0.91
Relevant countries	India	Kenya, Nepal, Tanzania, Bangladesh, Morocco, The Philippines, Pakistan	China, Tanzania, Zambia, India, Indonesia, Thailand, Nepal, Bangladesh, Tunisia, Pakistan	Malawi, Mali, Ethiopia, Sierra Leone, Niger, Uganda, Gambia, Rwanda, Guinea-Bissau, Tanzania, Tajikistan, Mozambique, Chad, Nepal, Ghana	As in 2008

Source Ferreira et al. (2015). *A global count of the extreme poor in 2012: Data issues, methodology and initial result* (Policy Research Working Paper 7432). World Bank Group

poor population dropped to 57 million, with a poverty incidence of 4.2%, reducing its share to 8.18% of the global total. There is no doubt that China has made remarkable achievements in poverty reduction (Table 2.13). If China's achievements in poverty reduction are not included, the global poor population increased between 1981 and 2002 (Fig. 2.7).

Table 2.12 Global poverty in 2012 (USD1.9/day poverty line)

Region	Poverty incidence (%)	Poverty gap (%)	Poverty gap squared	Poor population (in millions)	Total population (in millions)
East Asia and the Pacific	7.21	1.47	0.48	147.20	2,041.56
Europe and Central Asia	2.11	0.58	0.28	10.14	480.78
Latin America and the Caribbean	5.58	2.64	1.82	33.68	603.58
Middle East and North Africa	–	–	–	–	–
South Asia	18.75	3.73	1.12	309.23	1,649.25
Sub-Saharan Africa	42.65	16.47	8.56	388.76	911.51
Developing world	14.88	4.35	1.98	896.70	6,026.23
World total	12.73	3.72	1.69	896.70	7,043.07

Note "–" indicates that the sample size of the survey in the area is too small to report the corresponding poverty data
Source World Bank PovcalNet, accessed March 22, 2016

Table 2.13 Comparison of Chinese and global poverty (USD1.9/day poverty line)

Year	Poor population (in millions)			Poverty incidence (%)	
	Global	China	Percentage (%)	Global	China
1981	1,997.28	877.80	43.95	44.30	88.32
1984	1,955.26	785.40	40.17	41.16	75.75
1987	1,864.55	659.53	35.37	37.25	60.84
1990	1,958.57	755.81	38.59	37.10	66.58
1993	1,916.70	671.71	35.05	34.65	57.00
1996	1,715.79	511.98	29.84	29.69	42.05
1999	1751.45	507.86	29.00	29.08	40.54
2002	1645.12	409.09	24.87	26.29	31.95
2005	1401.01	244.45	17.45	21.59	18.75
2008	1253.90	194.06	15.48	18.65	14.65
2010	1119.75	149.56	13.36	16.27	11.18
2011	983.33	106.19	10.80	14.12	7.90
2012	896.70	87.39	9.75	12.73	6.47
2015	702.00	57.00	8.18	9.60	4.20

Source World Bank PovcalNet, accessed March 22, 2016. Data for 2015 are World Bank projections

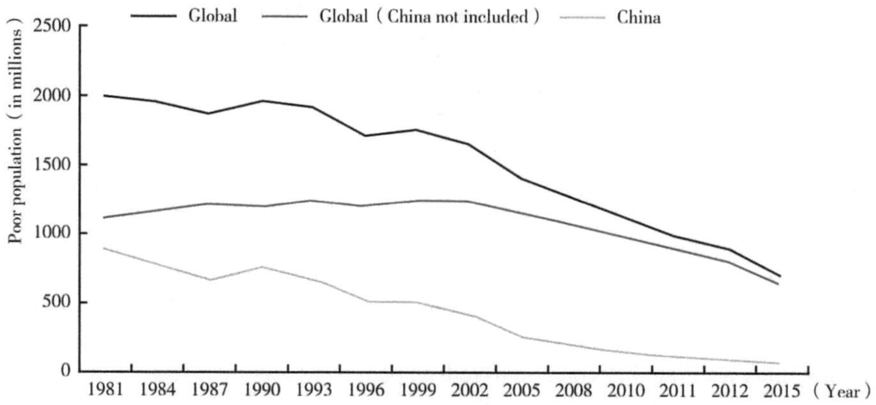

Fig. 2.7 Global poverty (USD1.9/day). *Source* World Bank, PovcalNet, accessed March 22, 2016. Data for 2015 are World Bank projections

2.2 Multidimensional Poverty Index

2.2.1 Why Measure Multidimensional Poverty

Previously, both international organizations and countries across the world have traditionally measured poverty in a single dimension, usually using income or consumption indicators to measure monetary poverty. This measure takes a "basket" of goods and services as the basic needs for survival, which is then converted into a poverty line expressed in monetary terms at current prices. People are identified as poor when they have insufficient funds to meet these basic needs. While the monetary poverty criterion does provide useful information, it is a far cry from what the poor themselves feel. The character, Jean Valjean, in *Les Miserables* provides a much more vivid expression of the feelings of the poor than the economist's measurement of poverty using money. Valjean suffers from multidimensional poverty.

> Please listen to me. My name is Jean Valjean. I'm a prisoner of hard labor. Spent nineteen years in prison. Four days out of prison, and now I'm going to Pontallier, that's where I'm going. I've been walking from Tulun for four days, and I've walked twelve miles today. I arrived in this place only at dark, and I went to a guest house and was thrown out just because I had asked for a yellow passport examination at the town hall. That again had to be asked for a check. I went to another shop. They said to me, 'Get out!' No one wanted me. I went back to the prison, and the gatekeeper wouldn't open the door. I also went to the kennel, and the dog bit me and threw me out, as if it were a human being, as if it knew who I was. I ran out into the field, intending to spend the night in the open air. But there were no stars in the sky. I thought it was going to rain, and there was no good weather to prevent it, so I went back to the city, and tried to find a doorway. And there, in the open space, was a slate. I was lying down, and an old woman showed me your house, and said to me, 'Go and knock on that door.' I knocked. What is this place? Is it a guest shop? I have money. I've got savings. One hundred and nine francs and fifteen sous, which I earned by working in prison for nineteen

years. I can pay the bills. What's that got to do with it? I have money. I'm sleepy, I've walked twelve miles and I'm hungry. Will you let me rest?

Amartya Sen, who proposes the capability approach, believes that poverty is the deprivation of basic human capabilities and that poverty reduction is about extending the real freedoms that are of value to people. The basic viable capabilities include equitable access to education, health, drinking water, housing, sanitation, and markets. Multidimensional poverty is derived from Sen's capability approach and is defined as the multiple deprivations from which the poor suffer, such as poorer health; lack of education, income, and empowerment; inadequate standard of living; poor working conditions; and threats from violence. Alkire and Foster argue that multidimensional poverty measurement associated with the capability approach can provide more accurate information to reduce people's capability deprivation.[9]

In existing theoretical studies, multidimensional poverty is measured for several reasons. First, as argued by Sen, multidimensional poverty is measured because the deprivations suffered by the poor are multifaceted and each aspect is important.[10] Second, any single dimension of poverty measurement is not matched by the multidimensionality of poverty itself. Studies in India and Peru have shown that many people who are impoverished in terms of education opportunities and health are not necessarily poor in income. Third, even though income is a good proxy for multidimensional poverty, alone it is not sufficient to capture other dimensions of deprivation and social exclusion. Fourth, although the Human Development Index (HDI) is a major complement to the measurement of income poverty, it only includes three dimensions—income, health, and education—which is far from adequate compared to the many basic viable capabilities that Sen proposes to influence human development. Fifth, multidimensional measurement of poverty enables public policy to identify priority areas for intervention. Sixth, this measurement is a vital complement to, rather than a substitute for, income poverty measurement. Expressed in the Chinese term "*pinkun*" (literally "poverty"), income measurement of poverty is essentially a measurement of "*pin*" (literally "insufficiency"), and multidimensional measurement of poverty can capture "*kun*" (literally "hardship").

2.2.2 How to Measure Multidimensional Poverty

After Sen's capability approach was proposed, many scholars criticized the theory, arguing that it is too abstract to be applied in practice and that the biggest challenge is how to measure multidimensional poverty. Currently, an increasing number of household-based statistical survey data are available worldwide, making it possible to measure multidimensional poverty.[11] In addition to Bourguignon and Chakravarty's exploration of multidimensional poverty measurement using the social welfare

[9] Alkire and Foster (2007).

[10] Sen (1992).

[11] Alkire (2011).

approach, in May 2007, Sen founded the Oxford Poverty and Human Development Initiative (OPHI) in the Department of International Development at the University of Oxford, aiming to measure multidimensional poverty. In 2007–2008, Alkire and Foster published the article "*Counting and Multidimensional Poverty Measurement*," pioneering the counting approach to multidimensional poverty measurement. This approach was the first method to widely apply multidimensional poverty measurement to that of global multidimensional poverty and has been adopted by an increasing number of countries. In 2007–2010, Alkire's team measured the multidimensional poverty of countries worldwide, including Wang and Alkire's measurement of multidimensional poverty in China in 2009.[12] In 2010, the United Nations Development Programme adopted and officially published the MPI for 104 countries in its *Human Development Report*.

The MPI can be divided into two categories: a global multidimensional poverty index for global measurement and country comparison, that is, MPI or G-MPI, and a national multidimensional poverty index to measure a single country's poverty levels, that is, C-MPI. The C-MPI can identify dimensions, indices, and weights of poverty according to the stage of economic and social development of a country and the focus of its poverty reduction strategies and policies. This section adopts the G-MPI (MPI) to outline how multidimensional poverty can be measured using the AF counting approach.

2.2.2.1 MPI

The MPI is a composite index used to measure acute poverty. Acute poverty has two features: one is the failure of the poor to meet internationally accepted minimum standards as defined by indicators of basic functions, such as access to adequate nutrition, a certain number of years of schooling, and clean drinking water; the other is the failure of the poor to meet internationally accepted minimum standards of several aspects simultaneously. Therefore, the MPI measures the multidimensional deprivations that people experience, for instance, a person who is malnourished and also lacks access to clean drinking water and decent sanitation.[13]

The MPI consists of two key components: poverty incidence and poverty intensity. Poverty incidence is the proportion of the population undergoing multidimensional poverty and is denoted by H (i.e., *headcount ratio*), while poverty intensity is the average (weighted) proportion of deprivation experienced by the poor, that is, how poor they are on average, and is denoted by A (i.e., *average deprivation share*). The MPI can thus be expressed as $\text{MPI} = \text{H} \times \text{A}$.[14] When a person is measured as suffering from poverty with a weighted indicator of one-third and above, they are considered multidimensionally poor, according to the 33.3% multidimensional poverty threshold (k).

---

[12] Wang and Alkire (2009).

[13] Alkire et al. (2016).

[14] Wang and Alkire (2009).

Poverty incidence and poverty intensity are crucial for the formulation of anti-poverty policies. For instance, take a multidimensional poverty incidence of 20% in both Area A and Area B. However, the poverty intensity in Area A is an average deprivation of one-third of the five dimensions, while that in Area B consists of an average deprivation of two-thirds of the five dimensions. Clearly, people in Area B are poorer than those in Area A.

2.2.2.2 Identification of Dimensions and Indicators

The G-MPI consists of three dimensions—health, education, and standard of living—with a total of ten indicators. The health dimension contains two indicators on nutrition and child mortality; the education dimension includes two indicators on years of schooling and children enrolled in school; and the standard of living dimension comprises six indicators: cooking fuel, toilet, drinking water, electricity, house flooring, and consumer durables (Table 2.14). The ten indicators for these three dimensions identify the superimposed deprivation at the household level and demonstrate the average number of poor people who are deprived and the dimensions of deprivation in impoverished households.

2.2.2.3 Measurement of MPI

In multidimensional poverty measurement, the deprivation of each dimension is first determined and then tallied to obtain the MPI. Therefore, first, the level of the indicators' deprivation must be measured.

To do so, first a cutoff or a poverty line needs to be determined. For each dimension, if the observed value is below the cutoff, the indicator is considered deprived or poor. For example, assume a cutoff of 5 years of schooling. A person who has an observed value of 4 years of schooling is identified as being deprived. Table 2.15 lists the cutoff

Table 2.14 Dimensions and indicators of the G-MPI

Index	Dimension	Indicator
MPI	Health	Nutrition
		Child mortality
	Education	Years of schooling
		Children enrolled in school
	Standard of living	Cooking fuel
		Toilet
		Drinking water
		Electricity
		House flooring
		Consumer durables

Table 2.15 Dimensions, indicators, and cutoffs used in the G-MPI

Dimension	Indicator	Cutoff	Rationale	Relative weight
Education	Years of schooling	Population aged more than 10 years and not completing 5 years of schooling	MDG2	1/6
	Children enrolled in school	School-age children not enrolled in school	MDG2	1/6
Health	Child mortality	Death of a child in the family	MDG4	1/6
	Nutrition	Malnutrition in adults less than 70 years of age or in children	MDG1	1/6
Standard of living	Electricity	No electricity at home		1/18
	Sanitary toilet	Toilet facilities are not improved (as per MDG guidelines), or improved toilet facilities are shared with other households	MDG7	1/18
	Safe drinking water	Lack of access to safe drinking water at home (as per MDG guidelines) or access at least at a 30-min walk from the home	MDG7	1/18
	House flooring	Dirty, sandy, fecal, or other types of flooring		1/18
	Cooking fuel	Use of dung, wood, charcoal, or other solid fuels for cooking	MDG7	1/18
	Consumer durables	No radio, TV, telephone, bicycle, motorcycle, or refrigerator at home and no car or truck	MDG7	1/18

Source Alkire et al. (2016). *The Global Multidimensional Poverty Index (G-MPI): 5-year methodological note* (OPHI Briefing 37)

for each indicator of the G-MPI, along with their rationale and relative weights.

In the adding-up process, the weights of each dimension and indicator need to be determined. Currently, health, education, and standard of living are given equal weight in the MPI calculation, while the same applies for the indicators within each dimension. Calculating the MPI with the same weights has been criticized by Ravallion, a poverty measurement expert at the World Bank, as being too arbitrary in its approach of assigning equal weights to each indicator.

The MPI is calculated by summing the three levels of the indicator-dimension-multidimensional poverty index. The calculation method of MPI can be found in Alkire and Foster's article "*Counting and Multidimensional Poverty Measurement*," Wang and Alkire's article "*Multidimensional Poverty Measurement in China: Estimates and Policy Implications*," or Chapter 4 of this book, "*Multidimensional Poverty Measurement of China*." Deprivation in any three of the ten MPI indicators as currently published in the *Human Development Report* indicates that the person or family is multidimensionally poor. Thus, the multidimensional poverty incidence can be calculated. Multidimensional poverty intensity is the average percentage of deprivation suffered by a multidimensionally poor person.[15]

2.2.3 Global Multidimensional Poverty

The OPHI released the Global Multidimensional Poverty Index 2015 in June 2015. The index covered 101 countries and 75% of the global population, approximately 5.2 billion. Of these, 29.8% (1.6 billion) were found to be multidimensionally poor (Table 2.16), 54% of whom lived in South Asia and 31% in sub-Saharan Africa; 70% of them lived in middle-income countries.

South Asia and sub-Saharan Africa remain the regions with both the highest number of people living in multidimensional poverty and with the highest incidence worldwide. They may live in a family where people are malnourished, children have died young, no one in the household has over 5 years of schooling, and school-age children cannot go to school. They may also be in a family where cooking fuel, sanitation, drinking water, electricity, house flooring, and consumer durables fail to meet the internationally accepted minimum living standards.

In 2012, China's MPI ($k = 33.3\%$) was 0.023, with a 5.2% incidence of multidimensional poverty and 43.2% intensity. When the cutoff for multidimensional poverty was set at $k = 20$–33.3%, the proportion of vulnerable poor was 19.8%, that is, 19.8% of Chinese people were likely to be multidimensionally poor ($k = 33.3\%$). The proportion of people in severe poverty ($k = 50\%$) was 1.0%, suggesting that approximately 13 million people in China were in severe poverty. These people were poor in more than half of the indicators set by the G-MPI. Figure 2.8 shows that China has better performance in multidimensional poverty reduction relative to income poverty. This may be related to the fact that the Chinese notion of poverty itself is multidimensional and that China's poverty reduction government agencies are set up across more than 40 departments to promote development-oriented poverty alleviation across all dimensions.

[15] UNDP (2011).

Table 2.16 Global multidimensional poverty in 2015

Region	MPI	H (multidimensional poverty incidence %)	A (multidimensional poverty intensity)	Multidimensionally poor population (million)	Total population (million)
Region (101 countries)	0.157	29.8	52.6	1,558.4	5,222.7
Europe and Central Asia	0.008	2.0	38.1	3.0	152.1
Latin America and the Caribbean	0.022	5.2	42.5	26.0	499.3
East Asia and the Pacific	0.031	7.1	43.46	26.0	499.3
Arabian countries	0.109	20.7	52.7	54.4	263.3
South Asia	0.275	52.5	52.3	844.0	1,607.5
Sub-Saharan Africa	0.343	61.1	56.2	496.0	811.5
Income group (101 countries)	0.157	29.8	52.6	1,558.4	5,222.7
High income: Non-OECD countries	0.017	4.8	35.1	0.1	1.6
Upper middle-income countries	0.021	4.9	42.1	101.0	2,063.5
Lower middle-income countries	0.212	40.5	52.5	983.0	2,428.7
Low-income countries	0.359	65.0	55.2	474.1	729.0

Source Alkire et al. (2015). *Global Multidimensional Poverty Index 2015* (Oxford Poverty and Human Development Initiative)

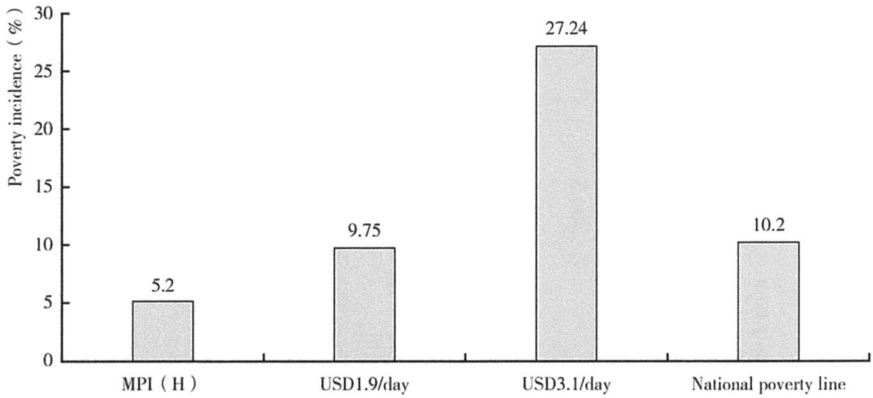

Fig. 2.8 Multidimensional poverty and income poverty in China in 2015. *Note* The national poverty line refers to the per capita net income of rural residents in 2010 at constant prices of RMB2,300, and the poverty incidence only covers rural areas, not urban areas. *Sources* MPI data (OPHI), USD1.9 and USD3.1 data (World Bank), and national poverty line data (NBS)

2.2.4 Pros and Cons of MPI

First, the MPI is an important complement to the World Bank's income poverty measure and provides a more vivid picture of the deprivation being suffered by the poor.

Second, the MPI provides a deeper understanding and measurement of environmental deprivation. The MPI comprises three indicators—cooking fuel, drinking water, and sanitation—that highlight the environmental deprivation of the poor. The MPI 2011 shows that in developing countries, six out of ten people experience at least one type of environmental deprivation, while four out of ten experience two types or more. For the multidimensional poor population, environmental deprivation is even more severe, with 80% experiencing two or more types of environmental deprivations and 29% experiencing all three types.[16]

Third, the MPI incorporates an indicator of consumer durables. The deprivation of consumer durables is present when a household does not own a car and owns, at most, either a bicycle, motorcycle, radio, refrigerator, telephone, or TV. The deprivation of consumer durables essentially reveals the asset poverty of households, which is a manifestation of persistent poverty.

Fourth, the MPI is based on existing household statistical surveys. Many indicators that reflect the extension of human viable capabilities have not yet been included in the measurement due to the unavailability of data. Moreover, the setting of weights needs improvement.

Fifth, the MPI is limited by the availability of statistical data across countries, and some countries have very old data that do not reflect the current poverty situation.

[16] UNDP (2011).

For instance, the multidimensional poverty measure for India is based on data from the World Health Survey (WHS) 2005, making it outdated from the current situation in India.

2.3 Conclusion and Discussion

Humanity's understanding of poverty is evolving, as is its measurement. The two types of poverty criterion used for global poverty monitoring, namely, the income/consumption principle and the MPI, are the most sophisticated methods for reflecting human poverty. They can be used as a reference for strengthening China's poverty monitoring and implementing the Outline for Development-Oriented Poverty Alleviation for China's Rural Areas (2011–2020).

The income/consumption principle captures the economic status of the poor from a simple monetary perspective and is an easy-to-understand poverty measurement method for formulating anti-poverty strategies and policies. The MPI expands poverty measurement to a more comprehensive range of dimensions and indicators, with more variables to reveal the quality of human life. The emergence of MPI is a tremendous advance in human measurement of poverty and fills a gap in previous poverty measurements of well-being. It is particularly useful in determining priorities for anti-poverty public policy interventions. Not only does it allow for accurate poverty monitoring, but it also provides a clear direction for anti-poverty strategies and policies.

References

Ahluwalia, M., Carter, N., & Chenery, H. (1978). Growth and poverty in developing countries. *Journal of Development Economics, 6*(3), 299–341.

Alkire, S., & Foster, J. E. (2007). *Counting and multidimensional poverty measures* (OPHI Working Paper No. 7). Oxford Poverty and Human Development Initiative, University of Oxford.

Alkire, S. (2011). *Multidimensional poverty and its discontents* (OPHI Working Paper No. 46).

Alkire S., Jindra, C., et al. (2015). *Global multidimensional poverty index, 2015*. Oxford Poverty & Human Development Initiative.

Alkire S., Conconi, A., et al. (2016). *The global multidimensional poverty index (MPI): 5-year methodological note* (OPHI Briefing 37).

Chen, S., & Ravallion, M. (2001). How did the world's poor fare in the 1990s? *Review of Income and Wealth, 47*(3), 283–300.

Fan, X. (2011, December 2). Director of the Office of the State Council for Development-Oriented Poverty Relief, Explains in Detail the RMB2,300 Poverty Alleviation Principle. *Xinhua News*.

Ferreira, F. H. G., Chen, S., et al. (2015). *A global count of the extreme poor in 2012: Data issues, methodology and initial results* (Policy Research Working Paper 74321). World Bank Group.

Kanbur, R., & Squire, L. (1999). *The evolution of thinking about poverty: Exploring the interactions.*

Ravallion, M., Datt, G., & Van de Walle, D. (1991). *Quantifying the magnitude and severity of absolute poverty in the developing world in the mid-1980s* (World Development Report, WPS 587).

Ravallion, M., Chen, S., & Sangraula, P. (2008). *Dollar a day revisited* (Policy Research Working Paper 4620). World Bank.
Sen, A. (1992). *Inequality re-examined*. Russell Sage Foundation.
UNDP. (2011). *Human development report*. United Nations Development Programme.
Wang, X., & Alkire, S. (2009). Multidimensional poverty measurement in China: Estimates and policy implications. *China's Rural Economy*, No. 12.
Wang, P., Fang, H., & Li, X. (2006). Comparison between China's poverty criterion and international poverty criterion. *Chinese Rural Economy*, No. 12.

Chapter 3
Dynamic Change Measurement of Poverty in China

3.1 Introduction

According to the World Bank, China succeeded in reducing the poor population who consume less than USD1.25 a day (PPP 2005) by 662 million between 1981 and 2008; this was done through sustained, rapid economic growth brought about by its reform and opening up, as well as development-oriented poverty alleviation and social security systems.[1] In line with the World Bank's poverty criterion of consuming less than USD1.25 a day, China had reduced its poor population to 173 million by the end of 2008,[2] an achievement which has attracted worldwide attention. Based on the subsequent poverty alleviation principle established in 2011 (i.e., an annual per capita net income of RMB2,300 for rural residents), there remain 128 million rural poor population.[3] Eliminating poverty and narrowing the development gap remain the major issues facing China's economic and social development. Therefore, on November 30, 2011, the General Secretary of the Chinese Communist Party Hu Jintao stated at the Central Poverty Alleviation Work Conference that, "Pushing forward development-oriented poverty alleviation and doing a good job in its new stage are of great significance for safeguarding the fundamental interests of the people, consolidating the Party's ruling base, ensuring long-term peace and stability in the country, and realizing the ambitious goal of building a moderately prosperous society in all respects and socialist modernization."

---

[1] The data were from the World Bank poverty database.

[2] Please refer to Chapter Two for the latest data on poverty in China according to the World Bank's poverty criteria of USD1.25, USD1.90, and USD3.10.

[3] Based on the new national poverty criterion, at the end of 2015 there were 55.75 million rural poor population remaining in China according to the poverty monitoring data from the National Bureau of Statistics.

© Social Sciences Academic Press 2022

X. Wang, *Multidimensional Poverty Measurement*,
International Research on Poverty Reduction,
https://doi.org/10.1007/978-981-19-1189-7_3

The scientific and objective measurement of poverty is the foundation for succeeding in the new stage of development-oriented poverty alleviation and building a harmonious society. However, in comparison to the tremendous achievements in poverty reduction, China's measurement has always been its weak link. The reason for this is, on one hand, the lack of theoretical research on poverty measurement and, on the other, difficulty in obtaining data. Poverty measurement requires household survey data, and it is extremely expensive to conduct such specialized surveys. This book measures the dynamic change of poverty over a 20-year period and contributes to the analysis of both rural and urban poverty, the latter being of utmost, possibly even more, importance. To date, China has implemented a system of anti-poverty policies based on the urban-rural divide and attached little importance to the measurement of urban poverty. There is no uniform national standard for measuring urban poverty, with each region setting its own minimum standard of living.

This book uses data from the China Health and Nutrition Survey (CHNS), conducted by the Carolina Population Center at the University of North Carolina and the Chinese Center for Disease Control and Prevention (CCDC). The data consist of panel data between 1989 and 2009. The analysis unit is individual, and the effective sample size is 48,954, including 32,693 rural residents (66.78 percent) and 16,261 urban ones (33.22 percent). The samples covered nine provinces (regions): Jiangsu, Shandong, Liaoning, and Heilongjiang in the east; Henan, Hunan, and Hubei in the center; and Guangxi and Guizhou in the west.

3.2 Methods and Models

The poverty measure used in this chapter is the Foster-Greer-Thorbecke (FGT) method, and the indicators measured include poverty incidence (P_0), the poverty gap index (P_1), the squared poverty gap index (P_2), the Sen index, the Sen-Shorrocks-Thon index, and Watts index. Inequality is measured using the Gini coefficient and Theil index.[4]

3.2.1 Poverty Measurement

The poverty incidence (P_0) simply measures the proportion of the poor in the total population, calculated as follows:

$$P_0 = \frac{1}{N}\sum_{i=1}^{N} I(y_i < z) \tag{3.1}$$

[4] For the definition of poverty and inequality measures used in this chapter, please refer to Haughton and Khandker (2009).

In the formula, P_0 denotes the poverty incidence as measured by the headcount ratio. When income y_i is lower than the poverty line z, it is defined as poverty.

The poverty gap index (P_1) is a measure of the ratio of the gap between the income of the poor to the poverty line (poverty gap), calculated as follows:

$$P_1 = \frac{1}{N}\sum_{i=1}^{N}\frac{G_i}{z} \tag{3.2}$$

In the formula, $G_i = (z - y_i) \times I(y_i < z)$. G_i denotes the poverty gap, z is the poverty line, and y_i is the real income of the poor. I is the variable 0 or 1; if $y_i < z$, then I is 1, otherwise I is 0 (i.e., the gap is 0).

The squared poverty gap index (P_2) assigns a higher weight to the poor, calculated as follows:

$$P_2 = \frac{1}{N}\sum_{i=1}^{N}\left(\frac{G_i}{z}\right)^2 \tag{3.3}$$

The Sen index was proposed by Amartya Sen in 1976 to combine the number, depth of poverty, and the intra-group distribution of the poor population, calculated as follows:

$$P_s = P_0\left[1 - \left(1 - G^P\right)\frac{\mu^P}{Z}\right] \tag{3.4}$$

In the formula, P_0 is the headcount index of poverty, μ^P is the mean income (or consumption) of the poor, and G^P is the Gini coefficient for the poor.

The Sen-Shorrocks-Thon (SST) index is a modification of the Sen index, defined as follows:

$$P_{SST} = P_0 P_1^P\left(1 + \hat{G}^p\right) \tag{3.5}$$

The SST index includes the headcount index of poverty, the poverty gap index, and the Gini coefficient of the poverty gap ratio. Thus, the SST index can be decomposed according to these components.

The Watts index is calculated as follows:

$$\begin{aligned} W &= \frac{1}{N}\sum_{i=1}^{q}[In(z) - In(y_i)] \\ &= \frac{1}{n}\sum_{i=1}^{q} In\left(\frac{z}{y_i}\right) \end{aligned} \tag{3.6}$$

3.2.2 Inequality Measurement

Economic growth and income distribution are two important aspects that affect poverty. For the same per capita income, a more equitable income distribution indicates a lower poverty incidence, and vice versa. The model for defining the inequality measurement is as follows.

The Gini coefficient (Gini) is a basic measure of inequality derived from the Lorenz curve, ranging from 0 to 1. A larger value indicates a more unequal income distribution.

$$Gini = 1 - \frac{1}{N}\sum_{i=1}^{N}(x_1 - x_{i-1})(y_t - y_{t-1}) \quad (3.7)$$

In the formula, x_i represents the cumulative percentage of the population and y_i represents the cumulative percentage of income (consumption).

The Gini coefficient measures inequality as a whole, but it is flawed in that the coefficient cannot be decomposed. Therefore, the cause of inequality cannot be identified. The Theil index and its decomposition are further used to analyze the causes of inequality.

Generalized entropy measures (GEM) essentially measure the logarithmic mean deviation of the per capita income or consumption. The calculation formula is as follows:

$$GE(\alpha) = \frac{1}{\alpha(\alpha - 1)}\left[\frac{1}{N}\sum_{i=1}^{N}\left(\frac{y_i}{\overline{y}}\right)^{\alpha}\right] - 1 \quad (3.8)$$

In the formula, y is the income or consumption of each individual, and $\overline{y}$ is the mean value of per capita income or consumption. α is the weight, which is usually 0, 1, or 2, and is used to assign weight to the deviation of per capita income or consumption. When GE is 0, it indicates that the income distribution is absolutely fair; moreover, a larger GE suggests a less fair income distribution.

When $\alpha = 0$, in Theil's L index, it indicates the logarithm of the mean deviation of personal income (consumption) from average income (consumption). The calculation formula is as follows:

$$GE(0) = \frac{1}{N}\sum_{i=1}^{N} \text{In}\left(\frac{\overline{y}}{y_i}\right) \quad (3.9)$$

When $\alpha = 1$, Theil's T index is calculated as follows:

$$GE(1) = \frac{1}{N}\sum_{i=1}^{N}\frac{y_i}{\overline{y}} In\left(\frac{y_i}{\overline{y}}\right) \quad (3.10)$$

The advantage of the Theil index is that it can be decomposed. Using Theil's T index as an example, T denotes GE(1), and the decomposition formula is

$$T = \sum_{i=1}^{N} \frac{y_i}{N\overline{y}} \ln\left(\frac{y_i N}{\overline{yN}}\right)$$

$$= \sum_{i=1}^{N} \frac{y_i}{\overline{Y}} \ln\left(\frac{y_i N}{\overline{Y}}\right) \tag{3.11}$$

$$= \sum_{j}\left(\frac{Y_j}{\overline{Y}}\right)T_j + \sum_{j}\left(\frac{Y_j}{\overline{Y}}\right) \cdot \ln\frac{y_j/n}{N_j/N} \tag{3.12}$$

Formula (3.11) decomposes Theil's T index into two parts: intra-group inequality and inter-group inequality.

3.2.3 *Definition of Poverty Lines*

This book defines the poverty line in two ways. First, it is defined as 25 percent of the median per capita net income for urban and rural residents, specifically between 1993 and 2009. Second, it is defined as 25 percent of both urban and rural per capita net incomes in 2009, which is then deflated by the consumer price index for both to derive the absolute poverty line for each year between 1989 and 2009.

The two poverty lines are significant for analyzing the changes in poverty. The relative poverty line focuses on changes in people whose per capita net income was below 25 percent of the median between 1989 and 2009, whereas the second definition fixes 25 percent of the median per capita net income in 2009 as the absolute poverty line, emphasizing its constant monetary amount. Table 3.1 presents the

Table 3.1 Poverty lines in urban and rural China

Year	Median income (yuan)		Relative poverty line (yuan)		Absolute poverty line (yuan)	
	Urban	Rural	Urban	Rural	Urban	Rural
1989	1180	1087	295	272	1433	972
1991	1434	980	359	245	1525	1040
1993	2072	1207	518	302	1923	1238
1997	4200	2846	1050	712	3150	1985
2000	5828	3220	1457	805	3115	1934
2004	7650	3727	1913	932	3237	2067
2006	9600	5210	2400	1303	3338	2144
2009	14,600	9595	3650	2399	3650	2399

median income and relative and absolute poverty lines for the sample data by year. In 2009, the median per capita net income of rural residents was RMB9,595 and the absolute poverty line was RMB2,399.

3.3 Poverty and Inequality

3.3.1 Relative Poverty

In accordance with the FGT measurement, the dynamic changes in relative poverty in China's nine provinces between 1989 and 2009 are shown in Table 3.2. Income distribution was very fair in 1989, so the incidence of relative poverty was quite low, at 1.8 percent and 3.0 percent in urban and rural areas, respectively. Urban relative poverty peaked at 13.6 percent in 2004, while rural relative poverty peaked at 19.1 percent in 2006. This was because after 2004, the social security system continued to improve for urban workers and residents, while after 2006, various government transfer payments to rural areas continued to increase, and the minimum living standard guarantee system and the new rural cooperative medical system continued to expand their coverage, all of which were conducive to the improvement of income distribution. After 2006, China also intensified its efforts in development-oriented poverty alleviation in impoverished areas. These policies have worked together to reduce relative poverty.

The poverty gap index is the ratio of the poverty gap to the poverty line, suggesting the depth of poverty. The squared poverty gap index is the ratio of the squared poverty gap to the poverty line, indicating the poverty intensity by assigning a higher weight to the poor. The measurement results of the poverty gap index and squared poverty gap index indicated that the depth and intensity of poverty were higher for rural than

Table 3.2 Dynamic changes in relative poverty in China (1989–2009)

Year	Poverty incidence (P_0)			Poverty gap index (P_1)			Squared poverty gap index (P_2)		
	Urban	Rural	Total	Urban	Rural	Total	Urban	Rural	Total
1989	1.8	3.0	2.3	4.0	5.9	4.7	28.6	96.4	54.2
1991	7.7	13.0	11.3	5.2	9.1	7.8	5.8	13.8	11.2
1993	8.0	13.9	12.0	6.6	9.5	8.6	17.8	12.0	13.8
1997	11.3	14.9	13.7	6.8	10.8	9.5	7.1	17.0	13.9
2000	12.6	15.7	14.7	7.9	9.7	9.1	7.8	12.4	10.9
2004	13.6	17.9	16.5	9.2	14.0	12.4	9.9	28.8	22.4
2006	10.1	19.1	16.1	6.2	13.7	11.2	5.3	21.3	16.0
2009	6.6	13.6	11.4	4.1	10.7	7.6	5.7	104.2	73.0
Change (1989–2009)	4.8	10.6	9.1	0.2	4.8	3.9	−22.9	7.8	18.8

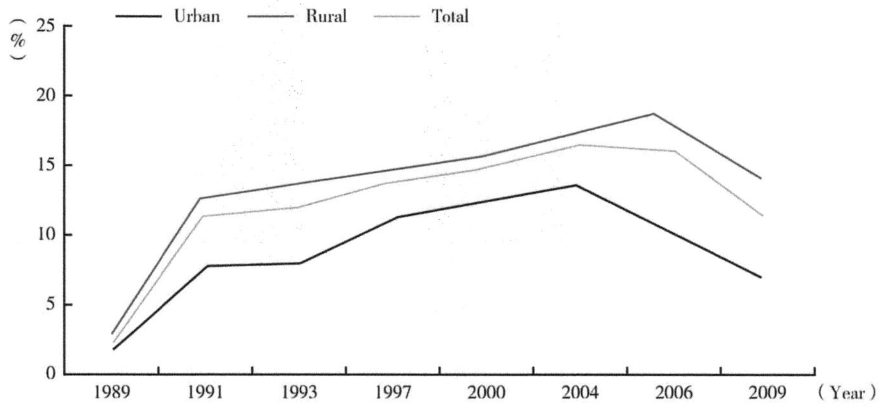

Fig. 3.1 Incidence of relative poverty in urban and rural China (1989–2009)

for urban residents. In particular, the rural poverty gap index was 104.2 in 2009, much higher than in previous years, which could be due to the impact of the 2008 financial crisis.

Figure 3.1 clearly shows the trend in relative poverty over a 20-year period. The incidence of relative poverty shows an inverted U-shaped trend. After rising over a decade, the incidence of relative poverty in urban areas began to decline after 2004 and in rural areas after 2006.

3.3.2 *Absolute Poverty*

Table 3.3 and Fig. 3.2 show the dynamic changes of poverty as measured by the absolute poverty line. Both urban and rural areas have made significant progress in absolute poverty reduction, with the incidence in urban areas falling from 67.9 percent in 1989 to 6.6 percent in 2009 and, correspondingly, from 38.2 percent to 13.6 percent in rural areas. The year 1993 was a turning point in the incidence of absolute poverty in both urban and rural areas. Prior to this, the incidence of absolute poverty was much higher in urban than in rural areas, which agreed with the national conditions in the early 1980s when rural areas were the first to implement the reform and opening-up policy. In the early days of reform and opening up, the income and quality of life for rural residents improved at a much higher rate than for urban residents. After 1993, however, with the advance of industrialization and urbanization, the cities rapidly prospered. Accordingly, absolute poverty among urban dwellers was rapidly reduced, at a faster rate than among their rural counterparts.

Recent studies have revealed that urban poverty is becoming more pronounced. However, it must be noted that since this book adopts the household registration for the division of urban and rural areas, a large number of urban migrant workers are counted as farmers in the measurements. The measurement of absolute urban and

Table 3.3 Dynamic changes of absolute poverty in China (1989–2009)

Year	Poverty incidence (P_0)			Poverty gap index (P_1)			Squared poverty gap index (P_2)		
	Urban	Rural	Total	Urban	Rural	Total	Urban	Rural	Total
1989	67.9	38.2	56.6	21.7	12.3	18.1	11.2	14.5	12.4
1991	55.2	53.1	53.8	22.1	27.5	25.8	13.4	19.5	17.5
1993	45.3	51.1	49.3	19.5	27.3	24.9	13.4	19.6	17.7
1997	34.7	37.4	36.6	17.7	21.0	20.0	12.4	16.6	15.2
2000	22.9	35.1	31.0	13.2	19.0	17.0	10.2	14.5	13.0
2004	19.8	32.2	28.0	12.5	20.1	17.5	10.6	19.6	16.6
2006	13.2	26.5	22.1	7.8	17.3	14.1	6.2	17.7	13.9
2009	6.6	13.6	11.4	4.1	10.7	8.6	5.7	104.2	73.0
Change (1989–2009)	−61.2	−24.6	−45.2	−17.5	−1.7	−9.5	−5.5	89.7	60.6

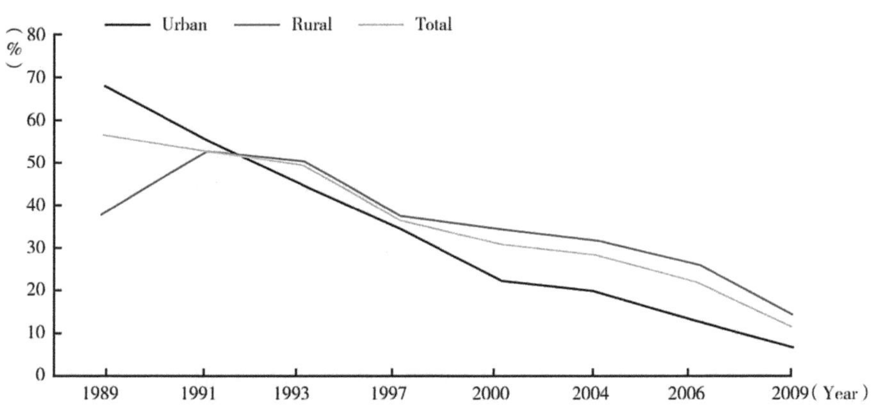

Fig. 3.2 Incidence of absolute poverty in urban and rural China (1989–2009)

rural poverty divided by household registration does not support the conclusion that urban poverty is prominent; rather this should be attributed mainly to the poverty of migrant farmers in cities.

The squared absolute poverty index also shows that the intensity of poverty among rural residents has increased since 2004. This implies that while the absolute poverty headcount is declining rapidly, the remaining poor are finding it increasingly difficult to reduce poverty.

Proposed by Amartya Sen in 1976, the Sen index combines the number, depth of poverty, and the intra-group distribution of the poor population.[5] The SST index is a further modification of the Sen index, which includes the headcount index of

[5] The Sen index is calculated as $P_s = P_0[1-(1-G^P)\frac{\mu^P}{z}]$, where P_0 is the headcount index of poverty, μ^P is the mean income (or consumption) of the poor population, and G^P is the Gini coefficient.

Table 3.4 Other poverty measurement indexes

Year	Sen index			SST index			Watts index		
1993	0.301	0.388	0.364	0.337	0.453	0.415	0.301	0.494	0.434
1997	0.249	0.288	0.276	0.314	0.368	0.349	0.318	0.317	0.318
2000	0.172	0.268	0.236	0.243	0.336	0.305	0.244	0.322	0.296
2004	0.156	0.263	0.228	0.233	0.360	0.318	0.186	0.325	0.278
2006	0.102	0.223	0.282	0.150	0.316	0.262	0.128	0.269	0.222
2009	0.052	0.122	0.100	0.081	0.206	0.167	0.066	0.115	0.099
Change (1989–2009)	−0.313	−0.115	−0.224	−0.258	−0.016	−0.123	−0.216	−0.045	−0.137

poverty, the poverty gap index, and the Gini coefficient of the poverty gap ratio; thus, it can be decomposed according to these three components. The Watts index has the advantage of being distribution sensitive and satisfies the three basic axioms of poverty measurement. The intuitive meaning of the three indexes is unclear but decomposing the contribution of each component leads to a deeper understanding of poverty. Table 3.4 reports the measurement results of the three indexes.

Table 3.5 shows that a higher education level has a positive effect on poverty reduction. In 2009, for instance, the poverty incidence among urban and rural residents with only primary education was 15.4 percent, compared with 0.8 percent for those with post-secondary education and above.

Figure 3.3 shows that poverty incidence declines with age but increases after middle age. In 2009, for instance, the poverty incidence was 22.2 percent among those aged 15–19, much lower at a minimum of 7.1 percent among those aged 45–49, but 16.3 percent among those aged 60–64. Therefore, attention needs to be paid to poverty among the youth and the elderly.

Table 3.5 Incidence of absolute poverty by education level

Year	Primary school	Junior high school	High school	Technical secondary school	College and above	Total
1989	48.0	59.6	61.7	52.0	56.5	56.6
1991	52.6	48.7	44.5	28.3	30.8	53.8
1993	49.2	45.0	37.6	37.6	20.9	49.3
1997	40.8	30.1	20.5	14.3	18.7	36.6
2000	37.3	28.9	12.6	5.3	3.9	31.0
2004	35.5	27.4	16.9	5.3	1.9	28.0
2006	27.2	21.5	11.4	4.2	0.9	22.1
2009	15.4	11.0	4.4	2.9	0.8	11.4
Change (1989–2009)	−32.6	−48.6	−57.3	−49.1	−55.6	−45.2

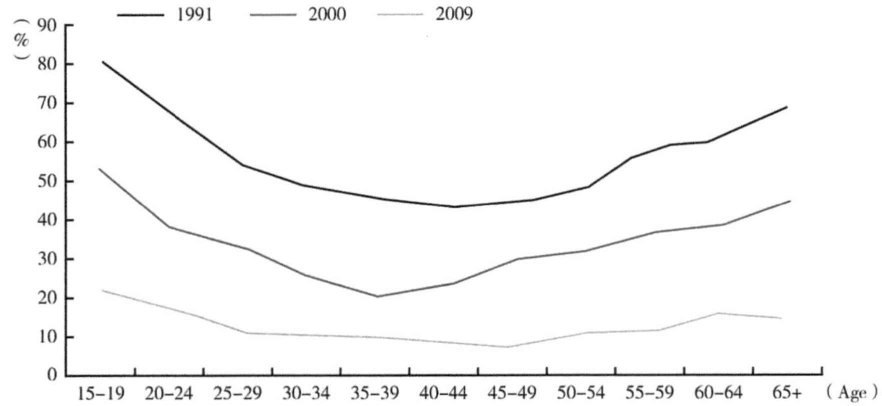

Fig. 3.3 Poverty incidence by age

3.3.3 Inequality

According to the calculations in this book, the Gini coefficients of per capita net income for urban and rural residents increased from 1989 to 2006 but decreased slightly in 2009, peaking in 2006 at 44.35 and 53.69, respectively. Mixing urban and rural areas, the Gini coefficient was 51.19 in 2006, exceeding the internationally accepted warning line (Table 3.6).

The Theil index can be better decomposed to account for the contribution of inequality. Table 3.7 demonstrates that all three Theil indexes significantly elevated between 1989 and 2009. In 2009, for example, Theil's L index of per capita net income for urban and rural residents, namely GE(0), was 50.2, with 56.1 for rural and 34.1 for urban residents, respectively. The decomposition of Theil's L index in 2009 indicated that inequality within groups was the main cause of disparity.

Poverty reduction can be divided into three aspects: income growth, income distribution, and the interaction between the two. Between 1989 and 2009, the incidence of rural poverty decreased by a massive 24.56 percentage points from 38.15 percent to

Table 3.6 Gini coefficient of per capita net income for urban and rural residents

Year	Total	Urban	Rural
1989	36.96	31.94	44.06
1991	41.8	35.06	44.53
1993	47.04	41.23	48.44
1997	45.82	41.98	47.12
2000	47.27	41.43	48.71
2004	49.82	43.13	51.55
2006	51.19	44.35	53.69
2009	48.92	40.92	51.96

Table 3.7 Theil's L index of per capita net income for urban and rural residents and its decomposition

Region	1989			2009		
	GE (0)	GE (1)	GE (2)	GE (0)	GE (1)	GE (2)
Urban	19.5	30.6	112.0	34.1	33.0	61.69
Rural	35.4	52.1	148.69	56.1	57.1	142.7
Intra-group inequality	25.5	39.2	128.0	49.1	47.7	107.3
Inter-group inequality	0.1	0.1	0.1	1.1	1.2	1.2
Total	25.6	39.3	128.1	50.2	48.8	108.6

13.59 percent. The positive effect of income growth decreased the poverty incidence by 36.95 percent, the negative effect of income distribution increased the poverty incidence by 44.68 percent, while the interaction between the two decreased the poverty incidence overall by 32.29 percent (Table 3.8).

The above analysis suggests that the income distribution in 1989–2009 was not conducive to poverty reduction. To further examine the effect of inequality on poverty reduction, Table 3.9 displays the elasticity of inequality to the FGT poverty reduction

Table 3.8 Contribution of growth and distribution to changes in poverty incidence (Unit: percent)

Region	Poverty incidence		Change	Income growth	Income distribution	Interaction
	1989	2009				
Urban	67.89	6.64	−61.25	−67.16	28.53	−22.62
Rural	38.15	13.59	−24.56	−36.95	44.68	−32.29
Total	56.64	11.39	−45.25	−55.50	33.03	−22.78

Table 3.9 Elasticity of inequality to poverty

Year	Poverty incidence (P_0)			Poverty gap index (P_1)			Squared poverty gap index (P_2)		
	Urban	Rural	Total	Urban	Rural	Total	Urban	Rural	Total
1989	0.04	1.68	0.43	1.06	2.89	1.56	1.97	2.80	2.36
1991	0.07	0.20	0.18	1.19	1.40	1.38	5.42	4.69	5.20
1993	0.46	0.48	0.55	1.87	1.69	1.87	2.86	2.81	3.03
1997	0.83	0.92	0.87	2.20	2.59	2.58	3.43	3.83	3.85
2000	1.10	1.23	1.40	3.00	3.19	3.44	4.43	4.51	4.77
2004	1.14	1.62	1.74	4.01	3.62	4.07	3.72	-0.26	0.30
2006	2.42	2.21	2.49	5.33	4.79	5.35	6.81	5.70	6.26
2009	4.24	5.01	5.25	6.58	5.72	6.07	5.69	2.54	2.66

measurement, that is, the elasticity of the Gini coefficient to the poverty incidence (P_0), the poverty gap index (P_1), and the squared poverty gap index (P_2).

The policy implication of the above decomposition results is that, given constant income growth, poverty incidence could have been lower between 1989 and 2009 if income distribution had improved. This suggests that improving income distribution should be a vital policy for achieving poverty reduction in the coming period. Table 3.9 shows that in 2009, for every 1 percentage point increase in the Gini coefficient, urban poverty increased by 4.24 percentage points and rural poverty increased by 5.01 percentage points.

3.4 Growth Rate Curve

The growth rate curve reflects whether the income of the poor is growing at a rate higher than the average social growth rate. If higher, it is called "pro-poor growth," and the reverse applies: a lower rate is not pro-poor. The overall goal of *the Outline for Development-oriented Poverty Reduction in China's Rural Areas (2011–2020)* was that "By the year 2020, rural poor populations will have no concerns about food and clothing and will be guaranteed compulsory education, basic medical services, and housing. The per capita disposable income of farmers in impoverished areas will grow at a rate higher than the national average, and the indicators in major areas of basic public services will be close to the national average, reversing the trend of widening development gaps." From a national perspective, this *Outline* proposed that the growth rate of per capita net income of farmers in impoverished areas should be higher than the national average, which would be deemed "growth of pro-impoverished areas."

In the current national conditions, not only is there a wide development gap between regions but the gap within rural areas is also widening. The calculations of the Gini coefficient of per capita net income and the Theil index for rural residents in this book reveal a large gap within rural areas. To reverse the widening trend of income disparity in these areas, there is a need to promote "pro-poor growth." The growth rate curve clearly displays whether the growth is pro-poor.

Figure 3.4 shows the growth rate curve of the per capita net income of rural residents calculated using data from 1989 to 2009, with the horizontal axis indicating the percentage of per capita net income from low to high and the vertical axis the corresponding growth rate of per capita net income. It is clear that the poorer the population, the lower the income growth rate when compared to the average. This suggests that the income growth rate of the poor population was lower than the average in that 20-year period.

China has implemented numerous policies to strengthen agriculture and benefit farmers and has increased direct subsidies to farmers since 2006. Moreover, the government has raised financial investment in development-oriented poverty alleviation in rural areas. In 2007, the State Council decided to establish a rural minimum living standard guarantee system nationwide. To examine whether these policies

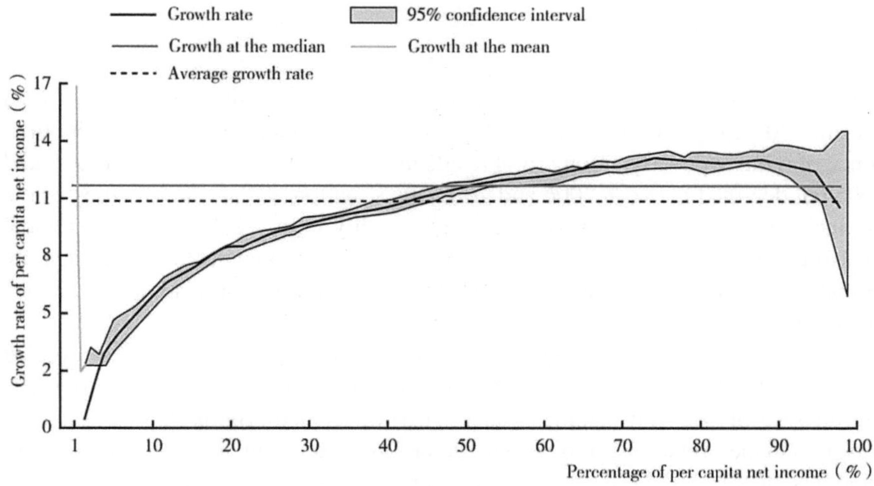

Fig. 3.4 Growth rate curve of net income of rural residents in 1989–2009

have succeeded in directly improving income growth for the poor, this book plots the growth rate curve of per capita net income of rural residents between 2006 and 2009 (Fig. 3.5). The results clearly show that the growth rate of per capita net income of the poor was higher than the average, revealing that the aforementioned policies implemented by the government for impoverished areas and poor populations were effective.

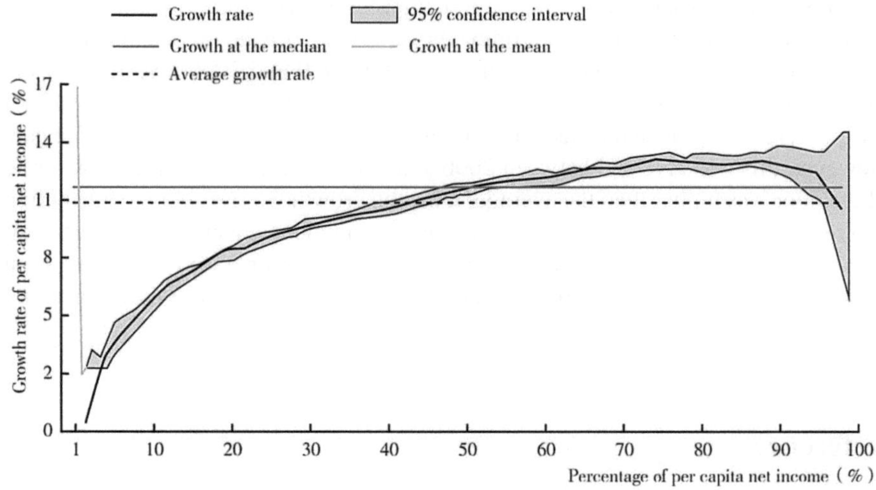

Fig. 3.5 Growth rate curve of per capita net income of rural residents in 2006–2009

3.5 Conclusion

This chapter analyzed the dynamic changes of poverty in urban and rural China over the 20-year period between 1989 and 2009. The results suggest that the incidence of relative poverty among rural residents increased steadily between 1989 and 2006 but declined between 2006 and 2009; the situation was similar in cities where the incidence of relative poverty increased steadily until 2004 and then declined. Measurements of absolute poverty showed that incidence had declined significantly in both urban and rural areas. Therefore, China has made significant achievements in its elimination.

An analysis from two demographic characteristics, education and age, revealed that the higher the level of education, the lower the incidence of absolute poverty. The analysis of data from samples over 16 years of age in this book showed that there was a U-shaped relationship between age and poverty incidence, with the poverty incidence decreasing with age but increasing after reaching middle age.

The Gini coefficient showed that between 1989 and 2009, urban and rural income inequality peaked in 2006 at 44.35 and 53.69, respectively, and declined slightly in 2009. This suggests that the pressure to improve income distribution remained intense. The Theil L index likewise indicated the presence of inequality, and decomposition of this index revealed that inequality in income distribution within rural areas contributed predominantly to the disparity in income distribution between urban and rural areas, whereas this was less so between urban and rural areas.

The elasticity of the Gini coefficient to poverty incidence demonstrated that, in 2009, an increase of 1 percentage point in the Gini coefficient would have increased the poverty incidence by 4.24 and 5.01 percentage points, respectively, for urban and rural residents. Thus, in the coming period, improving income distribution should be regarded as a foremost policy to promote poverty reduction and reduce inequality.

The analysis of the growth rate curve between 1989 and 2006 revealed that the income growth rate of the poor was lower than the average; thus, the growth was not pro-poor, resulting in an increase in the Gini coefficient and a widening income gap. However, this was reversed between 2006 and 2009, where the income growth rate of the poor was higher than the average; thus, the growth was pro-poor, contributing to a reduction in the Gini coefficient and a narrowing income gap. This, in part, is an indication that after 2006, both the rural development-oriented poverty alleviation policy to strengthen agriculture and benefit farmers and the rural minimum living standard guarantee system played a positive role.

Reference

Haughton J., & Khandker, S.R. (2009). *Handbook on poverty and inequality*. The World Bank.

Chapter 4
Multidimensional Poverty Measurement of China

As the Chinese term "*pinkun*" (literally "poverty"), which comprises both "*pin*" (literally "insufficiency") and "*kun*" (literally "hardship"), conveys, poverty is multidimensional. Usually, we can measure "poverty" by income. However, there has been little discussion on the meaning of "hardship" and its measures. Chapter Three adopted the FGT method to measure income poverty in China over a 20 year period, while this chapter uses the multidimensional poverty Alkire-Foster (AF) method to measure "hardship." Chapter Four will examine the relationship between income poverty and multidimensional poverty in China.

4.1 Literature Review

4.1.1 International Research

In 1983, Atkinson and Bourguignon studied multidimensional comparisons of economic inequality;[1] in 1985, Amartya Sen systematically articulated the "capabilities approach" in *Commodities and Capabilities.* In the capabilities approach, Sen expanded five crucial aspects of human development and improvement in quality of life that have long been left out of traditional welfare economics: (1) Consider the importance of real freedom when assessing a person's strengths, (2) individuals differ in their ability to convert the resources they possess into activities of value that they can realize, (3) activities that produce happiness are multifaceted, (4) balance between material and immaterial factors when assessing human well-being, and (5) care about the distribution of opportunities within society.[2] In the capabilities approach, which is the theoretical basis for multidimensional poverty measurement, emphasis is placed

[1] Atkinson and Bourguignon (1983).

[2] Sen (1985).

© Social Sciences Academic Press 2022

X. Wang, *Multidimensional Poverty Measurement*,
International Research on Poverty Reduction,
https://doi.org/10.1007/978-981-19-1189-7_4

on key elements that contribute to the improvement of quality of life, such as "extension of real freedom," "multidimensionality," "individual differences in capabilities," "material (objective) and immaterial (subjective)," and "opportunities."

In 1986, Esfandiar discussed the multidimensional measurement and decomposition of inequality.[3] In 1990, the Human Development Report (HDR) team, with Amartya Sen on board, wrote and published the HDR1990. The report clearly stated that people are the real wealth of a nation and the basic goal of development was to create a living environment for people to enjoy longevity, health, and creativity. The report released the Human Development Index (HDI) within the framework of the capabilities approach.

In 1993, Nussbaum traced the ideas in *The Theory of Moral Sentiments* in her article, "Non-Relative Virtues: An Aristotelian Approach." Following the capabilities approach proposed by Amartya Sen, she set out to construct a list of basic capabilities for human development (pp. 242–269)[4] and, in 2000, proposed 10 capabilities. (1) Life. To be able to live a normal life expectancy, without either dying or ending life prematurely because it is not worth living. (2) Physical health. To have good health, including reproductive health, adequate nutrition, and proper housing. (3) Physically healthy. To be able to move freely; to be free from violence, including sexual assault and domestic violence; and to have access to sexual gratification and reproduction-related choices. (4) Reason, imagination, and thinking. To be able to sensibly imagine, think, and act in a "truly human" way. This characteristic features decent education, including but not limited to literacy, basic math, and science training. This involves being able to imagine and think in relation to productive work and to make their own religious, literary, and musical choices; ensure freedom of expression in political and artistic speech; and enjoy pleasant experiences and avoid suffering. (5) Emotions. To have emotional attachments with outside affairs and people, to love those who love and care for us, and to grieve in their absence. (6) Practical reasoning. To be able to form worthy ideas and reflect critically on one's own life plans. (7) Friendship. To be able to live with others, be aware of and care about the existence of others, and engage in a great deal of social interaction and to have a social foundation for self-respect and be free from discrimination on the grounds of race, gender, sexual orientation, ethnicity, caste, or religion. (8) Other species. To be able to coexist with animals, plants, and nature. (9) Recreation. To be able to enjoy recreational activities. (10) To have control over one's own environment. Politically, to be able to participate in political activities and having the freedom of speech and assembly. Materially, to be able to own property (land and movable property) and have the same property rights as others; to live in a political environment which has fair employment rights; to be free from unfounded searches and seizures; and to be able to work as a human being and establish meaningful and mutually recognized relationships with others (Nussbaum, 2000).[5]

---

[3] Esfandiar (1986).

[4] Nussbaum (1993).

[5] Nussbaum (2000).

Alkire (2002) conducted a more thorough discussion of the dimension of human development, arguing that if human development is "multidimensional," the latter's meaning needs to be clarified. She provided a systematic review of existing discussions of "dimensions" in poverty research, cross-cultural psychology, moral philosophy, quality of life indicators, participatory development, and basic needs theory (pp. 181–205).[6] In 2003, Bourguignon and Chakravarty discussed in detail the measurement of multidimensional poverty and its mathematical properties, which is referred to as the "Bourguignon-Chakravarty approach" in this book.

Launched by Amartya Sen, the Oxford Poverty and Human Development Initiative (OPHI) was founded in May 2007 in the Department of International Development, at the University of Oxford. Alkire served as the Director of OPHI and built a research team dedicated to multidimensional poverty measurement. She argued that the measurement of multidimensional poverty along with the capabilities approach can provide more accurate information and facilitate the reduction of people's capability deprivation (Alkire & Foster, 2007a).[7] In 2007, Alkire and Foster published a working paper, "*Counting and Multidimensional Poverty Measurement*," and proposed the "Alkire-Foster method" for calculating the multidimensional poverty index (MPI),[8] which is referred to as the "AF method."

The *HDR 2010* of the United Nations Development Programme (UNDP) officially released the MPI for 104 developing countries, which was measured by Alkire's research team. In 2011, the *HDR* increased this to 109 countries. The MPI consists of 10 indicators in three dimensions: education, health, and standard of living. The index captures multiple dimensions of deprivation that exist simultaneously for individuals or households (UNDP, 2011).[9] Moreover, the index can be decomposed by region, dimension, and indicator, assisting policymakers in identifying areas for priority intervention under the 10 deprivation indicators. The MPI is a crucial complement to the traditional poverty measurement by income or consumption as well as to the HDI, contributing to a more comprehensive understanding of poverty. In 2011, Nussbaumer et al. applied the AF method to construct a multidimensional energy poverty index to measure energy poverty in several African countries (p. 42).[10] In 2011, Alkire and Roche applied the AF method to child poverty measurement (p. 45).[11] In 2012, the United Nations Children's Fund (UNICEF) examined child poverty from a multidimensional poverty perspective in *Child Poverty and Inequality: New Perspectives* (Ortiz et al., 2012).[12] In 2013, Alkire founded the "Multidimensional Poverty Peer Network (MPPN)" at the University of Oxford, which was committed to, first, improving the global multidimensional poverty index; second, providing technical support for countries in the development of national multidimensional poverty

---

[6] Alkire (2002).

[7] Alkire and Foster (2007a).

[8] Alkire and Foster (2007b).

[9] UNDP (2011).

[10] Nussbaumer et al. (2011).

[11] Alkire and Roche (2011).

[12] Ortiz et al. (2012).

indexes; and third, developing an MPI that reflects the Sustainable Development Goals set by the United Nations in the 2030 Agenda.[13]

Since 2011, President Santos of Colombia has personally promoted the application of the MPI in Colombia's national anti-poverty strategy, spearheading the development of the Colombian Multidimensional Poverty Index (C-MPI). The C-MPI comprises 15 indicators in 5 dimensions: education, childhood and youth conditions, employment, health, and access to public facilities and housing conditions. Based on the C-MPI, the Colombian government has formulated multisector public policies to implement targeted poverty reduction and alleviation in various dimensions and has achieved good results in poverty reduction.[14] In Mexico, in accordance with the legal requirements to guarantee the economic welfare and social rights of citizens, the *Independent Commission for the Evaluation of Social Policies* has invited national and international experts to analyze the main challenges of poverty reduction and social development throughout the country. They have conducted repeated discussions on the dimensions and indicators for identifying multidimensional poverty and have finally confirmed the dimensions, indicators, criteria, and weights for accurately identifying poverty, as well as its classification, by carrying out poverty identification every two years. Subject to *Mexico's General Law on Social Development*, the Mexican Multidimensional Poverty Index (M-MPI) includes eight dimensions: educational gap, health services, social security, basic housing services, housing quality, food, per capita income, and social integration. These are divided into two categories: economic welfare, which includes per capita income, and social rights, which includes the other seven dimensions, all of which are given equal weight (Wang, 2014).[15] In terms of the setting of C-MPI and M-MPI, large differences exist between countries. This is the strength of the MPI as it can be tailored to a country's stage of development and to the core concerns of national public policy. More than 40 countries worldwide have developed or are developing national MPIs appropriate to their stage of development.

4.1.2 Chinese Research

The research on multidimensional poverty in China is primarily an application of foreign multidimensional poverty methods. Shang and Yao (2005) discussed the measurement of multidimensional poverty using the "Bourguignon-Chakravarty" method; set equal weights on life expectancy, adult literacy rate, and GDP per capita as used in the HDI; and measured and compared poverty in Africa, Asia, North America, Oceania, South America, and Europe between 1998 and 2000. Zhang and Chen (2006) introduced five multidimensional poverty measures from abroad.[16]

[13] See http://www.mppn.org for details.

[14] Angulo (2016).

[15] Wang (2014).

[16] Zhang and Chen (2006).

Chen (2008) used the Watts MPI to measure multidimensional poverty in China in the dimensions of income, knowledge, and health and performed the Shapley decomposition.[17] On October 17, 2008, at the High-Level Forum on Poverty Reduction and Development, Hu stated that the deprivation of abilities, rights, and benefits was at the core of poverty (Hu, 2008). Poverty is not just income poverty but a multidimensional phenomenon that can be classified into four types: income, human, knowledge, and ecological poverty.[18]

Using the AF method, Wang and Alkire (2009) measured multidimensional poverty in China with data from the *CHNS 2006* and performed regional, dimensional, and urban-rural decompositions.[19] The results showed that both urban and rural households in China had multidimensional poverty beyond the income dimension; 19.8% of urban and rural households had poverty in any 3 of the 8 indicators beyond income. In 2009, Cao and Wang organized and implemented a multidimensional poverty survey of rural households in 13 counties in Aba Prefecture and applied the multidimensional poverty analytical framework to analyze poverty in particular types of impoverished areas in China. The book *Multidimensional Poverty Measurement and Intervention in Special Types of Impoverished Areas* was published in 2011, detailing the deprivation of such dimensions as income/consumption, education and health, asset poverty, sanitation, and vulnerability among rural households in Aba Prefecture. Following this analytical framework, Li (2010) carried out a poverty analysis of such dimensions as income, consumption, sanitation, education and health, and vulnerability for rural households in 30 poor counties in S Province.[20] Using the multidimensional poverty analytical framework, Wang (2011) performed a poverty analysis of dimensions such as drinking water for children, cooking fuels, and sanitation, using data from a survey of children in child welfare demonstration areas in five provinces in China.[21] Wang and Zhou (2015b, pp. 109–193) applied the AF method to measure and examine multidimensional child poverty in China.[22]

Zou and Fang measured dynamic multidimensional poverty using the AF method and data from the *CHNS*.[23] Ye and Wang (2010) conducted a literature review on the progress of multidimensional poverty measurement.[24] Between 2010 and 2011, as a technical advisor for the World Bank's TCC5 "*Study on Shanxi Fiscal Support to Agriculture and Poverty Reduction Policy Effects*," the author guided the research team to conduct an analysis using the multidimensional poverty analytical framework to measure poverty in 35 national key counties for development-oriented poverty alleviation in Shanxi. A member of the research team, Guo (2012),

---

[17] Chen (2008).

[18] Hu (2008).

[19] Wang and Alkire (2009).

[20] Li (2010).

[21] Wang (2011).

[22] Wang and Zhou (2015b).

[23] Zou and Fang (2011).

[24] Ye and Wang (2010).

published "*Multidimensional Poverty Levels and Characteristics of Rural Households*,"[25] and Sun et al. (2012) published "*Research on Poverty Measurement of Rural Residents in China—A Case Study of Shanxi*."[26] Shang and Wang (2012) used the multidimensional poverty analytical framework to examine child poverty in China.[27]

Between 2012 and 2015, with the support of the National Science and Technology Support Program, Wang et al. developed GIS software for multidimensional poverty measurement.[28] In 2015, Zhang measured the dynamic changes of multidimensional poverty in China.[29] In 2016, Wang et al. investigated the relationship between income poverty and multidimensional poverty in China.[30] An increasing number of Chinese scholars are engaged in the research into multidimensional poverty measurement, which will promote the establishment of more comprehensive poverty evaluation criteria in China.

Since 2013, China's development-oriented poverty alleviation strategies and policies have undergone major adjustments. The central government has proposed the implementation of a targeted poverty alleviation strategy that is required to replace the previous mechanism of targeting regional poverty (e.g., concentrated, contiguous extremely poor areas, poor counties, and poor villages) with a specific poverty alleviation mechanism that directly targets the poor. The Chinese government's goal for poverty eradication by 2020 was set as "The rural poor under the current standards will be lifted out of poverty" and "Rural poor populations will have no concerns about food and clothing and will be guaranteed compulsory education, basic medical services, and housing,"[31] indicating that the goal of poverty reduction has been defined as multidimensional in government policy. In accordance with the central government's requirements, every household in poverty has been registered and recorded in the information system. In this process, as rural residents derive most of their income from agriculture and informal employment, which is difficult to accurately calculate, local governments have developed a multidimensional poverty indicator system that comprehensively evaluates income, education, sanitation, housing, assets, and other production and living conditions to identify the poor population more objectively. However, China has yet to develop a national multidimensional poverty index.

In summary, multidimensional poverty is moving from theory to application. Nevertheless, due to the lack of data, the MPI, which is currently widely measured, only comprises material dimensions, whereas major non-material dimensions that

[25] Guo (2012).

[26] Sun et al. (2012).

[27] Shang and Wang (2012).

[28] Wang et al. (2015a).

[29] Zhang (2015).

[30] Wang et al. (2016).

[31] The national principle for poverty alleviation was RMB2,300 (in constant prices) of per capita net income of rural residents in 2010. See *The CPC Central Committee and the State Council's Decision on Winning the Battle Against Poverty*, 2015.

affect quality of life have not been studied. With respect to material dimensions, assets as a major measure of chronic poverty and the ability of poverty relief have not been included in the MPI in the *HDR*. In China, the MPI has been extensively and thoroughly studied, the multidimensional poverty indicator system has been widely used at grassroots level to identify the poor, and the central government has made it clear that the goal of poverty reduction is multidimensional, with the exception of the lack of an officially published composite index that identifies and aggregates multidimensional poverty.

4.2 AF Method

The AF method, developed by Alkire and Foster (2007a, b) and adopted by the UNDP, is the most established and widely used among various multidimensional poverty measures. An in-depth discussion of the AF method can be found in Alkire and Foster (2007a, b). In this book, the method is summarized in five steps: the welfare achievement of each dimension, identification of poverty for each dimension, aggregation of multiple dimensions, setting of weights for the aggregation, and decomposition, which are briefly described as follows.

(1) Welfare achievement of each dimension. $M^{n,d}$ represents an $n \times d$ dimensional matrix, and the matrix element $y \in M^{n,d}$ represents the value obtained by n individuals in d different dimensions. In the formula, any element y_{ij} in y denotes the value taken by individual i in dimension j, $i = 1, 2, \ldots, n$; $j = 1, 2, \ldots, d$.

The row vector $y_i = (y_{i1}, y_{i2}, \ldots, y_{id})$ includes the values of individual i in all dimensions. Similarly, the column vector $y_j = (y_{1j}, y_{2j}, \ldots, y_{nj})$ represents the distribution of values for different individuals of dimension j.

(2) Poverty identification

i. Poverty identification of each dimension. z_j ($z_j > 0$) indicates the cut-off value or poverty line of deprivation for the j dimension.

For any matrix y, a deprivation matrix can be defined as $g^0 = \left[g_{ij}^0\right]$, whose typical element g_{ij}^0 is defined as when $y_{ij} < z_j$, $g_{ij}^0 = 1$, and when $y_{ij} \geq z_j$, $g_{ij}^0 = 0$. The ij-th element is assigned a value of 1 when an individual i is poor in the j-th dimension (e.g., years of schooling) and a value of 0 when the individual is not poor in that dimension. Specifically, the cut-off z_j of an adult's years of schooling (j) can be set at 5. If individual i has 8 years of schooling, $y_{ij} = 8 > z_j = 5$, $g_{ij}^0 = 0$; if the individual has 4 years of schooling, $g_{ij}^0 = 1$.

For this deprivation matrix g^0, a column vector can be defined to represent the total dimensions of poverty suffered by individual i, that is, the value of the i-th element i-th is $c_i = \left|g_i^0\right|$.

ii. Identification of multiple dimensions (k) of deprivation. Each element of the above deprivation matrix $g^0 = \left[g^0_{ij}\right]$ represents whether there is deprivation for each individual in each dimension, which is a single-dimensional method. A multi-dimensional method is introduced below, that is, whether deprivation exists for the individual when k dimensions are considered simultaneously. Assuming that the total of the dimensions measured is 9, $k \geq 1/3$ means that the individual is deprived of any 1/3 of the total dimensions at the same time.

$k = 1, \ldots, d$. ρ_k is a function of identifying the poor when considering k dimensions: $\rho_k\ (y_i; z) = 1$ when $c_i \geq k$, and $\rho_k\ (y_i; z) = 0$ when $c_i < k$. ρ_k defines individual i as poor when the total dimensions of deprivation c_i are greater than or equal to k; otherwise, ρ_k defines individual i as non-poor in dimension k when the total dimensions of deprivation c_i are less than k. Thus, ρ_k is influenced both by z_j (deprivation within dimensions) and c_i (deprivation across dimensions) and thus called the dual cut-off method. ρ_k includes two extreme values: when $k = 1$, namely the union method, it is considered deprived as long as there is deprivation of any one dimension out of d dimensions, which is the most strict definition of multidimensional poverty; when $k = d$, namely, the intersection method, it is considered deprived in d dimensions only when there is deprivation in all dimensions, which is the most lenient definition of multidimensional poverty. Generally, the dimensions of multidimensional identification are between the extreme values 1 and d.

(3) Aggregation of poverty. After identifying the deprivation in various dimensions, the latter need to be aggregated to obtain a multidimensional composite index. The simplest aggregation method is the multidimensional poverty incidence (H) on a headcount basis. That is, (H): $H = H\ (y; z)$; $H = q/n$, where q is the number of individuals in poverty below z_k (i.e., the number of individuals with k dimensions of poverty). This method is known as the Foster-Greer-Thorbecke (FGT) method which, although simple and straightforward, is insensitive to the distribution of poverty and the depth of deprivation.

To overcome the shortcomings of the FGT method, Alkire and Foster (2007a, b) proposed a new measure of multidimensional poverty that modified the FGT. The formula is as follows:

$$M_0(y; z) = \mu\left[g^0(k)\right] = HA \tag{4.1}$$

M_0 is the adjusted multidimensional poverty index and consists of two components: H (poverty incidence) and A (average share of deprivation), where $A = |c(k)|\big/(qd)$.

M_0 in Formula (4.1) is further adjusted using average poverty gap (G), leading to the following:

$$M_1 = \mu\left[g^1(k)\right] = HAG \tag{4.2}$$

In Formula (4.2), $G = \left|g^1(k)\right| / \left|g^0(k)\right|,\ \ g_{ij}^1 = \left(z_j - yij\right)/zj.$

If M_0 is adjusted using the average severity of poverty (S), then

$$M_2 = \mu\left[g^2(k)\right] = HAS \tag{4.3}$$

In Formula (4.3), $S = \left|g^2(k)\right| \Big/ \left|g^0(k)\right|,\ \ g_{ij}^2 = \left(g_{ij}^1\right)^2.$

In summary, the multidimensional poverty index takes different forms such as M_0, M_1, and M_2, which can be chosen as needed in practice.

(4) Weight. Another issue to consider when aggregating dimensions is the weight of each dimension. Equal weights are used in the current HDR. The setting of weights is a controversial issue in MPI. Many experts have argued that it is impossible to determine which dimension was more important for human development, education, or health. Therefore, equal weights are often used, but they are too simplistic. In academic research, entropy weight method has been used, but in practice, it is difficult for policymakers to accept such a sophisticated method.

(5) Decomposition. The MPI can be decomposed by dimensions, regions, and provinces. Taking the decomposition by regions (urban and rural) as an example, u denotes the urban data matrix and r the rural data matrix, then

$$M(u, r; z) = \frac{n(u)}{n(u, r)} M(u; z) + \frac{n(r)}{n(u, r)} M(r; z) \tag{4.4}$$

4.3 Dimensions and Indicators Setting

4.3.1 Dimensions Setting

The MPI captures the number of people in multidimensional poverty (the share of people in multidimensional poverty) and the average number of deprivations suffered by each multidimensionally poor household (the poverty level). In the *HDR 2010* released by the UNDP, the MPI was calculated for 104 developing countries worldwide using three dimensions (health, education, and standard of living) with a total of 10 indicators. The health dimension is comprised of two indicators: nutrition and child mortality. The education dimension includes years of schooling for adults and school attendance for children. The standard of living covers six indicators: cooking fuels, toilets, drinking water, electricity, housing flooring, and assets.

The analytical framework used in this book consists of 10 indicators in four dimensions: health, education, assets, and standard of living, that is, assets have been added as a dimension in response to China's experience of poverty reduction. The dimension of assets contains indicators of both productive assets and housing. Assets exhibit a household's wealth after years of income accumulation and consumption smoothing.

Productive assets more accurately display whether a family is in chronic poverty and its ability to eliminate poverty. Housing can be acquired through inheritance, transfer, and conversion, which better reflects the social status of a family or an individual. The *Outline for Development-oriented Poverty Reduction in China's Rural Areas (2011–2020)* clearly states that "the overall goal of China's development-oriented poverty alleviation work in the next decade is that: By the year 2020, poor populations will have no concerns about food and clothing and will be guaranteed compulsory education, basic medical services, and housing." It is thus essential to include housing in the analysis of multidimensional poverty. In this chapter, two circumstances in the category of housing are regarded as the poverty alleviation: First is owning one's own house, regardless of the form in which it is acquired, such as purchase, planned allocation, inheritance, or transfer. Second, given the reality of more mobile people renting (some rent large apartments, while others live in crowded shantytowns with their families), a housing area per capita greater than 9 m^2 is seen as poverty alleviation in the housing dimension or category. This definition considers the availability of data, despite the difference between this housing indicator and the national goal of ensuring housing security.

On the whole, the inclusion of assets in multidimensional poverty analysis is a vital dimensional expansion of the multidimensional poverty analytical framework used in the *Human Development Reports* 2010 and 2011. This dimension reveals the multidimensional poverty status of the poor in greater depth, providing a reliable basis for government to formulate asset accumulation policies for poor households. More importantly, it takes into account the poverty reduction target of housing security designed by the Chinese government.

4.3.2 Interpretation of Indicators

Since this book uses data from the *CHNS 2009*, the design of the indicators for each dimension considers the availability of data. Table 4.1 shows the cut-off values for each indicator.

Table 4.1 Setting of 10 indicators in the four dimensions of Chinese MPI

Dimension	Indicator	Cut-off value
Education	Years of schooling for adults	Over 5 years of schooling
	School attendance for children	Children aged 6–16 in school
Health	Health insurance	With any kind of health insurance

(continued)

Table 4.1 (continued)

Dimension	Indicator	Cut-off value
Assets	Productive assets	One means of transportation, agricultural machinery, or household commercial equipment in the house. Transportation includes tricycles, bicycles, motorcycles, and automobiles. Agricultural machinery includes tractors of any size, walking tractors, irrigation equipment, electric threshers, and domestic water pumps. Household commercial equipment includes cookers, woodworking appliances, hairdressing utensils, metal shop utensils and equipment, and other apparatus which may be used in a commercial business
	Housing	Self-owned housing or a housing area per capita greater than 9 m^2
Standard of living	Drinking water	By type of water source, groundwater (more than 5 m) or water plant
	Sanitation	Indoor flushing or outdoor flushing public toilets
	Electricity	Electricity in the house
	Cooking fuels	Use of modern fuels such as electricity, liquefied gas, or natural gas
	Consumer durables	Any durable goods such as VCR, color TV washing machine, refrigerator, air conditioner, computer, camera, telephone, mobile phone, VCD/DVD, or satellite receiver in the house

The unit of analysis in this book is the household, with a valid observed value of 6,295 households and 30,471 people in 2009. The sample data cover nine provinces and regions: Liaoning, Heilongjiang, Jiangsu, Shandong, Henan, Hubei, Hunan, Guangxi, and Guizhou.[32]

4.4 Estimation of Multidimensional Poverty

4.4.1 Multidimensional Poverty Index

Using the 2009 household survey data from nine provinces in China and the multidimensional poverty AF method in this book, the estimated results of multidimensional

[32] The author extends thanks to the Carolina Population Center at the University of North Carolina and the Chinese Center for Disease Control and Prevention for providing the data.

Table 4.2 Estimation of multidimensional poverty in China

k	MPI (M_0)	Poverty incidence (H, %)	Deprivation intensity (A, %)
1	0.093	56.0	16.6
2	0.058	21.4	27.2
3	0.034	9.1	37.0
4	0.019	4.0	45.9
5	0.009	1.7	54.1

poverty in China are shown in Table 4.2. In terms of the poverty of any one of the 10 indicators in the 4 dimensions, the national poverty incidence (H) was 56.0%, the deprivation intensity 16.6%, and the MPI (M_0) 0.093. Concerning the poverty of any three of the 10 indicators, the national poverty incidence (H) was 9.1%, deprivation intensity (A) 37.0%, and the MPI (M_0) 0.034.

4.4.2 MPI Decomposition

(1) Decomposition by indicators. Table 4.3 presents the MPI (M_0) at different values of k and the poverty contribution rate of 10 indicators in 4 dimensions at a given value of k. When $k = 3$, the MPI is 0.034. Sanitation makes the largest contribution to the MPI at 24.0%, followed by health insurance at 17.3%, consumer durables at 16.8%, productive assets at 12.4%, modern fuels at 12.3%, and years of schooling for adults at 7.8%.

The policy implications of this result are clear, suggesting that the policy objectives for urban and rural poverty reduction in China in 2009 should be as follows: first, address the sanitation of households; second, increase the health insurance coverage of residents; third, raise the consumption level of consumer durables in both urban and rural areas; fourth, innovate policies for the accumulation of productive assets and encourage households to make productive investments, enhancing their ability to eliminate poverty and increase wealth; fifth, modernize cooking fuels, reducing the use of animal dung and crop residues as well as increasing the use of modern domestic fuels to reduce carbon emissions and protect the ecological environment; sixth, reinforce vocational education, employment training, and skills training for adults to improve the human capital of the existing workforce.

(2) Urban-rural decomposition. Among the sample households in the 2009 survey, the urban population accounted for 34.2% and the rural population 67.54%. By weighting the MPI by urban and rural population and then decomposing it, the urban and rural contributions to multidimensional poverty at different k-values were obtained, as shown in Table 4.4.

Table 4.3 MPI by indicators

k	M_0	Education		Health	Assets		Standard of living				
		Adult education	Child education	Health insurance	Productive assets	Housing	Drinking water	Sanitation	Electricity	Modern fuels	Durables
1	0.093	4.7	1.6	14.0	11.4	1.9	2.4	46.3	0.5	9.6	7.6
2	0.058	6.6	1.8	17.9	12.2	2.1	3.5	30.7	0.8	12.8	11.7
3	0.034	7.8	1.7	17.3	12.4	1.9	4.5	24.0	1.3	12.3	16.8
4	0.019	8.7	1.5	15.5	12.1	2.2	6.1	20.6	2.2	12.8	18.2
5	0.009	9.9	1.0	14.1	12.9	2.6	7.9	18.3	4.0	12.2	16.9

Unit: %

Table 4.4 Multidimensional poverty incidence and MPI decomposed by urban and rural areas

k	Poverty incidence	Contribution rate (%)		MPI (M_0)	Contribution rate (%)	
		Urban	Rural		Urban	Rural
1	56.0	28.5	71.5	0.093	27.1	72.9
2	21.4	27.6	72.4	0.058	25.9	74.1
3	9.1	24.2	75.8	0.034	22.8	77.2
4	4.0	18.9	81.1	0.019	18.1	81.9
5	1.7	15.1	84.9	0.009	14.5	85.5

When $k = 3$, the poverty incidence was 9.1% and the MPI (M_0) was 0.034. The rural and urban contribution rates to the poverty incidence were 75.8% and 24.2%, respectively, and to the MPI (M_0) were 77.2% and 22.8%, respectively. The results revealed that the rural contribution rate to the MPI increased due to the increase in the selected dimensions and indicators. When $k = 5$, the contribution rate of rural poverty to multidimensional poverty was 85.5% and that of urban poverty was 14.5%.

4.5 Conclusion and Discussion

This chapter conducted a systematic literature review on the theory and measures of multidimensional poverty which provide a more accurate picture of the welfare deprivation of the poor than the traditional definition and measurement of poverty by income. This book incorporates assets as a crucial dimension into the multidimensional poverty analytical framework and uses the AF multidimensional poverty measure and data from the *CHNS 2009* to measure multidimensional poverty among urban and rural households in China. The measurement results indicated the following:

(1) Both urban and rural households in China suffered from multidimensional poverty besides the income dimension; 9.1% of households in both urban and rural areas suffered from any 3 of the 10 indicators in the 4 dimensions of poverty over and above the income dimension. Thus, the identification and targeting of the poor in China's new 10-year development-oriented poverty alleviation strategy (2011–2020) should be carried out from a multidimensional perspective.

(2) At the national level, the five indicators of sanitation, health insurance, consumer durables, productive assets, and modern fuels contributed the most to the MPI in 2009. Sanitation is a significant aspect of the UN's Millennium Development Goals (MDGs). Policies in place in China have paid adequate attention to rural drinking water, which has seen a marked decline in its poverty but little to sanitation. As stated by General Secretary Xi Jinping in 2015 during

a visit to rural households in Yanbian, Jilin Province, with the accelerating pace of agricultural modernization, new rural construction should also advance, and a "toilet revolution" was needed to provide rural people with sanitary toilets. To date, however, sanitary toilets have not been clearly set as a national target for poverty reduction. When formulating poverty alleviation policies, there is a need to raise awareness of the importance of sanitary toilets and include the indicator of sanitary toilets in rural poverty alleviation targets as soon as possible. Consumer durables can better demonstrate people's quality of life, and the future consumption capacity of households in consumer durables needs improvement. Productive assets are an essential resource for households to eliminate poverty, and China will need to innovate policies on the accumulation of productive assets. It is also important to encourage the use of modern fuels to reduce environmental damage.

(3) The contribution of rural poverty to the national MPI was significantly higher than that of urban poverty. While anti-poverty policies should prioritize rural areas, the contribution of urban poverty indicates that China should intensify urban poverty interventions. In particular, effective identification and targeting policies are needed for the multidimensionally poor among the 250 million migrant population.

(4) China has to establish a composite poverty indicator, or national MPI, that accurately reflects the multidimensional poverty reduction targets set by the national poverty reduction strategy to 2020. This should be led by the State Council Leading Group of Development-oriented Poverty Relief, with technical support from an expert advisory committee. The dimensions, indicators, and weights of the MPI should be set in accordance with the country's phased strategic objectives and measured and published by the National Bureau of Statistics on the basis of household survey data, thereby affording a more scientific and objective evaluation method for the targeted poverty alleviation work of registering poor households and lifting them out of poverty.

References

Alkire, S., & Foster, J. (2007b). *Counting and multidimensional poverty measurement.* Oxford Poverty & Human Development Initiative (Working Paper No. 7). OPHI.

Alkire, S., & Foster, J. (2007a). *Choosing dimensions: The capability approach and multidimensional poverty.* Chronic Poverty Research Centre.

Alkire, S. & Foster, J. (2009). *Counting and multidimensional poverty measurement*. Oxford Poverty & Human Development Initiative (Working Paper No. 32). OPHI.

Alkire, S., & Roche J. M. (2011). *Beyond headcount: Measures that reflect the breadth and components of child poverty.* Oxford Poverty & Human Development Initiative (Working Paper No. 45). OPHI.

Alkire, S. (2002). Dimensions of human development. *World Development, 30*(2), 00–00.

Angulo, R. (2016). *From multidimensional poverty measurement to multisector public policy for poverty reduction: Lesson from the Colombian case.* Oxford Poverty & Human Development Initiative (Working Paper No. 102). OPHI.

Atkinson A. B., & Bourguignon, F. (1983). The comparison of multi-dimensioned distributions of economic status. *Review of Economic Studies* 49(2).

Chen, L. (2008). Multidimensional poverty measurement and its decomposition in China during the transition period. *Economic Review Issue, 5*, x.

Esfandiar, M. (1986). The measurement and decomposition of multidimensional inequality. *Econometrica, 54*(2), 991–997.

Guo, J. (2012). Multidimensional poverty levels and characteristics of rural households. *Rural Economy,* (3).

Hu, A. (2008). From a poverty-stricken big country to a well-off society: How to eliminate four types of poverty in China. *China Old Regions Construction,* (12).

Li, J. (2010). Multidimensional poverty measurement for rural households—A case study of 30 national key counties for development-oriented poverty alleviation in S province. *Finance and Trade Economics,* (10).

Nussbaum, M. (2000). *Women and human development: The capabilities approach.* Cambridge University Press.

Nussbaum, M. (1993). Non-relative virtues: An Aristotelian approach. In M. Nussbaum & A. Sen (Eds.), *The quality of life* (pp. 00–00). Oxford Clarendon Press.

Nussbaumer, P., Bazilian, M., Modi, V., & Yumkella, K. (2011). Measuring energy poverty: Focusing on what matters (Working Paper No. 42). Oxford Poverty & Human Development Initiative. OPHI.

Ortiz, I., Daniels, L. M., & Engibertsdottir, S. (2012). *Child poverty and inequality: New perspectives.* UNCEIF.

Sen, A. (1985). *Commodities and capabilities.* Oxford University Press.

Shang, W., & Yao, Z. (2005). Research on multidimensional poverty measures. *Journal of Finance and Economics,* (12).

Shang, X., & Wang, X. (2012). *Discovery report: Emerging issues and findings for child welfare and protection in China.* Social Science Academic Press.

Sun, X., & Tian, G., et al. (2012). Research on poverty measurement of rural residents in China—A case study of Shanxi. *On Economic Problems,* (4).

UNDP. (2011). Human Development Report.

Wang, X., & Alkire, S. (2009). Measurement of multidimensional poverty in China: Estimation and policy implication. *China Rural Economy,* (12).

Wang, X. (2011). On the guarantee of Chinese children's survival, health, and development rights—Based on a survey of five provinces (regions). *People's Tribune,* (14).

Wang, X. (2014). *Implications of multidimensional poverty identification in Mexico for China's 'Targeted Poverty Alleviation'.* International Poverty Reduction Center in China, Poverty Reduction Research Reference, (1).

Wang, X., Feng, H., et al. (2016). *On the relationship between income poverty and multidimensional poverty in China.* Oxford Poverty & Human Development Initiative (Working Paper No. 101). OPHI.

Wang, X., Zhou, L., et al. (2015b). Child poverty in rural China: Multidimensional perspective. *Asian Social Work and Policy Review, 9*(2), 109–193.

Wang, Y., Wang, X., et al. (2015a). *GIS-based accurate identification and evaluation of multidimensional poverty.* Science Press.

Ye, C., & Wang, H. (2010). Recent progress in the study of multidimensional poverty and its measurement: issues and methods. *Economic Research Journal,* (6).

Zhang, J., & Chen, L. (2006). Review of research on aggregate poverty measurement. *China Economic Quarterly,* (4).

Zhang, Q. (2015). Dynamic changes of multidimensional poverty in China (1991–2011). *Journal of Finance and Economics,* (4).

Zou, W., & Fang, Y. (2011). A multidimensional study of the dynamic changes of poverty in China. *Chinese Journal of Population Science,* (6).

Chapter 5
On the Relationship Between Income Poverty and Multidimensional Poverty in China

5.1 Introduction

Poverty is usually defined as deprivations in well-being resulting in an inability to meet the basic needs of the individual or family (World Bank, 2000). The measurement of poverty is, therefore, a kind of measurement of the income or consumption necessary to meet certain basic needs (poverty line), including food and non-food needs (Haughton & Khandker, 2009). The food poverty line is usually based on the market price of 2100 cal per person per day. Non-food needs include the basic needs for clothing, housing, etc. Engel's coefficient of the poor is usually above 60%. Based on the food poverty line and Engel's coefficient of 60%, one can estimate the non-food poverty line and then obtain the income poverty line (Ravallion, 2012).

Poverty or lack of well-being covers both monetary and non-monetary aspects. Nobel Laureate Amartya Sen believes that poverty is not the mere lack of income to meet basic needs, but deprivations in basic human capabilities (Sen, 1992). An income poverty line well captures the monetary aspect of poverty but cannot accurately reflect the non-monetary aspects. There is no doubt that under normal circumstances, with an increase in people's income, well-being in both monetary and non-monetary domains will be improved to some extent. It is undeniable, however, that non-monetary well-being problems are usually related to market failure or incomplete markets. For a poor illiterate person, for example, even if s/he lives above the income poverty line, her/his educational status will remain unchanged; a person with physical disabilities needs more income to maintain life and mobility than other people. Not only can health and basic education make it easier for people to shake off poverty, but it also makes their lives more meaningful and helps them participate in social activities (Sen, 1999). Improvements in non-monetary well-being (such as education and health care) mainly involves the improvement of public goods and services (Bourguignon & Chakravarty, 2003).

Correspondingly, two major international standards have been developed for poverty measurement. The first is the World Bank's poverty line based on income

© Social Sciences Academic Press 2022

X. Wang, *Multidimensional Poverty Measurement*,
International Research on Poverty Reduction,
https://doi.org/10.1007/978-981-19-1189-7_5

level, i.e., USD1.25 or USD2 a day (PPP), and the other is the Multidimensional Poverty Index (MPI) put forward by the United Nations Development Programme (UNDP, see also Alkire & Santos, 2014).

Then, what on earth is the relationship between income poverty and multidimensional poverty? When a country develops its MPI, should it take income as a dimension and include it in the MPI system? What is the cause of multidimensional poverty? This is what this paper attempts to study.

In order to answer the above questions, this paper attempts to explore the linkages and discrepancies between the income poverty and multidimensional poverty in China using Alkire-Foster (AF) multidimensional poverty measurement and logit models with 2011 China Health and Nutrition Survey (CHNS) data. It aims to provide a reference for the measurement of multidimensional poverty in China and a basis for the improvement of the national poverty reduction strategies and policies as well. Part two of this paper is the study of relevant literature and presents the conceptual framework of this paper; the third part describes the models, data, and relevant variables; the fourth part analyzes the empirical results; and the fifth part is the summary and policy implications based on the empirical results.

5.2 Conceptual Framework

What on earth is the relationship between income poverty and multidimensional poverty? From the perspective of basic needs, the World Bank defines poverty as deprivations in well-being and defines the poverty line as the income needed to meet the basic needs of the "shopping basket" (World Bank, 2000). According to Amartya Sen, however, poverty refers to deprivations in basic capabilities of the individual or family; the deprivation of basic capabilities is multidimensional and includes premature death, obvious malnutrition, persistent disease, widespread illiteracy, etc. One should understand deprivations in basic capabilities with reference to people's actual living and empowerment. Such capabilities are intrinsically and also instrumentally valuable: enhancing poor people's basic capabilities through education and health care will increase their productivity and income (Sen, 1999). Therefore, multidimensional poverty measurement based on basic capability can more accurately reflect the real circumstances of poverty, and the measurement of poverty should be multidimensional (Alkire, 2002; Alkire & Foster, 2007, 2011; Wang & Alkire, 2009).

Income poverty is based on the basic needs approach while multidimensional poverty is based on the basic capabilities approach. The former well reflects monetary poverty while the latter more accurately reflects the non-monetary aspects of poverty. However, there are certain different opinions in the academic world on the measurement of poverty by income or a multidimensional standard. Those who insist on income poverty measurement believe that income poverty is not the single standard since the regression model covers both food and non-food aspects, and it is just putting all dimensions of well-being together as a single monetary dimension (World

Bank, 2009). Those who persist in using the MPI to measure poverty fall into two categories. The first group believes that income is a dimension of multidimensional poverty and it constitutes multidimensional poverty together with education, health, and living standards (Dhongde & Haveman, 2014; Santos, 2013; Whelan et al., 2012). The other group believes that multidimensional poverty is a complement to income poverty, focusing on the non-tradable aspects of individual or family poverty, i.e., the non-monetary aspects (Haughton & Khandker, 2009).

Many countries now have official national MPIs. Mexico is the only country to include income inside its MPI. The MPI in Mexico, which was the pioneering measure launched in 2009, includes income, weighted at 50%, and six social rights.[1] The rest of the countries report MPI alongside traditional monetary poverty statistics.[2] For example, the MPI in Columbia covers five dimensions, namely family education condition, children and youth condition, employment, health, access to public facilities and housing condition, using 15 indicators (Salazar et al., 2013). Colombia's MPI is reported alongside a separate income poverty measure, and both guide policy. Bhutan's MPI has the same three dimensions as the global MPI, uses 12 indicators, and informs allocation and targeting. Chile's MPI has four dimensions—education, health, labor and social security, and housing—and 12 indicators. Costa Rica's has five dimensions: education, health, housing, work, and social protection, and 20 indicators; El Salvador has a different five dimensions: Childhood and adolescence, housing, access to work, health and food security, and surroundings and 20 indicators. Ecuador's MPI has four dimensions: education, work and social security, health water and nutrition, and housing and lived environment, and 12 indicators.

The Chinese notion of poverty may help us understand the relationship between income poverty and multidimensional poverty. The *Analytical Dictionary of Chinese Characters* defines poverty (*pinkun*) as "little wealth."[3] The Xinhua Dictionary defines "poor (*pin*)" as "little income and difficulties in life" and defines "predicament (*kun*)" as "falling into a harsh environment or any environment that one cannot shake off."[4] Thus, the "poor" aspect of poverty mainly refers to the lack of income and the "predicament" aspect of poverty emphasizes the social environment. According to the Chinese notion, "poverty" can be defined as "falling into a harsh environment or any environment that one cannot shake off due to little income or wealth" (Wang, 2012). Similarly, this paper believes that poverty includes not only the lack of income but also social predicaments (Fig. 5.1).

Poverty is multidimensional and includes not only a shortage of income to maintain basic living, but also social exclusion, expressed as a lack of access to education,

[1] See http://www.coneval.gob.mx/rw/resource/coneval/med_pobreza/MPMMPshortversion100903.pdf.

[2] Links to all relevant national documents are found at www.mppn.org.

[3] *Analytical Dictionary of Chinese Characters* is an ancient Chinese dictionary written by Shen Xu in the year 121 when China is in the East Han dynasty, in which 'poverty (*pinkun*)' is defined as "little wealth".

[4] The *Xinhua Dictionary* is the modern Chinese dictionary, in which 'poor (*pin*)' is defined as "little income and difficulties in life" and 'predicament (*kun*)' is defined as "falling into a harsh environment or any environment that one cannot shake off".

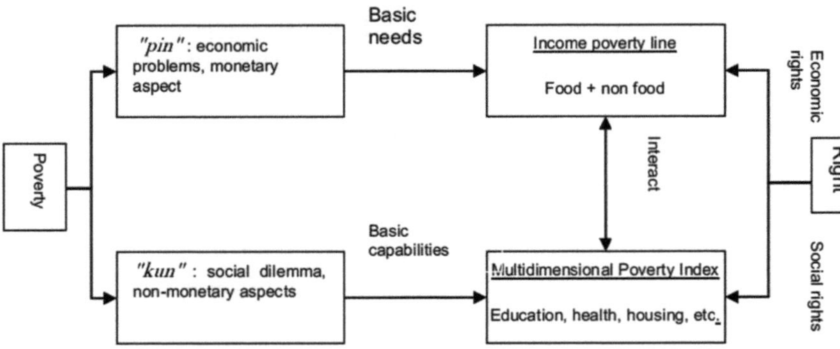

Fig. 5.1 The conceptual framework for poverty analysis

health, and housing due to a social predicament. It is obvious that income poverty measures cannot well capture the "predicament" aspect of poverty. If the MPI does not cover the dimension of income, it can hardly capture the "poor" aspect of poverty. But if we include income in the MPI, it will be affected by market prices, exchange rate, and PPP, so the comparison of poverty between regions and countries is not so accurate.

This paper argues, therefore, that setting up the income poverty and MPI measures separately in order to measure the economic and social aspects of poverty will help in the development of a more comprehensive pro-poor strategy and policy system.

Economists are accustomed to using currency (income or consumption) to measure poverty. They divide the income (consumption) poverty line into the basic food needs and non-food needs and convert the basic non-food needs into income according to Engel's coefficient (Ravallion, 2012). In such a way, only one income poverty line needs to be set for a country to identify the poor (Sen, 1976) and work out the incidence of poverty so as to provide simple policy instruments for anti-poverty policies. However, many aspects of "predicament" involve the supply of basic public goods and services by a government and society, and the private sector seldom provides such goods and services, leading to the phenomenon of market failure; thus, the "predicament" in this aspect cannot be accurately captured by currency. "Predicament" is a kind of social exclusion to a large extent, so it is necessary to analyze the problem from the perspective of sociology and social policy. According to Saunders (2003), social exclusion is what happens to some people or regions when they are facing a series of complex problems such as unemployment, lack of skills, low income, housing difficulties, high incidence of crime, loss of health, and family breakdown.

Being "poor" and facing a social "predicament" often influence each other. Many people cannot afford to attend school, see a doctor, or improve their living conditions due to being poor and then falling into a predicament. On the contrary, in a "predicament" situation, without access to good education or health care, it is difficult to accumulate effective human or material capital, thereby aggravating the "poor" situation and causing people to fall into the "poverty trap." With the improvement of overall income level and of ensuing social policies, education, health, and other social welfare will improve accordingly.

Public policy that is based on the concept of income poverty puts more emphasis on using income support policy to achieve poverty reduction. However, using data across developing countries and across time, Bourguignon et al. (2010) did not find empirical evidence that a reduction in monetary poverty was associated with a reduction of non-monetary deprivations. Social policy based on deprivations in capabilities, stresses poverty reduction through active social policy and social intervention. From the perspective of policy implementation, if no social policy for building basic human capabilities is implemented while eliminating income poverty, it will be very easy for those out of poverty to fall into poverty again. On the contrary, if we implement social policies that stress building basic human capabilities while eliminating income poverty, the population or families who have risen out of poverty, obtaining education and some other basic capabilities, will rarely fall into poverty again (Drèze & Sen, 2013). As long as they receive a good education, the originally poor will have the chance to become the elites and hence improve social mobility and inclusiveness.

According to Amartya Sen (1981), the root cause of poverty is an inequality of rights. When some people have too much to eat while some others are starving in a country, a famine takes place. It is a result of the inequality in rights and distribution. To eliminate famine, therefore, we should first eliminate the inequality of rights. Amartya Sen believes that for a poor person to live a decent life, the government needs to empower him/her in many aspects such as production, exchange, and transfer.

According to Wang (2012), the fundamental experience of China's success in poverty reduction is empowering the poor, including through the property rights brought by land reform and the social rights brought by population flow. Thus, according to the conceptual framework of this paper, the key to eliminating poverty lies in giving economic and social rights to the poor. The core of "teaching a man to fish" is empowering people and developing their capabilities.

Let's take the world's two most populous developing countries China and India as examples. The land system launched since the founding of New China, especially the land contract system launched since the economic reform, avoided the phenomenon of women's and children's malnutrition in poverty-stricken families due to lack of food. Also, universal nine-year compulsory education has greatly raised the literacy rate and education level of children from poor families in less-developed areas. Since the resumption of college entrance examinations in 1977, tens of millions of young people (including many children from rural poor families) have received higher education.

Amartya Sen (1999) believes that New China's popularization of nine-year compulsory education and countrywide basic medical services before economic reform laid a human capital foundation for the rapid economic growth after the reform. In India, private land ownership, on the one hand, led to the accumulation of a large quantity of grain, and, on the other hand, the high food prices won by large farmer groups lobbying the government led to the malnutrition of a large number of women and children (Gragnolati et al., 2005; IFPRI 2011). In the field of basic education, India lags far behind China (Drèze & Sen, 2013). To a large extent, the difference in economic and social development between India and China lies in the difference in the policies for building basic human capabilities.

As for poverty reduction in China, since the economic reform, China has not only achieved sustained and rapid economic growth, but also disproven the prejudice that economic growth in developing countries does not necessarily lead to poverty reduction (Kuznet, 1955). China achieved a sustained significant decline in urban and rural poverty rates (Ravallion, 2007), thereby achieving the Millennium Development Goal of halving poverty by 2015 ahead of schedule (Wu, 2012). Due to differences in economic development between regions, and between urban and rural areas, a small number of Chinese people still live below the poverty line (the rural poor accounted for 2.8% of the total rural residents in 2010) (NBS 2011), but the "survival, food and clothing problems of the rural residents in China have been basically solved." Thus the Chinese anti-poverty goal has changed from simple income growth to a systematic anti-poverty strategy to eradicate poverty (CPAD, 2011). Specifically, while increasing the income of low-income groups, China now aims to promote the implementation of anti-poverty measures under an inclusive growth strategy covering development, education, health, pension insurance, human survival, the environment, and financial services (CPAD, 2011).

In addition, poverty measurement simply from the perspective of income or consumption has limitations, and the definition of a poverty line also has a certain degree of arbitrariness. Moreover, beyond food and shelter, human survival and development also require certain conditions for education, medical treatment, and living environment (Sen, 1999). Thus, research based on a multidimensional perspective on poverty helps make clear the complex root causes of poverty.

Multidimensional poverty measurement methods include fuzzy set (FS), totally fuzzy and relative (TFR), Alkire-Foster (AF), etc. (see Alkire et al., 2015, Chs 3 and 4, for a survey). The FS method, put forward by Cerioli and Zani (1990), is a way to study the problem of poverty with fuzzy sets. To be specific, set a poverty line (such as 60% of the median of family income per capita) higher than the national one and take into account the poverty of low-income groups living above the low poverty line but below the higher one while calculating the poverty rate (determining the weight of poverty based on its distance to the low poverty line). On this basis, Cheli and Lemmi (1995) put forward the TFR method for the study of poverty problem; Betti and Verma (1998) applied the TFR method to the study of dynamic multidimensional poverty by using the multidimensional poverty and panel data. In recent years, an increasing number of studies have used the TFR method to analyze the problem of poverty and even the European Union has used the TFR method to report its poverty index (Giorgi & Verma, 2003).

Based on the theory of basic capabilities, Alkire and Foster (2007, 2011) put forward the AF method to establish the MPI and the global MPI. The AF method first sets the "dimensional cutoff" for each dimension and then judges whether a person is poor through a calculation using a "poverty cutoff" similar to that used for the calculation of "incidence of poverty." Deprivations may be weighted using a vector of relative weights. When a person is poor in at least some proportion of the dimensions (as specified by the poverty cutoff), s/he has fallen into multidimensional poverty.

The global MPI includes three dimensions, namely education, health, and living standards, and ten weighted indicators, with a poverty cutoff of one-third (Alkire & Santos, 2010, 2014; Wang, 2012). The UNDP adopted the global MPI and began to publish the global multidimensional poverty status in their 20th Anniversary Human Development Report in 2010. Compared to the FS and TFR method, the AF method is adopted more often in studies of China's multidimensional poverty because it is simple and easy to operate and the conclusion is persuasive (Yu 2008, Wang & Alkire, 2009, Zou & Fang, 2011, Guo & Wu, 2012; Wang & Wang, 2013, among others).

Most scholars have used the AF method in building the MPI system, but there is a big difference in the poverty dimensions they use, especially with respect to whether the poverty dimensions of MPI should include an income dimension or not. However, the income dimension and other non-monetary dimensions are closely related. In the process of building the MPI system, the linkages and discrepancies between income poverty and multidimensional poverty measurement cannot be ignored. In China, in the context of advocating for exact poverty targeting and building a well-off society, the implementation of multidimensional poverty reduction is of great practical significance. However, should China implement the multidimensional poverty reduction strategies with two poverty measures (income and multidimensional) complementing each other, or give income a certain weight and implement a unified multidimensional poverty line including the dimension of income? It is not only a basic issue for the study of multidimensional poverty, but a premise and the key for developing a unified, standardized MPI. On this basis, this paper attempts to study this issue from an empirical perspective through statistical analysis using the rural sample data of CHNS in 2011, aiming to provide a basis for the establishment of a national multidimensional poverty reduction strategy and policy.

5.3 Model, Methods, and Data

5.3.1 Model and Methods

Multidimensional poverty identification and aggregation method. The AF method, used by the UNDP's Human Development Reports to measure MPI, is the most mature and most widely used method for multidimensional poverty measurement. The multidimensional poverty measurement in this paper is mainly based on the AF identification, aggregation, and decomposition methods. First, we set the deprivation line for each indicator and identify the deprivations of each unit (usually person or household); second, we work out the MPI based on the dimensions of poverty, weights, and a poverty cutoff; and third, we break the MPI down by indicators and partial indices, and disaggregate by groups. The study is carried out to explore the linkages and discrepancies between multidimensional poverty and income poverty measures. Here, we do not discuss the AF identification, aggregation, and decomposition methods. Details of the AF method are described in Alkire and Foster (2007, 2011).

The method to analyze the relationship between income poverty and multidimensional poverty. For further quantitative analysis of the relationship between income poverty and multidimensional poverty, the measurement models below are defined in the spirit of Alkire and Foster (2007, 2011):

$$y_i^j = \beta_0^j + \beta_1^j ln(X_i) + \beta_2^j Z + \mu_i^j \tag{5.1}$$

$$y_i^m = \beta_0^m + \beta_1^m ln(X_i) + \beta_2^m Z + \mu_i^m \tag{5.2}$$

where y_i^j in formula (5.1) represents rural household i's deprivation in the dimension j, i = 1, 2, …, n; j = 1,2,…,d. When rural household i is deprived in the dimension j, $y_i^j = 1$, otherwise, it is zero. y_i^m in formula (5.2) refers to multidimensional poverty. If C, C = 1,2,…, d refers to the total (weighted) dimensions of deprivation of rural household i, $c_i = C/d$, is the percentage of dimensions. If the poverty threshold k is $k = 1/3$, then when ci > 1/3, $y_i^m = 1$, otherwise, it is zero. x_i represents the per capita annual disposable income of households. Z is a vector of the family's characteristic variables, including the number of family members of rural households and the provinces to which they belong.

It should be noted that the purpose of this chapter is to investigate the linkages and discrepancy between income poverty and multidimensional poverty; therefore, we are not reporting and analyzing the MPI separately or in detail. Rather, we focus on the identification of who is poor and its analysis. As the explained variables in formulas (5.1) and (5.2) are both binary variables, a logit model is used for regression.

Poverty classification. We regard the rural households who are deprived in one-third of the dimensions as multidimensionally poor (Alkire & Foster, 2007, 2011; Wang & Alkire, 2009). We further divide the multidimensionally poor into the ordinary and extreme multidimensionally poor using a second cutoff of 2/3, and define those with deprivations of more than 0 and less than 1/3 as the vulnerable poor—who are not multidimensionally poor at the moment but will easily fall into multidimensional poverty if there is a slight decline in their circumstances. These four types can be defined by the following formula[5]:

$$y_i^k = \sum_{j=1}^{d} y_i^j = y_i^1 + y_i^2 + \ldots + y_i^d \tag{5.3}$$

where y_i^k represents the sum of total deprivations of rural household i. When i is deprived in the dimension j, $y_i^j = 1$, otherwise, it is zero. Thus, $0 \leq y_i^k \leq$ d. The

[5] The indicators in Table 1 are given equal weights when calculating j_i in formula (5.3).

specific definitions of the four types of poverty are as follows: When $y_i^k = 0$, i is not multidimensionally poor; when $0 < y_i^k < 1/3$, i is a vulnerable poor household; when $1/3 \leqq y_i^k < 2/3$, i is multidimensionally poor, but its poverty dimension does not exceed 2/3, we define such groups as ordinary multidimensionally poor households; when $y_i^k \geq 2/3$, i is in extreme multidimensional poverty.

In addition, according to the official national poverty line (2300 yuan of per capita net income of rural households based on 2010 constant price), we divide the rural poor into two groups: rural households in income poverty and those in non-income poverty.

5.3.2 *Dimensions, Indicators, and Poverty Descriptions*

The dimensions and indicators of a country's MPI are usually set according to the country's economic and social development stage and the level of economic and social welfare protected by its relevant laws and development strategies. In this paper, six equally weighted dimensions have been set for China's MPI, namely education, health, housing, water and sanitation, energy, and consumer durable goods. The selection of indicators under each dimension is limited by the CHNS data, and a total of nine indicators have been selected (Alkire & Foster, 2007, 2011; Wang & Alkire, 2009).

"China's Rural Poverty Alleviation and Development Program (2011–2020)" clearly stipulates that the overall objective of China's poverty alleviation and development in the next decade is to address the food and clothing problem of the poor and guarantee their access to compulsory education, basic medical care, and housing by 2020 (CPAD, 2011). We assume that income poverty determines whether the food and clothing problem is addressed and the MPI indicates the education, health, and housing situation. According to the definition of energy poverty given by the United Nations Department of Energy, this paper adds the dimension of energy poverty and uses electricity and cooking fuel as indicators. In rural China, "three major items" are usually used to measure the living standard of a family, although the definition of these items has evolved over time.[6] Therefore, this paper increases the dimension of durable consumer goods to further reflect the quality of life.

In this chapter, we use the rural sample data of 2011 CHNS and take the household as the unit of analysis, covering a total of 3784 sample households in 12 provinces (or municipalities at provincial level), namely Beijing, Liaoning, Heilongjiang, Shanghai, Jiangsu, Shandong, Henan, Hubei, Hunan, Guangxi, Guizhou, and Chongqing. According to the relevant technical provisions of the UN Millennium

---

[6] In the 1970s, "three major items" referred to the sewing machine, wristwatch, and bicycles. In the 1980s, "three major items" indicated the refrigerator, color TV, and washing machine. In the 1990s, "three major items" were a computer, air conditioner, and motor bike. Since the new century, the "three major items" further changed to house, car, and a large bank deposit sum.

Development Goals on specific indicators and the data availability, we set the dimensions and indicators as shown in Table 5.1.

Figure 5.2 describes the deprivation incidence of rural households' nine indicators. Figure 5.2 shows that the coverage rate of electricity and durable consumer goods and children's school enrollment rate are generally high among rural households. The electricity poverty rate is 0.8%, the durable consumer goods poverty rate is 1.72%, and the incidence of poverty of children's enrollment rate is 3.81%. But rural households' problem of deprivation in sanitation, cooking fuel, and adult education level is relatively prominent. Fully 50.03% of the surveyed rural households have no outdoor or indoor flush toilets; 20.56% have no access to electricity, liquefied gas,

Table 5.1 Multidimensional poverty index dimension and indicator setting and their descriptive statistics

Dimension	Indicators	Mean	Std.Dev	Definition of indicator (dimensions are equally weighted)
Education	Years of schooling	0.258	0.437	When the best-educated member of a household has received less than five years of school education, the deprivation index is 1; otherwise, the index is 0
	Children's enrollment	0.043	0.202	Families with children aged 6–16 out of school are regarded as deprived, the deprivation index is 1; otherwise, the index is 0
Health	Health insurance	0.061	0.238	When at least one household member has no health insurance, the household is regarded as poor with a deprivation index of 1; otherwise, the index is 0
Housing	Housing conditions	0.103	0.303	When a household does not have its own housing or has a housing area per capita of less than 9 sq.m., the deprivation index is 1; otherwise, the index is 0
Water and sanitation facility	Drinking water	0.070	0.256	Households without access to tap water or water plant water, or without underground water within less than 5 m, the deprivation index is 1; otherwise, the index is 0

(continued)

Table 5.1 (continued)

Dimension	Indicators	Mean	Std.Dev	Definition of indicator (dimensions are equally weighted)
	Sanitation facility	0.357	0.479	Households without indoor or outdoor flush toilet are regarded as deprived and the deprivation index is 1; otherwise, the index is 0
Energy	Electricity	0.008	0.091	Households with no access to electricity are regarded as deprived and the deprivation index is 1; otherwise, the index is 0
	Cooking fuel	0.245	0.430	Households with no access to electricity, liquefied gas, or natural gas for cooking are regarded as deprived and the deprivation index is 1; otherwise, the index is 0
Consumer durables	Consumer goods	0.003	0.058	Households without transportation means, household appliances, or any information communication tool are regarded as deprived and the deprivation index is 1; otherwise, the index is 0; transportation means include tricycles, motorcycles, and vehicles; house hold appliances include color TV set, washing machine, refrigerator, air conditioner; information communication tools include computer, telephone, and mobile phone

or natural gas; and 19.65% have no family members who have completed 5 years of education.

Tables 5.2 and 5.3 respectively describe the distribution of rural households' income poverty and multidimensional poverty. We can see from Table 5.2 that, according to the national poverty line (2300 yuan of per capita net income of rural households based on 2010 constant price), the poverty incidence in rural China was

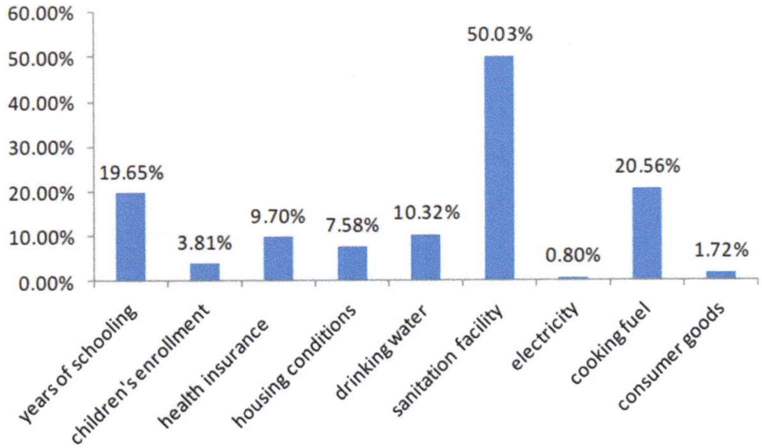

Fig. 5.2 Poverty incidental rates of rural households by each dimension

Table 5.2 Distribution of rural households' income poverty (N = 3784)

Income poverty (X)	Number of samples	Proportion (%)	Cumulative total (%)
Under poverty line X < 2536	495	13.08	13.08
At and above poverty line X ≧ 2536	3289	86.92	100

Note After CPI adjustment, the national poverty line of 2300 yuan in 2010 equals 2536 yuan in 2011

13.08% in 2011, slightly higher than the national rural low-income poverty rate of 12.7% and far below the low-income poverty rate of 29.2% in key counties for poverty reduction (NBS 2011). In accordance with this poverty line, the poverty rate in rural China was 35% in 2002, indicating that China's large-scale poverty alleviation and development achieved good results in reducing poverty.[7]

In rural China, however, the multidimensional poverty rate is far higher than the incidence of income poverty. Table 5.3 shows that when taking 1/3 of dimensions (K = 2) as the threshold, the incidence of multidimensional poverty among rural households is 33.21%, and this rate reaches 66.96% when the vulnerable poor are included (poor in at least one dimension), which is roughly the same as the estimated result of Wang and Alkire (2009) and Zou and Fang (2011). In addition, the multidimensionally poor are mainly those vulnerable to multidimensional poverty

[7] With the inflation factors deducted, the poverty line of 2300 yuan in 2010 equals 1796 yuan in 2002. According to this poverty line and Fig. 2 in Xia et al. (2010), the rural poverty rate in 2002 was estimated to be about 35%.

Table 5.3 Distribution of rural household poverty

Dimensions of poverty (k)	Number in sample	Proportion (%)	Cumulative total (%)
Non-multidimensional			
Poverty (k = 0)			
K = 0	1136	30.04	30.04
Vulnerable poverty			
(0 < k < 1/3)			
K = 1	1390	36.75	66.79
Ordinary multidimensional			
Poverty (1/3≦k < 2/3)			
K = 2	918	24.27	91.06
K = 3			
Extreme multidimensional	279	7.38	98.44
Poverty (k≧2/3)			
K = 4	57	1.51	99.95
K = 5	2	0.05	100

and the ordinary multidimensionally poor, involving few in extreme multidimensional poverty. Among them, 1390 belong to the vulnerable groups, accounting for 36.75% of the total population; 1197 or 31.65% were ordinary multidimensionally poor households; and only 59 or 1.56% were extremely poor in at least four dimensions. However, only 1136 or 30.04% households were not poor measured by these multidimensional poverty standards, far below the 86.92% of rural households living above the income poverty line (Table 5.2). Thus, there is a big difference in the identification of income poverty and multidimensional poverty. It also shows that the elimination of income poverty is not necessarily equal to the end of poverty although income growth helps reduce multidimensional poverty. Multidimensional poverty as well as deprivations in education, health insurance, electricity, water, and energy are, however, a result of the undersupply of public goods by the government and society. Simple income growth will not necessarily improve the situation of deprivation in these aspects. Thus, while eliminating income poverty, we should also eliminate multidimensional poverty and deprivation by providing more public products.

5.4 Comparative Analysis of Income Poverty and Multidimensional Poverty

5.4.1 *Statistical Analysis*

5.4.1.1 Linkages and Discrepancies Between Income Poverty and Multidimensional Poverty

Table 5.4 compares the linkages and discrepancies between income poverty and multidimensional poverty in the form of a matrix. According to the national poverty line, 39.77% of households have shaken off income poverty and are not the targets of poverty reduction, but they are multidimensionally poor in at least at one-third of the dimensions. In other words, 46% (39.77/86.92%) of non-income-poor rural families are actually in multidimensional poverty. In terms of the multidimensional poverty measurement standard, only 5.39% of households have shaken off multidimensional poverty but are still in income poverty (41% of the income poverty-stricken rural households have shaken off multidimensional poverty). Therefore, there is a big discrepancy in the measurement of income poverty and multidimensional poverty—up to 45.16% (39.77 + 5.39%); and the discrepancy (39.77%) when using income poverty measurement alone is far higher than the discrepancy (5.39%) caused by multidimensional poverty measurement. In other words, if the poverty-reduction policies target only at those in income poverty, then about 40% of rural households will still live in multidimensional poverty to various degrees. Therefore, the poverty-reduction policies should cover not only income poverty but also multidimensional poverty and deprivation.

In addition, the measurement results of income poverty and multidimensional poverty are consistent to a large extent. Fifty-nine percent (7.67/13.08%) of rural households in income poverty are also multidimensionally poor; 54% (47.17/86.92%) of non-income-poor households are not in multidimensional poverty. In other words, the measurement results of income poverty and multidimensional poverty are consistent up to 54.84% (7.67 + 47.17%), and the rural households not in either income poverty or multidimensional poverty account for 47.17% of the total, far higher than the 7.67% of rural households in both income poverty and

Table 5.4 Comparison of income poverty and multidimensional poverty (N = 3776)

Multidimensional poverty	Income poverty	
	Poor (X < 2536)	Non-poor (X≧2536)
Poor (ci≧1/3 and k = 1/3)	7.67	39.77
Non-poor (0 < ci < 1/3; k = 0.0001)	5.39	47.17

Note Figures in the table are the proportions of various samples in the total. After CPI adjustment, the national poverty line of 2300 yuan in 2010 equals 2536 yuan in 2011

Table 5.5 Income poverty's coverage and ignorance of the rural households in multidimensional poverty to varying degrees (N = 3776)

Multidimensional poverty	Income poverty	
	Poor (X < 2536)	Non-poor (X≧2536)
Non-poor (ci = 0)	1.59	19.14
Vulnerable poverty (0 < ci < 1/3)	3.81	28.02
Ordinary multidimensional	7.11	38.08
Poverty (1/3 ≤ ci < 2/3)		
Extreme multidimensional poverty	0.56	1.69
(ci ≥ 2/3)		

Note Figures in the table are the proportions of various samples in the total. After CPI adjustment, the national poverty line of 2300 yuan in 2010 equals 2536 yuan in 2011

multidimensional poverty. Thus, income still plays a basic and critical role in poverty measurement.

To further analyze the relationship between income poverty and multidimensional poverty, Table 5 shows income poverty's coverage and the situation of rural households in multidimensional poverty to varying degrees in the form of a matrix. It can be seen from Table 5.5 that 28.02% of rural households have shaken off income poverty but are still vulnerable poor in terms of multidimensional poverty, 38.08% of rural households have shaken off income poverty but are in ordinary multidimensional poverty, and 1.69% of rural households have been lifted out of income poverty but are still in extreme multidimensional poverty. In other words, according to the national poverty line, 67.79% (28.02 + 38.08 + 1.69%) of poor households are lifted out of income poverty but they are in vulnerable or ordinary or extreme multidimensional poverty. The fact that 75% of the extreme multidimensionally poor (1.69/2.25) are not income poor is particularly surprising. Thus, in poverty identification, income can hardly capture the comprehensiveness and complexity of poverty. The trends of multidimensional poverty are important and cannot be replaced by income poverty.

In addition, Table 5.5 shows that 11.48% (3.81 + 7.11 + 0.56%) of rural households are not only incomepoor, but also multidimensionally poor in at least one dimension. A total of 19.14% of rural households have shaken off not only income poverty but also multidimensional poverty. In other words, the overlap of income poverty with multidimensional poverty is only up to 30.62% (11.48 + 19.14%), ignoring 68.69% of multidimensionally poor households.

5.4.1.2 Linkages and Discrepancies Between Income Poverty and Each of the Dimensions of Poverty

In this paper, the degree of deprivation of each dimension is indicated by the mean of that deprivation dimension, or its headcount ratio. The larger the mean (from 0 to 1), the higher the degree of deprivation in that dimension. Table 5.6 describes the linkages

Table 5.6 Comparison of income poverty and the dimensions of poverty: households in multidimensional poverty (N = 2167)

Dimensions of poverty	Share who are income poor by deprivation in each dimension	
	Deprived	Non-deprived
Health insurance	0.155	0.149
Education	0.831	0.783
Housing	0.131	0.111
Water and sanitary facility	0.893	0.860
Energy	0.415	0.378
Consumer durables	0.058	0.025

Note Figures in the table are the average share of income poor in each deprivation group. Each row includes the whole sample, partitioned into deprived and non-deprived by dimension

and discrepancies between income poverty and each dimension of multidimensional poverty for the households in multidimensional poverty (at least 1/3 of dimensions). We can see from Table 5.6 that every dimension of multidimensional poverty has a positive correlation with income poverty. In other words, the degrees of deprivation in various dimensions of these income-poor households are higher than that of those non-income-poor households. It is worth noting that this positive correlation is not obvious. Taking health insurance, which has an obvious positive correlation with income poverty, as an example, the degree of deprivation in health insurance of rural households in income poverty is 15.5%, and the degree of the non-income-poor households is 14.9%, with only a slight difference of 0.6%. The difference between these two groups in other dimensions is even less.

5.4.2 Estimation Results and Robustness Tests of the Logit Model

5.4.2.1 Analysis of the Estimation Results of the Logit Model

To further analyze the linkages and discrepancies between income poverty and multidimensional poverty, we use 2011 CHNS data and the logit model for regression of multidimensional poverty and each dimension of it on household income per capita and other characteristic variables. The results, as seen in Table 5.7, show that, with the improvement of income level, the incidence of multidimensional poverty fell. The increase of one unit in the log of income per capita will lead to a decline in the probability of an incidence of multidimensional poverty by 41.34% ($e^{0.346}$–1). However, the pseudo R2 is only 7.9%. That is to say, rural household income per capita and other household characteristic variables explain only 7.9% of the variation in the MPI, leaving about 92% unexplained.

Table 5.7 The logit regression results

Explanatory variable		Explained variable					
	Multidimensional poverty	Health poverty	Education poverty	Housing poverty	Water & sanitation poverty	Energy poverty	Consumer durables poverty
Log of household income per capita	−0.346 (0.026)	−0.162 (0.023)	−0.454 (0.019)	−0.036 (0.022)	−0.387 (0.028)	−0.124 (0.019)	−0.504 (0.029)
Prob > z	0.000	0.000	0.000	0.054	0.000	0.000	0.000
Number of obs	3750	3750	3750	3750	3750	3750	3750
Pseudo R2	0.079	0.075	0.067	0.012	0.048	0.039	0.03

Note Figures in the brackets are robust standard errors

In addition, rising income levels significantly decreased the probability of incidence of various dimensions of poverty. The increase of one unit in the log of income per capita will lead to a decline of 17.59% ($e^{0.162}$–1) in the probability of incidence of health insurance poverty and a decline of 57.46% ($e^{0.454}$–1) in the probability of incidence of educational poverty. Among the other dimensions, income has the largest impact on consumer durables and water and sanitation, and the least impact on energy and housing. The increase of one unit in the log of income per capita will lead to a decline of 65.53% ($e^{0.504}$–1) in the probability of incidence of consumer durables poverty, a decrease of 47.25% ($e^{0.387}$–1) in the probability of incidence of water and sanitation poverty, a decline of 13.20% ($e^{0.124}$–1) in the probability of incidence of energy poverty, and a decrease of 3.67% ($e^{0.036}$–1) in the probability of incidence of housing poverty.

It is worth noting that an increase in income can significantly reduce the probability of incidence of multidimensional poverty and each dimension of it, but the impact is small. When the log of income per capita increases by one unit, the incidence of multidimensional poverty and each dimension of it will fall by no more than 70%.

5.4.2.2 Robustness Tests of the Estimation Results of Logit Model

To test the robustness of the regression results in Table 5.7, we use the CHNS data in 2009 and the same model, methods, and variables for regression again and obtained the results as shown in Table 5.8. Regression analysis shows that an increase in income can significantly reduce the probability of incidence of multidimensional poverty and each dimension of it. Thus, the regression results in Tables 5.7 and 5.8 are basically the same. This once again demonstrates the reliability of our model setting and the robustness of the model results.

Table 5.8 Robustness tests of logit model

Explanatory variable	Explained variable						
	Multidimensional poverty	Health poverty	Education poverty	Housing poverty	Water and sanitation poverty	Energy poverty	Consumer durables poverty
Log of household income per capita	−0.324 (0.024)	−0.038 (0.022)	−0.448 (0.023)	−0.164 (0.025)	−0.299 (0.031)	−0.100 (0.021)	−0.593 (0.030)
Prob > z	0.000	0.000	0.000	0.052	0.000	0.008	0.000
Number of obs.	2946	2946	2946	2946	2946	2946	2946
Pseudo R2	0.069	0.046	0.097	0.008	0.043	0.019	0.078

Note Figures in the brackets are robust standard errors

5.5 Conclusions and Policy Implications

This paper attempts to discuss the theoretical correlation between income poverty and multidimensional poverty, focusing on an analysis of the linkages and discrepancies between income poverty and multidimensional poverty using the AF method with 2011 CHNS data. Based on the existing literatures, this paper summarizes poverty as not the mere lack of income, but the deprivation of basic human capabilities, covering both monetary and non-monetary poverty. The income poverty line well captures the monetary aspects of poverty but cannot accurately reflect the non-monetary aspects of poverty. Under normal circumstances, with an increase in people's income and with good social policies, both monetary and non-monetary well-being will be improved to some extent. It is a premise of this paper, however, that non-monetary well-being is usually related to market failure or incomplete markets, because a pure market can hardly provide adequate education and health services for low-income groups. Thus, the government and society of a country are required to provide public goods and public services (such as education and health care). This paper believes that, therefore, setting up the income poverty measure and MPI separately in order to measure the economic and social aspects of poverty will help in the development of a more comprehensive pro-poor strategy and policy system.

The statistical analysis of income and multidimensional poverty measurement shows that the coincidence of income poverty and multidimensional poverty is 30.62% (11.48 + 19.14%). In other words, 68.69% of the multidimensionally poor households are not considered as poor in terms of income poverty. According to the national poverty line, nearly 70% of households in multidimensional poverty are not covered by poverty-reduction programs, but they are in a state of vulnerable or ordinary or extreme multidimensional poverty. The regression results of the logit model

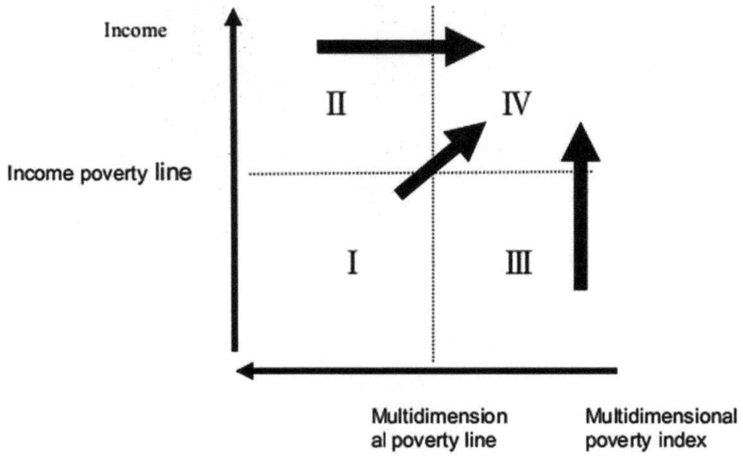

Fig. 5.3 Complementarity of income poverty and multidimensional poverty: two kinds of poverty

show that an increase in income can significantly reduce the incidence of multidimensional poverty and each dimension of it, but the impact is small. This implies that income-based poverty measurement can hardly reflect the comprehensiveness and complexity of poverty. Therefore, when measuring poverty, we must take into account various dimensions of multidimensional poverty and pay attention to the essential role of income poverty at the same time.

Based on the above research results, this paper makes the following policy recommendations. Given that income cannot fully reflect the quality of life and poverty, and that income measurement is not conducive to multidimensional poverty reduction and exact poverty targeting, this paper proposes to implement poverty alleviation policies with income poverty and multidimensional poverty measures complementing each other. Based on the conclusion of this paper, Fig. 5.3 indicates the poverty alleviation policies with the two poverty lines complementing each other.

Figure 5.3 divides rural households into four types—I: Rural households in both income poverty and multidimensional poverty; II: Rural households not in income poverty but in multidimensional poverty; III: Rural households in income poverty but not in multidimensional poverty; IV: Rural households in neither income poverty nor multidimensional poverty. According to Table 5.4 and Fig. 5.3, we'll ignore some poor rural households if we use either the income poverty line or the multidimensional poverty line. When we use the income poverty line exclusively, the households in Zone II should not be poor, but they are actually in multidimensional poverty. Table 5.4 shows that 39.77% of rural households are in Zone II. When a MPI is used as the poverty measurement standard, the households in Zone III should not be poor, but they are actually in income poverty. Table 5.4 shows that 5.39% of rural households are in Zone III. Thus, the aim of poverty alleviation policies should be to move those rural households in Zones I and II and III to Zone IV, in which rural households have shaken off not only income poverty but also multidimensional poverty. The best way

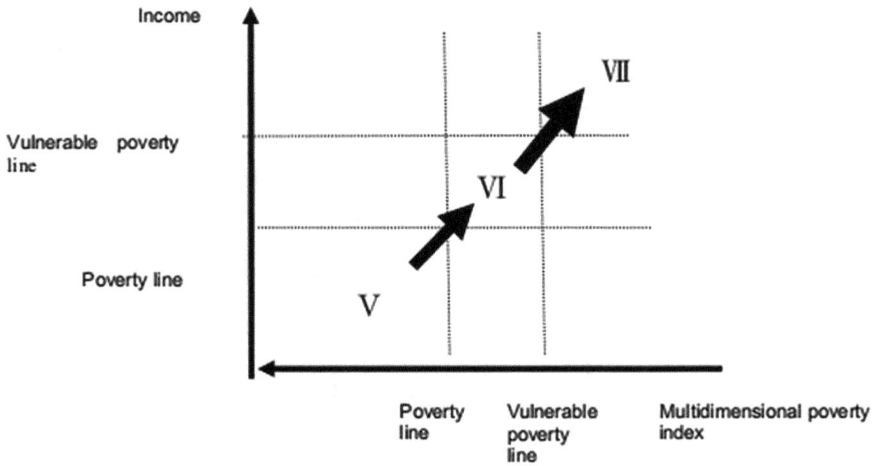

Fig. 5.4 Complementarity of income poverty and multidimensional poverty: three kinds of poverty

to achieve this poverty reduction goal is to combine these two poverty lines rather than ignore either.

Similarly, we divide income poverty and multidimensional poverty, respectively, into three types, namely non-poverty, vulnerable poverty, and poverty, and then analyze the poverty alleviation policies with the income poverty line and multidimensional poverty line complementing each other. Details are shown in Fig. 5.4. Zone V represents the rural households in both income poverty and multidimensional poverty who are the key targets of poverty alleviation. The short-term poverty alleviation goal is to lift them out of absolute poverty and make them jump to Zone VI, and the ultimate goal is to make them jump to Zone VII—shaking off not only short-term income poverty and multidimensional poverty, but also long-term and dynamic vulnerable poverty, and intergenerational poverty.

In summary, this paper advocates the implementation of poverty alleviation policies with income poverty measures and multidimensional poverty measures complementing each other. It will not only circumvent the shortcomings of income poverty measurement but also reflect the comprehensiveness and complexity of poverty. This will not only help relevant poverty alleviation departments achieve exact poverty targeting more effectively, but also improve the level of income, education, health, and quality of life of the poor.

References

Alkire, S. (2002). Dimensions of human development. *World Development, 30*(2), 181–205.

Alkire, S., & Foster, J. E. (2007). Counting and multidimensional Poverty measurement. *OPHI Working Paper, No. 7*, University of Oxford.

Alkire, S., & Foster, J. E. (2011). Counting and multidimensional poverty measurement. *Journal of Public Economics, 95*, 476–487.

Alkire, S., & Santos, M. E. (2010). Acute multidimensional poverty: A new index for developing countries. *OPHI Working Paper No. 38*, University of Oxford.

Alkire, S., & Santos, M. E. (2014). Measuring acute poverty in the developing world: Robustness and scope of the multidimensional poverty index. *World Development, 59*, 251–274.

Alkire, S., Foster, J. E., Seth, S., Santos, M. E., Roche, J. M., & Ballon, P. (2015). Multidimensional poverty measurement and analysis, Chapter 3. *OPHI Working Paper No. 84*, University of Oxford.

Betti, G., & Verma, V. (1998). Measuring the degree of poverty in a dynamic and comparative context: A multidimensional approach using fuzzy set theory. *Proceedings of the ICCS-VI, Lahore, Pakistan, 11*, 289–301.

Bourguignon, F., & Chakravarty, S. R. (2003). The measurement of multidimensional poverty. *Journal of Economic Inequality, 1*(1), 25–49.

Bourguignon, F., Bénassy-Queéré, A., Dercon, S., Estache, A., Gunning, J. W., Kanbur, R., Klasen, S., Maxwell, S., Platteau, J., & Spadaro, A. (2010). Millennium development goals: An assessment. In R. Kanbur & M. Spencer (Eds.), *Equity and growth in a globalizing world*. Washington, DC: World Bank.

Cerioli, A., & Zan, S. (1990). A fuzzy approach to the measurement of poverty. In C. Dagum & M. Zenga (Eds.), *Income and wealth distribution, inequality and poverty, studies in contemporary economics* (pp. 272–284). Springer.

Cheli, B., & Lemmi, A. (1995). A 'Totally' fuzzy and relative approach to the multidimensional analysis of poverty. *Economic Note by Monte dei Paschi di Siena, 24*(1), 115–134.

CPAD (China's State Council Leading Group Office of Poverty Alleviation and Development). (2011). China's Rural Poverty Alleviation and Development Program 2011–2020. (http://www.cpad.gov.cn).

Dhongde, S., Haveman, R. (2014). Multi-dimensional Poverty in the U.S. *Working Paper. No. 4*, University of Wisconsin-Madison's Institute for Research on Poverty.

Drèze, J., & Sen, A. (2013). *Uncertain glory: India and its contradictions*. Allen Lane.

Giorgi, L., & Verma, V. (2003). *European social statistics: Income, poverty and social exclusion, 2nd report*. Office for Official Publications of the European Communities.

Gragnolati, M., Shekar, M., Das, M., Bredenkamp, C., & Lee, Y. (2005). *India's undernourished children: A call for reform and action*. Health.

Guo, J. Y., & Wu, G. B. (2012). Measurement of multidimensional poverty based on different indicators and weights: A case study of poverty-stricken counties in Shanxi province. *Chinese Rural Economy*, No. 2 of 2012, 12–20.

Haughton, J., & Khandker, S. R. (2009). *Handbook on poverty and inequality*. World Bank.

IFPRI (International Food Policy Research Institute). (2011). *Global Hunger Index 2011: The Challenge of Hunger—Taming Price Spikes and Excessive Food Price Volatility*. http://www.ifpri.org/sites/default/files/publications/ar11.pdf.

Kuznet, S. (1955). Economic growth and income inequality. *American Economic Review, 45*(1), 1–28.

NBS (The National Bureau of Statistics). (2011). *Chinese rural poverty monitoring report*. China Statistics Press.

Ravallion, M., & Chen, S. (2007). China's (Uneven) progress against poverty. *Journal of Development Economics, 82*(1), 1–42.

Ravallion, M. (2012). Benchmarking global poverty reduction. *Policy Research Working Paper No. 6205*, World Bank.

Salazar, R. C. A., Díaz, B. Y., & Pinzón, R. P. (2013). A counting multidimensional poverty index in public policy context: The case of Colombia. *OPHI Working Paper No. 62*, University of Oxford.
Santos, M. E. (2013). Measuring multidimensional poverty in Latin America: previous experience and the way forward. OPHI *Working Paper No. 66*, University of Oxford.
Saunders, P. (2003). Can social exclusion provide a new framework for measuring poverty? *Social Policy Research Center Discussion Paper No.127*, New South Wales University.
Sen, A. (1976). Poverty: An order approach to measurement. *Econometrica, 44*(2), 219–231.
Sen, A. (1981). *Poverty and famines*. Oxford University Press.
Sen, A. (1992). *Inequality re-examined*. Oxford University Press.
Sen, A. (1999). *Development as freedom*. Oxford University Press.
Wang, S. X., & Wang, X. L. (2013). Measurement of multidimensional poverty in China. *China Agricultural University Journal of Social Sciences, 30*(6), 129–136.
Wang, X. L., & Alkire, S. (2009). Measurement of multidimensional poverty in China: Estimation and policy implications. *Chinese Rural Economy*, No.12, 4–23.
Wang, X. L. (2012). *Measurement of poverty: theory and methods*. Social Science Academic Press.
Whelan, C., Nolan, B., & Maitre, B. (2012). Multidimensional poverty measurement in Europe: An application of the adjusted headcount approach. *Geary Institute Discussion Paper No. 2012/11*, University College Dublin.
World Bank. (2000). *World development report 2000/2001: Attacking poverty*. World Bank.
World Bank. (2009). *World development report 2009: Reshaping economic geography*. World Bank.
Wu, H. (2012). *Inclusive development and poverty reduction*. 2012 International Poverty Reduction and Development Forum, The Presidential Hotel, Beijing, China, 17 October 2012.
Xia, Q. J., Song, L., & Appleton, S. (2010). Economic growth and rural anti-poverty. *China Economic Quarterly, 9*(3), 851–870.
Zou, W., & Fang, Y. F. (2011). A multidimensional study of China's poverty dynamics. *Chinese Journal of Population Science*, No. 6 of 2011, 49–59.

Chapter 6
Subjective Well-Being and Relative Poverty of Urban and Rural Residents in China

Over three decades of reform and opening up have achieved a massive reduction in China's poor populations. Particularly in the past decade, China has promoted theoretical, institutional, and policy innovation in development-oriented poverty alleviation and improved the national strategy and policy system for poverty alleviation. With economic development as the driving force enhancing the self-development capacity of the target population as the fundamental way, government leadership, social assistance, and the main role of farmers have been combined; inclusive and preferential policies have been put in place; and development-oriented poverty alleviation has been connected with social security. Consequently, the country has succeeded in following a path of development-oriented poverty alleviation with Chinese characteristics.[1] On November 30, 2011, General Secretary Hu Jintao stated at the Central Poverty Alleviation Work Conference that "China's development-oriented poverty alleviation has shifted from a stage where the main task is to provide for subsistence to a new stage of consolidating the gains of subsistence, accelerating poverty alleviation, improving the ecological environment, enhancing development capacity, and narrowing the development gap." This marks a shift from absolute poverty to relative poverty as the main issue of poverty in China. The scope of relative poverty goes far beyond absolute poverty. In addition to objective measures such as money and wealth, relative poverty also includes individuals' subjective evaluation of well-being. General Secretary Xi Jinping has repeatedly emphasized that "[we should be] making people have a greater sense of gain."[2] The term "sense of gain" encompasses both the acquisition of material wealth and the subjective feelings of people toward it. This chapter conducts a regression analysis of subjective well-being and relative poverty of urban and rural residents in China, which can be

[1] Fan (2012).

[2] Xi Jinping's speech at the tenth meeting of the Central Leading Group for Comprehensively Deepening Reform on February 27, 2016.

© Social Sciences Academic Press 2022

X. Wang, *Multidimensional Poverty Measurement*,
International Research on Poverty Reduction,
https://doi.org/10.1007/978-981-19-1189-7_6

used as a reference for decision-making about strategies and policies on China's new stage of development-oriented poverty alleviation.

6.1 Literature Review

Defining well-being is difficult, but measuring it is even more so. Its measurement can be divided into two broad categories: objective and subjective measurement. The former involves economic, social, and environmental indicators. People's objective well-being can be assessed indirectly using base measures. In the past, objective well-being was generally measured in a single dimension of per capita income or GDP per capita; in contrast, it is now increasingly measured using multidimensional indicators. The Human Development Index (HDI) and the Multidimensional Poverty Index (MPI), both published in the United Nations *Human Development Report*, measure well-being in multiple dimensions.[3]

The other measure used is subjective where individuals self-report their well-being or life satisfaction. Subjective well-being primarily reflects a person's cognitive and affective evaluations of their life.[4] The cognitive element indicates how people think about life satisfaction in a certain context (global, national, county, community, or unit). The affective element involves emotions, moods, and feelings. Affections are positive when emotions, moods, and feelings are pleasant (e.g., joy, excitement, and liking,) and negative when unpleasant (e.g., guilt, anger, and shame). Thus, subjective well-being relates to people's experiences of quality of life, including emotional reactions and cognitive judgments.[5]

Subjective well-being measurement attempts to directly capture people's feelings or real experiences through ordinal measurements.[6] Subjective well-being is often associated with happiness. Over the last few centuries, the discipline of "happiness" was the domain of theology and philosophy, but recently, the social sciences have become increasingly interested in this area. The study of happiness in psychology first moved into mainstream social sciences and economics after 1950.[7] According to McGillivray and Clarke (2006), "subjective well-being encompasses a multidimensional assessment of life, including cognitive judgments of life satisfaction and the effect of feelings and emotions." Some economists use the term "subjective well-being" as a synonym for "happiness," but in psychology, the term "happiness" is a much narrower concept than subjective well-being. Bruni and Porta (2007) made a distinction between happiness and subjective well-being. Psychologists believe that (1) life satisfaction is a cognitive element, (2) happiness reflects an affective element, and (3) subjective well-being is a state that is a long-term synthesis of

[3] United Nations Development Programme (UNDP) (2011).

[4] Diener et al. (2002).

[5] Diener (1984).

[6] McGillivray and Clarke (2006).

[7] Easterlin (2004).

affective and cognitive elements. Subjective well-being consists of four components: (1) pleasant emotions, (2) unpleasant emotions, (3) overall life judgments, and (4) areas of satisfaction (marriage, health, and leisure). Both happiness and life satisfaction are components of subjective well-being, yet the concept of happiness is narrower than subjective well-being and differs from life satisfaction. Whereas the latter demonstrates the difference between what individuals perceive and what they desire, happiness is the result of balancing positive and negative effects.[8]

Strictly speaking, although subjective well-being differs from happiness and life satisfaction, economists use the latter extensively to measure it. Currently, subjective well-being is being applied to various research topics. Diener et al. (2003) examined the implications of subjective well-being for empowerment.[9] Mavridis (2010) assessed the role of subjective well-being in the transformation of labor market. Petrovic (2010) investigated the subjective well-being of participants in social assistance public works in Serbia. Asdullah and Chaudhury (2012) studied the subjective well-being and relative poverty of rural residents in Bangladesh. Wang et al. (2012) researched the subjective well-being and poverty of the elderly in China in 2006.

It has been well documented that adopting life satisfaction to measure subjective well-being is the dominant method. This book analyzes the subjective well-being and relative poverty of urban and rural residents in China, using data from the *China Health and Nutrition Survey (CHNS) 2009.*

6.2 Conceptual Framework, Model, and Data

6.2.1 Conceptual Framework

(1) Income and subjective well-being—"Easterlin Paradox." "Modern economics is built on the central proposition that increased wealth will lead to increased well-being or happiness." However, according to Easterlin's findings in "Does Economic Growth Improve the Human Lot? Some Empirical Evidence," self-reported happiness grows as individual income grows within a country. Although the return to happiness declines rapidly as income grows, the relationship between income and happiness is not linear among individuals; especially, it has little to no effect on happiness for high-income earners. This accords with the typical assumption of utility function theory that "as consumption grows, marginal rewards diminish." In this way, Easterlin confirmed that income has a positive effect on happiness for some individuals. Nevertheless, when compared across countries, the level of happiness in poor countries is almost the same as in rich countries. Hence, citizens of the United States do not necessarily feel happier than those in North Korea. This is known as the

[8] Bruni and Porta (2007).

[9] Diener et al. (2002).

"Easterlin Paradox."[10] On this basis, we can conclude that happiness or satisfaction depends on relative income rather than absolute income. People tend to compare their income with others' income or their own past income and consumption; when they are worse off than their referent, they are less happy or satisfied.[11]

(2) Demographic characteristics and subjective well-being. Although demographic characteristics variables, such as age, gender, and marriage, may not be correlated with economic status, they have an impact on happiness and thus need to be placed in a regression model as control variables to avoid estimation bias.[12] It is generally assumed that younger people are happier than older people, but existing research suggests otherwise.[13]

(3) Social capital and subjective well-being. Levy (2007) argues that when utility indicates the satisfaction derived from consuming goods, happiness implies the non-monetary rewards received from social capital. This judgment builds on the assumption that an individual's happiness relies on the combination of their wealth and real social capital. Levy proposed an "inverted U-shaped" hypothesis for the relationship between individual happiness, wealth, and social capital, that is, individual happiness grows with wealth and social capital but starts to decrease when a certain level is reached.[14]

(4) Social policy. Social welfare policy is a crucial policy instrument to increase the level of individual well-being, although individuals facing the same social policy may have different levels of well-being. According to Sen (1999), this is due to differences in individual transformational capacity. Sen examined how national social policies affect human well-being, and cross-country comparisons revealed that the HDI increases as a country's public social spending as a percentage of GDP grows. This indicates the positive correlation between social policy and welfare. In addition, a study by Timofeyev and Timofeyeva (2012) suggests that effective social policies and wealth are not the only determinants of human well-being.[15]

6.2.2 *Model*

Based on the above conceptual framework, this chapter constructs the following model for the regression analysis of subjective well-being.

$$W = \beta_0 + \beta_1 I + \beta_2 D + \beta_3 S + \beta_4 P + \varepsilon \tag{6.1}$$

---

[10] Conceição (2008).

[11] Kingdon and Knight (2004).

[12] Frey and Stutzer (2003).

[13] Gentry (2006).

[14] Levy (2007).

[15] Timofeyev and Timofeyeva (2012).

In Eq. (6.2), W stands for subjective well-being, namely the dependent variable. The explanatory variables of subjective well-being are per capita income, demography, social variables, personal attitudes, and social policy. I stands for annual per capita income; D, demography that affects well-being, such as gender, age, and marriage; S, social capital, such as membership in social networks and cooperatives or associations and access to the Internet; P, social policy, such as access to health insurance; β, the parameter to be evaluated; and ε, the residual term.

6.2.3 Data

The data used in this study are from the CHNS 2009, with 6,556 valid observations. The samples consisted of adults aged 18 years and above, distributed in 9 provinces in the northeastern, eastern, central, and western regions of China.[16] This chapter takes individuals as the unit of analysis.

The study used a life satisfaction scale to assess the subjective well-being of urban and rural residents, and a self-rated well-being status could be poor, fair, or good, represented by 1, 2, and 3, respectively. Income was divided into five groups according to quintiles, with 1 representing the lowest income group and 5 the highest. Demography variables include age, gender, urban/rural areas, marital status, and education level. The variables were scored as follows: Age (18–44 years = 1, 45–59 years = 2, 60–74 years = 3, and 75 + years = 4), gender (1 = male and 2 = female), areas (1 = urban and 2 = rural), marital status (0 = unmarried and 1 = married), education level (1 = primary school, 2 = junior high school, 3 = senior high school, 4 = technical secondary school and vocational school, and 5 = secondary school or above). Social capital was indicated by access to the Internet, which was scored as follows: 1 = "No" and 2 = "Yes"; social policy was indicated by access to health insurance, which was scored as follows: 1 = "No" and 2 = "Yes" (Table 6.1).

6.2.4 Descriptive Statistics

Table 6.2 provides the descriptive statistics for subjective well-being evaluations and incidence of income poverty for the sample data. With respect to subjective well-being, overall, urban residents rated themselves better than rural residents. In terms of age group, urban and rural residents showed opposite results: the percentage of urban residents with good or very good subjective well-being ratings increased with age, whereas that of rural residents with poor or very poor subjective well-being ratings increased with age. Specifically, 12.9% of rural residents aged 75 or above

[16] The author extends thanks to the Carolina Population Center at the University of North Carolina and the Chinese Center for Disease Control and Prevention for providing the data.

Table 6.1 Variable definitions

Category	Name	Code	Variable definition
Dependent variable	Subjective well-being	W	What do you think of life now?
Economic variables	Per capita income	I	Per capita annual net income quintiles
	Employment	E	Unemployed/employed
Demography	Age	D_1	Group by Age
	Gender	D_2	Male/female
	Urban/rural	D_3	Urban/rural areas
	Marital status	D_4	Marital status
	Education	D_5	Education status
Social capital	Access to the Internet	S_1	Do you have access to the Internet?
Social policy	Access to health insurance	P_1	Do you have access to any type of health insurance?

had a poor or very poor subjective well-being rating, significantly higher than 5.9% of urban residents.

By gender, the subjective well-being of urban residents was lower for women than for men, while the opposite was true in rural areas. The incidence of income poverty was 12.7% in urban areas and significantly higher at 20.5% in rural areas. Poverty incidence decreased with age in urban areas but increased with age in rural areas. Notably, the incidence among rural senior citizens reached 29.5%, which may be due to the lack of a social security system for elderly rural residents. The poverty incidence among unmarried urban and rural residents was higher than that among married residents. In addition, it was higher among women than men.

Table 6.3 shows that in both urban and rural areas, subjective well-being was better among those who had a higher education level, who were employed, or who had access to health insurance. There was no significant difference between urban and rural residents when assessing subjective well-being.

6.3 Model Estimation and Test

Due to the non-linear relationship between subjective well-being and income, we regressed Eq. (6.1) using a logistic model. Since the variable W is a three-categorical ordinal variable, the model was estimated using ordered logit.

$$P_i = E(W = 1|X_i) = \frac{1}{1 + e^{-W}}$$

$$P_i = E(W = 2|X_i) = \frac{1}{1 + e^{-W}}$$

Table 6.2 Subjective well-being and incidence of income poverty among urban and rural residents in China (Unit: %)

Profile of residents		Subjective well-being				Incidence of income poverty
		Poor or very poor	Fair	Good or very good	Total	
Urban	Total	6.8	39.5	53.7	100.0	12.7
Age	18–44	8.2	42.9	49.0	100.0	14.1
	45–59	6.4	41.3	52.3	100.0	13.9
	60–74	6.2	36.7	57.1	100.0	11.0
	75 and above	5.9	31.9	62.2	100.0	6.8
Gender	Male	7.0	39.7	53.3	100.0	10.5
	Female	6.6	39.3	54.2	100.0	14.9
Marital status	Single	9.7	41.4	48.9	100.0	14.6
	Married	6.3	39.3	54.4	100.0	12.3
Rural	Total	7.2	44.9	47.9	100.0	20.5
Age	18–44	5.7	47.3	47.0	100.0	17.0
	45–59	6.6	45.0	48.4	100.0	20.4
	60–74	8.6	44.9	46.5	100.0	27.6
	75 and above	12.9	38.2	48.9	100.0	29.5
Gender	Male	6.4	43.8	49.8	100.0	15.9
	Female	8.1	46.1	45.8	100.0	25.2
Marital status	Single	11.2	45.4	43.4	100.0	22.6
	Married	6.7	44.8	48.5	100.0	20.2

Note The incidence of poverty in this table is calculated using the relative poverty line. The relative poverty line is 30% of the median net income of the residents. Based on this, the median income of urban residents is RMB15,000 and the relative poverty line is RMB7,500 and RMB9,600 and RMB4,800, respectively, for rural residents

$$P_i = E(W = 3|X_i) = \frac{1}{1 + e^{-W}}$$

$$L_i = ln\left(\frac{P_i}{1 - P_i}\right) = W = \beta_0 + \beta_1 I + \beta_2 D + \beta_3 S + \beta_4 P + \varepsilon \quad (6.2)$$

Table 6.4 shows the optimal estimation results of the model, with 6,299 valid observations. LR chi^2 (15) = 347.92, Prob > chi^2 = 0.0000, and the overall model is significant. As income grows, the directly estimated income coefficient of the O-Logit model changes from negative to positive. This indicates that as income grows, subjective well-being undergoes a transition from lower to higher evaluations; specifically, the coefficient for the high-income group was 0.647, indicating a 64.7% increase in the odds ratio of higher subjective well-being evaluations as residents' income increased from the middle to high level.

Table 6.3 Subjective well-being of urban and rural residents in China (Unit: %)

Profile of residents		Poor or very poor	Fair	Good or very good	Total
Urban					
Education level	Primary school	10.2	48.5	41.3	100.0
	Junior high school	7.7	44.3	48.0	100.0
	High school	5.7	37.8	56.5	100.0
	Technical secondary school	4.2	34.1	61.7	100.0
	College or above	0.8	25.9	73.3	100.0
Access to the Internet	No	8.0	41.4	50.6	100.0
	Yes	2.9	33.3	63.8	100.0
Access to health insurance	No	13.9	41.7	44.4	100.0
	Yes	5.6	39.1	55.4	100.0
Rural					
Education level	Primary school	5.7	47.3	47.0	100.0
	Junior high school	6.6	45.0	48.4	100.0
	High school	8.6	44.9	46.5	100.0
	Technical secondary school	12.9	38.2	48.9	100.0
	College or above	5.7	47.3	47.0	100.0
Access to the Internet	No	8.0	41.4	50.6	100.0
	Yes	2.9	33.3	63.8	100.0
Access to health insurance	No	13.9	41.7	44.4	100.0
	Yes	5.6	39.1	55.4	100.0

The coefficient for age was positive, suggesting that the older the person, the more likely residents will have a good subjective well-being rating. Females had a higher subjective well-being rating than males, with a 15.3% increase in odds ratio. Rural residents had a 23.2% higher odds ratio of a better subjective well-being rating than urban residents.

The coefficient of marriage was positive, indicating that being married has a positive effect on the subjective well-being of both urban and rural residents compared to being unmarried. The coefficient for married residents was 0.383, indicating a 38.3% higher odds ratio of a high subjective well-being rating compared to unmarried residents; the change in the odds ratio of married people is 46.7%.

The coefficient of education level was positive, and the value increased with a higher education level, indicating that those with a higher education level are more likely to have subjective well-being evaluations. Residents with access to health insurance had a 44% higher odds ratio of a high subjective well-being rating compared to those without access. Residents with access to Internet had a 35.6% higher odds ratio of a higher subjective well-being rating compared to those without, suggesting

Table 6.4 Model estimation results

Subjective well-being	Coefficient	z	> z	%	% StdX	SDofX
Income						
Low-income group	…	…	…	…	…	…
Low-middle-income group	−0.012	−0.121	0.904	−1.2	−0.4	0.339
Middle-income group	0.022	0.223	0.824	2.2	0.8	0.387
Middle-high-income group	0.195	2.044	0.041	21.5	8.6	0.423
High-income group	0.647	6.715	0.000	90.9	36	0.476
Age						
Youth	…	…	…	…	…	…
Middle-aged	0.130	2.080	0.038	13.9	6.5	0.481
Elderly	0.361	4.729	0.000	43.4	16.5	0.424
Elderly at an advanced age	0.444	3.221	0.001	55.8	9.5	0.205
Gender						
Male	…	…	…	…	…	…
Female	0.142	2.717	0.007	15.3	7.3	0.494
Urban/Rural						
Urban	…	…	…	…	…	…
Rural	0.209	3.645	0.000	23.2	10.6	0.481
Marital status						
Unmarried	…	…	…	…	…	…
Married	0.383	4.673	0.000	46.7	12.69	0.317
Education level						
Primary school	…	…	…	…	…	…
Junior high school	0.137	20,125	0.034	14.7	6.9	0.490
High school	0.368	4.252	0.000	44.4	14.1	0.359
Technical secondary school	0.452	4.402	0.000	57.1	14.7	0.303
College or above	0.818	6.606	0.000	126.7	25	0.273
Access to health insurance						
No	…	…	…	…	…	…
Yes	0.3648	4.459	0.0000	44	12.7	0.329
Access to the Internet						
No	…	…	…	…	…	…
Yes	0.3044	4.098	0.0000	35.6	13.2	0.407
Year						
2004	…	…	…	…	…	…
2006	−0.125	−0.384	0.701	−11.8	−4.8	0.395
2009	−0.517	−1.595	0.111	−40.4	−18.7	0.399

(continued)

Table 6.4 (continued)

Subjective well-being	Coefficient	z	> z	%	% StdX	SDofX
/cut1	−1.767	0.346	–	–	–	–
/cut2	1.051	0.344	–	–	–	–
N	6, 299	–	–	–	–	–

that Internet use is important for improving people's subjective well-being. The coefficient for year was negative, implying that over time, in the three survey years (2004, 2006, and 2009), the proportion of urban and rural residents more likely to have a high subjective well-being evaluation declined compared to the situation in 2004.

6.4 Conclusion and Discussion

6.4.1 Main Conclusions

The above analysis shows that income poverty is pronounced in urban and rural China and that subjective well-being assessment is better than income poverty. The incidence of income poverty was significantly higher among rural residents than in urban areas. As urban residents age, the incidence of income poverty drops, and the odds of having a poor or very poor subjective well-being assessment decline; as rural residents age, the incidence of income poverty rises, resulting in a poor or very poor subjective well-being assessment. Marital status had a significant impact on subjective well-being, with married residents having greater odds of a high subjective well-being rating compared to unmarried residents. Health care coverage and the Internet also had a positive effect on subjective well-being evaluations for both urban and rural residents, as did a higher education level. The Internet has a very clear positive effect on improving people's life satisfaction.

6.4.2 Discussion

(1) Development-oriented poverty alleviation for the rural poor needs to be intensified to effectively raise their development capacity. In particular, the income growth rate of the poor should be increased, so that their income is higher than the average income of the society, achieving pro-poor growth.
(2) Improving education level and health care can enhance human capital and the capacity of the poor for self-development as well as advance their subjective well-being evaluation. Equitable access to basic public services such as

education and health is conducive to improving subjective well-being, reducing relative poverty, and promoting harmonious development of the population.

(3) It is essential to establish and improve the rural security system for the elderly. The analysis in this chapter reveals that the incidence of income poverty among elderly rural residents is much higher than that among the urban elderly, which is closely related to the lack of a security system for the elderly in rural areas. Therefore, there is a need to improve this security system.

(4) Both marriage and the Internet have significant positive effects on subjective well-being. Strengthening information services in impoverished areas not only improves the subjective well-being of rural residents but also increases income. Attention needs to be paid to the increasing number of older men without spouses in remote and impoverished rural areas. This is a poverty issue as well as a social issue. With the rapid development of mobile Internet today, increasing online social networking is enhancing social capital. Future poverty alleviation policies should redouble efforts into the Internet + poverty alleviation, so that every poor person at least has access to a smartphone.

References

Asdullah, M. N., & Chaudhury, N. (2012). *Subjective well-being and relative poverty in rural Bangladesh* (Discussion paper No. 6569). The Institute for the Study of Labor in Bonn.

Bruni, L., & Porta, P.L. (2007). Introduction. In L. Bruni & P.L. Porta (Eds.), *Handbook on the economics of happiness*. Cheltenham, UK: Edward Elgar.

Conceição, P. (2008). *Measuring subjective well-being: A summary review of the literature*. Office of Development Studies, United Nations Development Programme (UNDP).

Diener, E., Oishi, S., & Lucas, R. E. (2002). Subjective well-being: The science of happiness and life satisfaction. In C.R. Snyder & S.J. Lopez (Eds.), *Handbook of positive psychology*. Oxford and New York: Oxford University Press.

Diener, ed. (1984). Subjective well-being. *Psychological Bulletin, 95*(3), 542–575.

Easterlin, R. (2004). The economics of happiness. *Daedalus, 133*(2), 26–33.

Fan, X. (2012, February 28). Striving to win a victory in a new round of development-oriented poverty alleviation. *People's Daily*, 00–00.

Frey, B. S., & Stutzer, A. (2003). *Happiness and economics: How the economy and institutions affect human well-being*. Princeton University Press.

Gentry, W. D. (2006). The demographics of happiness. In M. McGillivray & M. Clarke (Eds.), *Understanding human well-being* (pp. 00–00). UNU Press.

Kingdon, G.G., & Knight, J. (2004). *Subjective well-being poverty versus income poverty and capabilities poverty?* GPRG-WPS-003.

Levy, A. (2007). *Wealth, social capital and happiness: The case of status sensitive people* (Economics Working Paper Series). University of Wollongong. http://www.uow.edu.au/commerce/econ/wpapers.html.

McGillivray, M. & Clarke, M. (2006). Human well-being: Concepts and measures. In M. McGillivray & M. Clarke (Eds.), *Understanding Human Well-Being*. Basingstoke: Palgrave MacMillan.

Petrovic, M. (2010). *Subjective well-being of social assistance recipients in Serbia: Experience of public work participants*. Paper prepared for presentation at the World Bank International

Conference on Poverty and Social Inclusion in the Western Balkans. Brussels, Belgium, December 14–15, 2010.

Timofeyev, Y. V., & Timofeyeva, G. V. (2012). Does effective social policy guarantee happiness? *World Academy of Science, Engineering and Technology* (63).

United Nations Development Programme (UNDP). (2011). *Human development report 2011—sustainability and equity: A better future for all.* http://hdr.undp.org.

Chapter 7
Subjective Well-Being and Poverty of the Elderly in China

7.1 Introduction

The United Nations Millennium Development Goals (MDGs) have made poverty reduction the primary goal for national development measurement. Poverty reduction is the main objective to be taken into account in the design of social assistance policies as well as the major indicator for assessing policy performance. However, the principal indicators used to assess poverty worldwide are income-based, which inevitably leads to poverty reduction policies that focus on increasing people's purchasing power, thereby lowering the incidence of income poverty.[1]

From the perspective of poverty reduction and development, the well-being of China's elderly population has increasingly become a major social issue that the government must face. This is based on the following fundamental judgments about China's economic and social development. First, China is now an aging society, resulting in significant changes to China's economy and society in terms of the structure of the labor force and consumption. As the aging population increases, their well-being and poverty levels have an increasing impact on the well-being of society as a whole. Second, China's poverty alleviation has entered a development stage that primarily targets relative poverty. After over three decades of reform and opening up and the implementation of the government-led development-oriented poverty alleviation strategy, China's absolute poverty population has been drastically reduced with a decrease in the poor population from 250 million in 1978 to 40.07 million at the end of 2008.[2] With the rapid growth of national income, the urban-rural development gap is widening and the polarization between rich and poor is becoming more pronounced. In 2008, the income ratio between urban and rural residents in the country rose to 3.3:1, and the income gap between them exceeded RMB10,000 for the first time. If the disparity in access to public services is considered, the

[1] Rojas (2007).

[2] National Bureau of Statistics (2009).

© Social Sciences Academic Press 2022

X. Wang, *Multidimensional Poverty Measurement*,
International Research on Poverty Reduction,
https://doi.org/10.1007/978-981-19-1189-7_7

urban-rural gap is even greater. According to the World Bank's World Development Report (2006), among 127 countries, 94 have a Gini coefficient lower than that of China. Although the population in absolute poverty in China has been significantly reduced, people's self-evaluation of their subjective well-being (happiness or life satisfaction) and their sense of relative deprivation are becoming more prominent. If the relative poverty of a society cannot be effectively reduced, or if the subjective well-being of a society cannot be significantly improved, even if absolute poverty, as measured by income, is eliminated on a large scale, it still does not bring about an improvement in the overall well-being of society. It is also not conducive to the formation and sustainable development of a harmonious society. Finally, in China's social development, the elderly poor are considered to be a special group as they are more vulnerable to a certain degree in terms of both economic and social activities.

Therefore, the study of subjective well-being poverty and its influencing factors in China's urban and rural elderly populations has significant policy implications for the forthcoming establishment of a social welfare policy for the elderly in China's urban and rural areas, as well as for the poverty reduction strategy being implemented by the Chinese government which is driving development and security. The inclusion of subjective well-being in the indicators for monitoring poverty reduction will be more conducive to building a harmonious society. This chapter first builds a conceptual framework of subjective well-being poverty and its measurement methods. Second, it reports a descriptive statistical analysis of the subjective well-being of the elderly in China. Third, it uses ordered logit model to explain the factors influencing subjective well-being poverty among the elderly. Finally, the chapter outlines corresponding conclusions and policy recommendations.

7.2 Literature Review and Conceptual Framework

7.2.1 Multidimensionality of Poverty

Poverty eradication and the improvement of human well-being have been the primary objectives pursued by national development policies, but there has been no standard definition of these two essential concepts. Initially, well-being concerns were based on income, which was a unidimensional objective, while poverty concerns were also based on per capita income or consumption. In recent decades, well-being concerns have shifted to multiple dimensions. Sumner concluded that well-being concerns have expanded from a single income dimension to social, environmental, and human rights dimensions.[3] The multidimensional concept of well-being is now widely accepted, encompassing all aspects of human life.[4] Accordingly, people's

[3] Sumner (2006).

[4] McGillivray and Clarke (2006).

concern about poverty has also expanded from the traditional income-based dimension to multiple dimensions.[5] The core idea of multidimensional poverty is that human poverty covers not only income poverty but also poverty of other objective indicators, such as drinking water, roads, and sanitation, and of subjective perceptions of well-being.[6]

Based on multidimensional poverty research, there has been a gradual shift in the well-being and poverty criterion, namely from an objective well-being and absolute poverty criterion to a subjective well-being and relative deprivation principle. The study of poverty from a subjective well-being perspective is a new area of research in China, and this chapter attempts to explore this issue.

7.2.2 Subjectivity of Poverty

The well-being for measuring development has two dimensions: one is the objective well-being that each individual achieves in society, such as net per capita income, and the other is each individual's subjective assessment of their living conditions. At a time when there are large numbers of people living in absolute poverty, both governments and researchers are devoting more energy toward objective well-being improvements. As the incidence of absolute poverty decreases globally and the gap in income distribution widens, the assessment and research of subjective well-being have received increasing attention. Policymakers in some countries, such as Australia, Canada, France, Germany, Italy, New Zealand, and the United Kingdom, are attempting to measure life satisfaction as a component of well-being[7] and use this as a basis for formulating social policies.

Subjective well-being theory suggests that an individual's self-assessed level of well-being easily indicates their sense of well-being, whereas objective indicators, such as economic well-being, are usually selected by experts or policymakers arbitrarily, which are the same for everyone.[8]

Subjective well-being is defined as an individual's self-judgment of well-being, usually in terms of life satisfaction and happiness.[9] Psychologists make a detailed distinction between life satisfaction and happiness, while economists often interchange the two concepts.[10]

Judgments of life satisfaction or happiness depend on economic and non-economic factors. Four theories of subjective well-being have emerged from various influencing factors: absolute theory, relative theory, adaptation theory, and expectation theory (Table 7.1). The absolute and relative theories judge life satisfaction

[5] Alkire (2007).

[6] Wang Xiaolin and Alkire (2009).

[7] Samman (2007).

[8] Rojas (2003).

[9] Ravallion, Datt and Van de Walle (1991).

[10] World Bank (2010).

Table 7.1 Subjective well-being theories

Theory	Content	Main literature
Absolute theory	Higher incomes make it easier to meet basic needs and provide for higher subjective well-being	Venhoveen (1988, 1991)
Relative theory	The impact of income on subjective well-being depends on the changes in the level of individual expectations and on social comparisons. Regardless of an individual's income level, changes in their current and previous economic status can affect their well-being	Easterlin (1974)
Adaptation theory	Individuals with better adaptability are more likely to be happy	Brickman et al. (1978)
Expectation theory	An individual's level of satisfaction is related to their overall level of expectation. Regardless of the income level, individuals are happier when they perceive that their expectations have been met	Michalos (1985)

Source Easterlin, R. A., "Does Economic Growth Improve the Human Lot? Some Empirical Evidence", in P. A. David and W. R. Melvin, eds, *Nations and Households in Economic Growth*, Palo Alto. Alto, CA: Stanford University Press, 1974, pp. 98–125; Veenhoven, R., "The Utility of Happiness?", *Social Indicators Research*, 20, 1998, pp. 334–354; Veenhoven, R, "Is Happiness Relative?", *Social Indicators Research*, 24, 1991, pp. 1–34; Brickman, P., Coates, D., Janoff–Bulman, R., "Lottery Winners and Accident Victims: Is Happiness Relative?", *Journal of Personality and Social Psychology*, 36, 1978, pp. 917–927; Michalos, A. C., "Multiple Discrepancies Theory (MDT)", *Social Indicators Research*, 16, 4, 1985, pp. 347–413

or well-being from an income perspective, whereas the adaptation and expectation theories judge from a non-economic perspective.

Absolute theory. Happiness or life satisfaction grows with an increase in absolute income but not in proportion; rather, the proportion of increased happiness is diminishing.[11] The importance of income varies across countries.[12]

It is well documented that there is a correlation between life satisfaction and household income; however, an increasing income has only a short-term effect on an individual's life satisfaction. Long-term surveys conducted in many countries have found that there is little change in life satisfaction or well-being despite a large increase in per capita income.[13] For instance, looking at time series in the United States and Japan, even though real per capita income has grown over time, the happiness score remains the same.[14]

Relative theory. Happiness or satisfaction depends on the relative income. People tend to compare their income with that of others or their own past income and

[11] Fery and Stutzer (2002).

[12] Kingdon and Knight (2004).

[13] Krueger and Schkade (2007).

[14] Easterlin (2001).

consumption; when they are worse off than their referent, they are less happy or satisfied.[15]

Adaptation theory. An individual's affective ability to cope with positive and negative events is also a vital factor in happiness or satisfaction. Individuals who are more adaptable are more likely to be happy, even if they have a lower income.[16]

Expectation theory. An individual's happiness or satisfaction depends on their overall expectations. Regardless of income level, individuals feel happy if they believe that their expectations are being met and, conversely, unhappy if not.[17]

This study argues that since China is in a period of rapid economic and social change, living standards have improved rapidly in a short time frame. With the changing contextual factors affecting changes in social structure and attitudes, it is arduous to explain the complex phenomena facing China using a single theoretical framework. Therefore, this chapter introduces the analytical concept of "subjective well-being poverty," where subjective well-being is defined as an individual's judgment of life satisfaction and expressed by answering questions about their life satisfaction. The World Bank defines poverty as the deprivation of well-being, both subjective and objective. Traditionally, income or consumption poverty has been based on objective judgments of well-being, whereas subjective well-being poverty, as discussed in this chapter, is an individual's subjective perception or evaluation of a deprivation of well-being. The study classifies the subjective well-being of older people as "good or very good," "fair," "poor or very poor," with the last defined as the subjective well-being poverty line. Absolute theory was applied to develop presuppositions, and adaptation theory was applied to identify the factors influencing life satisfaction.

7.2.3 Conceptual Framework

On the basis of the above literature review, we hypothesized the following.

Hypothesis 1: The subjective well-being of the elderly grows with increasing income but not necessarily proportionately (absolute theory).

Hypothesis 2: In China, the subjective well-being of the rural elderly is rated lower compared to that of the urban elderly (absolute theory).

Hypothesis 3: Non-income factors, such as living with relatives, changes in psychological expectations, and personal attitudes toward life and adaptive capacity, have a significant impact on the subjective well-being of the elderly. Those with a spouse have a higher subjective well-being than those living alone; the elderly with a more positive attitude toward life have a better adaptive capacity and thus a higher level of subjective well-being.

---

[15] Michael Sherraden (2007).

[16] Brickman, Coates, and Janoff-Bulman (1978).

[17] Fuentes and Rojas (2001).

This chapter intends to test whether the above hypotheses are valid for subjective well-being poverty among older people in urban and rural China, using household survey data from China. In addition, it aims to test the impact of social policy, namely, health insurance, on the subjective well-being of the elderly.

7.3 Model and Data

7.3.1 Model

Based on the above basic hypotheses, the following measurement model is constructed:

$$W = \beta_0 + \beta_1 I + \beta_2 D + \beta_3 S + \beta_4 A + \beta_5 P + \varepsilon \tag{7.1}$$

Here, *W* stands for the subjective well-being of the elderly, namely, the dependent variable. The explanatory variables of subjective well-being are per capita income, demography, social variables, personal attitudes, and social policy. *I* stands for annual per capita income; *D*, demography that affects well-being, such as gender, age, and marriage; *S*, social capital, such as membership in social networks and cooperatives or associations; *A*, personal attitudinal variable; *P*, social policy, such as access to health insurance; β, the parameter to be evaluated; and ε, the residual term.

7.3.2 Data and Variables

The data used in this chapter were taken from the CHNS 2006, with a total sample of 2,344 elderly people from 9 provinces in northeast, east, central, and west China; in this chapter, elderly people are defined as citizens aged 60 years or above.[18] The chapter also uses individuals as the unit of analysis.

A life satisfaction scale was chosen to assess the subjective well-being of the elderly. The self-assessment of well-being can be categorized as follows: poor, fair, and good, represented by 1, 2, and 3, respectively. Demography variables were scored as follows: Age (1 = 60–69 years, 2 = 70–79 years, and 3 = 80 > years), gender (0 = female and 1 = male), areas (1 = urban and 0 = rural), marital status (0 = single and 1 = married), health (0 = poor, 1 = fair, and 2 = good or very good), and education level(1 = primary school, 2 = junior high school, 3 = high school and middle school, and 4 = college or above). The social capital variable was represented by whether they participated in social activities, which was scored as follows: 0 = no participation, 1 = dislike or very dislike, 2 = fair, and 3 = like or like very much.

[18] The author extends thanks to the Carolina Population Center at the University of North Carolina and the Chinese Center for Disease Control and Prevention for providing the data.

Table 7.2 Variable definitions

Category	Name	Code	Variable definition
Dependent variable	Subjective well-being	W	Self-assessed subjective well-being
Economic variable	Annual per capita income	I	Annual per capita income
Demographic variables	Age	D_1	Age group
	Gender	D_2	Gender
	Urban/Rural	D_3	Urban or rural
	Health	D_4	Health status
	Marital status	D_5	Marital status
	Education	D_6	Education level
Social capital	Social activity	S_1	Do you regularly participate in social activities?
Personal attitude	Personal attitude toward life	A_1	Are you as happy as when you were younger?
Social policy	Access to health insurance	P_1	Do you have access to health insurance?

The personal attitudinal variable was expressed by whether or not they feel happy, which was scored as follows: 0 = unhappy, 1 = fair, and 2 = happy or very happy. The social policy variable was indicated by whether or not they had access to health insurance, which was scored as follows: 0 = "No" and 1 = "Yes" (Table 7.2).

7.3.3 Profile of the Elderly in Urban and Rural China

Table 7.3 shows the descriptive statistics of income poverty and subjective well-being poverty among the elderly in urban and rural China, applying the sample data. The incidence of income poverty among the elderly in urban and rural areas was 8.23 and 9.73%, respectively, and thus higher in rural areas. According to the *2008 Poverty Monitoring Report of Rural China*, the incidence of poverty in rural areas was 2.3 and 1.6% in 2006 and 2007, respectively; at the end of 2007, the incidence of poverty among rural elderly aged 65 or above was 2.2%, while that among low- and middle-income elderly was 3.9%.[19] Such different results between this chapter and the report lie in the varying poverty criterion, calculation methods, and definitions of the elderly. However, regardless of which measure was used, both indicated that the incidence of poverty among the elderly was higher than that among other adults. With regard to age, the incidence of income poverty was highest among the elderly aged 70–79 years in urban areas, whereas this increased with age in rural areas.

[19] National Bureau of Statistics (NBS), Poverty Monitoring Report of Rural China, 2008, China Statistics Press, 2008.

Table 7.3 Income poverty and subjective well-being poverty of the elderly in urban and rural areas

		Income poverty (%)			Subjective well-being (status) (%)			
		Non-poverty	Poverty	Total	Poor or very poor	Fair	Good or very good	Total
Urban	Total	91.77	8.23	100	11.51	34.45	54.04	100
Age	60 – 69	92.49	7.51	100	7.62	33.58	58.80	100
	70 – 79	90.26	9.74	100	13.62	37.56	48.83	100
	80 & above	94.17	5.83	100	24.00	26.00	50.00	100
Gender	Male	93.57	6.43	100	8.30	33.98	57.72	100
	Female	90.07	9.93	100	14.49	34.88	50.63	100
Rural	Total	90.27	9.73	100	16.24	45.53	38.23	100
Age	60 – 69	91.67	8.33	100	11.97	47.04	40.99	100
	70 – 79	89.31	10.69	100	22.16	44.61	33.24	100
	80 & above	84.48	15.52	100	25.23	38.74	36.04	100
Gender	Male	91.11	8.89	100	12.78	46.80	40.41	100
	Female	89.56	10.44	100	19.15	44.46	36.39	100

Note The urban poverty line of RMB1,251 set by the World Bank in 2007 was used as the urban poverty line; adjusted for an inflation of 48% in 2007, the urban poverty line in 2006 was RMB1,194. The rural poverty line was based on the official poverty line of RMB693 yuan in 2006, as published by the Chinese government

By gender, the incidence of poverty was higher among female elderly than among elderly males.

Subjective well-being poverty among the elderly also revealed urban-rural, age, and gender differences. Such poverty occurs when the subjective well-being status is rated as "poor or very poor." From the subjective well-being rating of "poor or very poor," the proportion of rural elderly in subjective well-being poverty was higher than that of urban elderly; the proportion of female elderly in subjective well-being poverty was higher than that of elderly males; and the proportion of the elderly in subjective well-being poverty was greater with age.

Table 7.4 presents the descriptive statistics on the health, education, social activities, personal attitudes, and health insurance of the elderly in urban and rural China, applying the sample data in this chapter. There are obvious differences in the basic conditions of the elderly in urban and rural areas. A higher proportion of urban elderly rated their health as "good or very good" compared to their rural counterparts; the education level of urban elderly was higher than that of rural elderly; and a higher proportion of urban elderly "like or like very much" to participate in social activities and feel "happy or very happy."

Table 7.4 Profile of the elderly in urban and rural areas

Unit: %

Health status	Urban/Rural	Poor	Fair	Good or very good	Total	
	Urban	15.14	42.66	42.20	100	
	Rural	17.54	51.75	30.71	100	
Education level	Urban/Rural	Primary school	Junior high school	High school or technical secondary school	College or above	Total
	Urban	31.92	29.05	24.21	14.83	100
	Rural	64.66	30.14	3.84	1.37	100
Social activity	Urban/Rural	No participation	Like or like very much	Neither dislike nor like	Like or like very much	Total
	Urban	55.66	19.96	8.37	16.01	100
	Rural	72.47	19.80	4.25	3.48	100
Personal attitude	Urban/Rural	Happy or very happy	Neither happy nor unhappy	Unhappy or very unhappy	Total	
	Urban	53.21	20.70	26.09	100	
	Rural	33.19	26.48	40.33	100	
Access to health insurance	Urban/Rural	Yes	No	Total		
	Urban	58.19	41.81	100		
	Rural	46.11	53.89	100		

7.4 Model Estimation and Test

Due to the non-linear relationship between subjective well-being and income, we regress Eq. (7.1) using a logistic model. Since the variable W is a three-categorical ordinal variable, the model was estimated using ordered logit.

$$P_i = E(W = 1|X_i) = \frac{1}{1 + e^{-W}}$$

$$P_i = E(W = 2|X_i) = \frac{1}{1 + e^{-W}}$$

$$P_i = E(W = 3|X_i) = \frac{1}{1 + e^{-W}}$$

$$L_i = In\left(\frac{P}{1 - P_i}\right) = W = \beta_0 + \beta_1 I + \beta_2 D + \beta_3 S + \beta_4 A + \beta_5 P + \varepsilon \quad (7.2)$$

Maximum likelihood ordinal logit was used for model estimation, and Table 7.5 shows the optimal estimation results. The valid observations of the model are 2,200. The chi-square value is 736.52, Prob > $chi^2 = 0.0000$, and the model is significant overall. Asymptotic z-tests for the variables of gender (male), urban/rural (urban), marriage (married), and education level (junior high school) in the model indicate that these individual variables are not significant. However, in ordered logit regressions,

Table 7.5 Ordered logit optimal model estimation results

Explanatory variable	Coefficient	z	P > |z|
Gross income per capita	0.040	4.990	0.000
Age	– 0.126	– 1.750	0.080
Gender			
Male	0.023	0.250	0.804
Female	…	…	…
Urban/Rural			
Urban	0.047	0.470	0.636
Rural	…	…	…
Marital status			
Married	0.112	1.030	0.303
Unmarried	…	…	…
Health status			
Poor	– 0.985	– 7.720	0.000
Fair	…	…	…
Good or very good	0.966	9.250	0.000
Education level			
Primary school	…	…	…
Junior high school	– 0.152	– 1.110	0.266
High school or Technical secondary school	0.412	2.110	0.035
College or above	…	…	…
Social activity	0.412	2.110	0.035
Personal attitude			
Happy or very happy	1.516	13.570	0.000
Neither happy nor unhappy	0.425	3.760	0.000
Unhappy or very unhappy	…	…	…
Access to health insurance			
Yes	…	…	…
No	– 0.268	– 2.910	0.004
/cut1	– 1.237		
/cut2	1.307		

Note The unit of income is thousand yuan

the asymptotic z-test is imprecise and requires the more accurate likelihood-ratio test. After this test, the model as a whole was insignificant when any one of these variables was removed, suggesting that these variables have a significant effect on subjective well-being.

The estimated coefficient of per capita total income was 0.040, which is statistically significant. A positive sign indicates a positive relationship between income and subjective well-being. The income coefficient suggests that for every RMB1,000 increase in annual per capita household income, the odds ratio for a higher evaluation of subjective well-being of the elderly grew by 0.040, all else being equal. A small income coefficient implies that an increase in income will have a positive effect on the subjective well-being of the elderly, but the coefficient of the effect was small, supporting Hypothesis 1.

The coefficient of marriage was positive, which hints that compared to being single, having a spouse has a positive effect on the subjective well-being of the elderly. The urban-rural coefficient was positive, demonstrating that living in a city has a positive effect on the subjective well-being of the elderly; thus, Hypothesis 2 is confirmed. The coefficient of age was negative, that is, elderly seniors had lower subjective well-being ratings than non-elderly seniors, revealing that age has a negative effect on the subjective well-being of the elderly. The coefficient of poor health was negative, which indicates that poor health has a negative effect on subjective well-being in the elderly compared to fair health. The coefficient of education at the junior high school level was negative, implying that a lower education level has a negative impact on the subjective well-being of the elderly as does the lack of health insurance.

In terms of the impact of various factors on the subjective well-being of the elderly, personal attitudes had the greatest impact, followed by health status and education level. The coefficient of 1.516 for a personal attitude of "happy or very happy" and 0.425 for that of "fair" indicate a large difference in the impact of personal attitudes on the subjective well-being of the elderly, which confirms Hypothesis 3. The coefficient of 0.966 for "good or very good" health and –0.985 for "poor" health shows a large difference in the impact of health status on the subjective well-being of the elderly.

Coefficients of the explanatory variables in the logistic model represent odds ratios and therefore do not directly explain changes in the dependent variable. For instance, the coefficient of 0.040 per capita total income represents an increase of 0.040 in the odds ratio of a higher subjective well-being rating for each unit increase in income. The interpretation of the odds ratio does not intuitively explain the relationship between income and subjective well-being, and therefore, requires the probability of the impact of the independent variable on the dependent variable.

$$\Pr(w = 1) = P(W + \mu \leq \_cut1) = P(W + \mu \leq -2.000766) \quad (7.3)$$

$$\begin{aligned} P_r(w = 2) &= P(cut1 < W + \mu \leq \_cut2) \\ &= P(-2.000766 < W + \mu \leq 0.3179626) \end{aligned} \quad (7.4)$$

$$P_r(w = 3) = P(W + \mu > \_cut2) = P(W + \mu > 0.3179626) \quad (7.5)$$

From this, the probability values for subjective well-being were obtained, as shown in Table 7.6.

Table 7.6 shows the probability of the effect of each explanatory variable on the subjective well-being of the elderly. In terms of income poverty, Table 7.5 reveals the positive effect of per capita household income on the subjective well-being of the elderly, but the coefficient is not significant. In Table 7.6, the subjective well-being values for poor and non-poor elderly are 0.275 and 0.395 among rural elderly who rated their life satisfaction as "good or very good" and 0.345 and 0.549 for urban poor and non-poor elderly, respectively. In this way, irrespective of urban and rural areas, there are differences in the effect of poverty and non-poverty on the subjective well-being values of older people, showing that poverty has an impact on the subjective well-being of older people in terms of income poverty.

With respect to age, the subjective well-being of the elderly was lower at an older age, with the lowest value being 0.363 for senior citizens aged over 80 years. This indicates that the elderly have a lower life satisfaction at an older age. The subjective well-being values of the variables were higher for men than for women, for urban than for rural seniors, for those with a spouse than for those who are single, for those who enjoy social activities than for those who do not, and for those who are covered by health insurance than for those who are not.

In addition, subjective well-being values varied considerably among older persons depending on their health status, personal attitudes, and education level. The subjective well-being values for older persons in "poor" and "good or very good" health were 0.156 and 0.693, respectively, indicating that the life satisfaction of older persons depends to a large extent on their own health.

The subjective well-being values for older persons with a personal attitude of "happy or very happy" and "unhappy" were 0.695 and 0.235, respectively, indicating that the elderly have a greater life satisfaction when they take more positive personal attitudes.

Regarding educational level, elderly with a higher education level showed a greater life satisfaction. The subjective well-being values for education levels of "primary school" and "college or above" were 0.464 and 0.701, respectively.

Table 7.7 exhibits the interactions among variables.

7.5 Main Conclusion and Policy Recommendations

7.5.1 Main Conclusions

The analysis in this chapter shows that both income poverty and subjective well-being poverty are prominent among the elderly population in China, and this group of people has thus emerged as one among China's poor that requires special attention.

Table 7.6 Subjective well-being

	Probability of influence on life satisfaction judgments		
Explanatory variable	Poor or very poor	Fair	Good or very good
Rural			
Income poverty	0.242	0.484	0.275
Non-income poverty	0.165	0.440	0.395
Urban			
Income poverty	0.197	0.457	0.345
Non-income poverty	0.104	0.347	0.549
Age			
60 – 69	0.118	0.387	0.495
70 – 79	0.167	0.418	0.415
80 & above	0.206	0.431	0.363
Gender			
Male	0.123	0.382	0.495
Female	0.161	0.419	0.420
Urban/Rural			
Urban	0.11	0.356	0.533
Rural	0.172	0.44	0.383
Marital status			
Married	0.130	0.390	0.481
Unmarried	0.179	0.434	0.387
Health status			
Poor	0.361	0.482	0.156
Fair	0.145	0.475	0.380
Good or very good	0.041	0.266	0.693
Education level			
Primary school	0.131	0.405	0.464
Junior high school	0.109	0.374	0.517
High school or Technical secondary school	0.062	0.276	0.661
College or above	0.046	0.252	0.701
Social activity			
Like or like very much	0.163	0.426	0.411
Neither dislike nor like	0.131	0.391	0.477
Dislike or dislike very much	0.088	0.344	0.568
No participation	0.068	0.299	0.634
Personal attitude			

(continued)

Table 7.6 (continued)

	Probability of influence on life satisfaction judgments		
Explanatory variable	Poor or very poor	Fair	Good or very good
Happy or very happy	0.040	0.266	0.695
Neither happy nor unhappy	0.153	0.489	0.358
Unhappy or very unhappy	0.258	0.507	0.235
Access to health insurance			
Yes	0.107	0.367	0.526
No	0.182	0.439	0.379

This chapter shifts the poverty criterion from an objective dimension to a combined objective and subjective perspective and measures the subjective well-being poverty of China's growing elderly population, providing a new perspective for the analysis of poverty in China.

The empirical analysis also leads to some meaningful conclusions. From an angle of income and subjective well-being, these are positively correlated, that is, the higher the income, the greater the subjective well-being value of the elderly; however, the coefficient of the effect of income on subjective well-being is insignificant. According to the income poverty criterion, poverty has some effect on the subjective well-being of the elderly. Concerning income and subjective well-being, income is more sensitive to subjective well-being for seniors below the poverty line. Thus, the poverty line corresponds to an approximate threshold of the income-subjective well-being function curve, beyond which the probability of increasing income to improve subjective well-being is low. Using data from China, this also supports the hypothesis that although income and subjective well-being are positively correlated, this is not in a linear way.

Subjective well-being is lower for older women than men, lower in rural than in urban areas, and lower for older people living alone than for those with a spouse.

The coefficient of health status is the largest, which suggests that health is quite sensitive to subjective well-being poverty. There are important policy implications for the urban and rural health care system under construction in China in terms of improving the subjective well-being of the elderly.

The effect of personal attitudes on the subjective well-being of the elderly is evident, and enhancing positive and optimistic attitudes among older people will greatly raise their life satisfaction. For the elderly, the stock of education in the past cannot be changed, but community-run geriatric schools and other elderly oriented social activities play a crucial role in improving their subjective well-being.

Table 7.7 Interactions among variables

		Probability of influence on life satisfaction judgments		
Interactions among variables		Poor or very poor	Fair	Good or very good
Age and health				
Age (years)	Health status			
60 – 69	Poor	0.315	0.497	0.188
60 – 69	Fair	0.135	0.467	0.398
60 – 69	Good or very good	0.038	0.254	0.708
70 – 79	Poor	0.385	0.478	0.138
70 – 79	Fair	0.150	0.480	0.370
70 – 79	Good or very good	0.044	0.281	0.675
80 & above	Poor	0.430	0.451	0.119
80 & above	Fair	0.192	0.506	0.301
80 & above	Good or very good	0.054	0.308	0.637
Age and Marital status				
Age (years)	Marital status			
60 – 69	Married	0.114	0.378	0.508
60 – 69	Unmarried	0.144	0.431	0.426
70 – 79	Married	0.159	0.409	0.432
70 – 79	Unmarried	0.181	0.434	0.385
80 & above	Married	0.162	0.416	0.423
80 & above	Unmarried	0.236	0.441	0.324
Age and Urban/Rural				
Age (years)	Urban/Rural			
60 – 69	Urban	0.084	0.329	0.587
60 – 69	Rural	0.145	0.432	0.423
70 – 79	Urban	0.136	0.382	0.482
70 – 79	Rural	0.206	0.463	0.332
80 & above	Urban	0.163	0.394	0.443
80 & above	Rural	0.243	0.464	0.293
Age and Education level				
Age (years)	Education Level			
60 – 69	Primary school	0.119	0.396	0.485
60 – 69	Junior high school	0.097	0.367	0.536

(continued)

Table 7.7 (continued)

		Probability of influence on life satisfaction judgments		
Interactions among variables		Poor or very poor	Fair	Good or very good
60 – 69	High school or Technical secondary school	0.064	0.277	0.660
60 – 69	College or above	0.043	0.244	0.713
70 – 79	Primary school	0.152	0.423	0.425
70 – 79	Junior high school	0.138	0.390	0.472
70 – 79	High school or Technical secondary school	0.058	0.277	0.665
70 – 79	College or above	0.050	0.261	0.689
80 & above	Primary school	0.182	0.443	0.376
80 & above	Junior high school	0.138	0.394	0.468
80 & above	High school or Technical secondary school	0.064	0.270	0.666
80 & above	College or above	0.062	0.294	0.643

7.5.2 Policy Recommendations

(1) The Chinese government has been implementing the *Outline for Development-oriented Poverty Reduction in China's Rural Areas (2011–2020)*. With the massive reduction of the population in absolute poverty, the new phase of the national poverty reduction strategies should prioritize both the absolute poor and the relative poor populations.

(2) The elderly will be a special group among the poor in China. Within the elderly group, poverty reduction strategies and social assistance policies need to prioritize those at an advanced age, rural elderly, female elderly, and those with a low education level. Rural elderly women at an advanced age, especially those with a low education level, will be a particularly vulnerable group requiring special attention. For public policy, there is a need not only for old age insurance but also for the provision of appropriate care services. The current development-oriented poverty alleviation work will contribute to reductions in income poverty and subjective well-being poverty among the elderly in the future.

(3) To achieve the strategic goal of eradicating poverty by 2020, in new poverty reduction strategies and social policies, it has been essential to establish a multi-dimensional and targeted poverty identification mechanism for the elderly and to integrate poverty alleviation, security, and social service mechanisms for

poverty reduction. Overall, in the identification of the poor, multiple objective and subjective dimensions have been considered; in poverty reduction policies, multiple policy systems such as poverty alleviation, old age insurance, assistance, and care services for the elderly have been in place.

References

Alkire, S. (2007). The missing dimensions of poverty data: Introduction to the special issue. *Oxford Development Studies, 35*(4), 347–359.

Brickman, P., Coates, D., & Janoff-Bulman, R. (1978). Lottery winners and accident victims: Is happiness relative? *Journal of Personality and Social Psychology, 36*, 917–927.

Easterlin, R. A. (2001). Income and happiness: Towards a unified theory. *Economic Journal, 111*, 465–484.

Fery, B., & Stutzer, A. (2002). What can economists learn from happiness research? *Journal of Economic Literature, XL*, 402–435.

Fuentes, N., & Rojas, M. (2001). *Economic theory and subjective well-being: Mexico, social indicators research.* Kluwer Academic Press, Marzo.

Kingdon, G. G., & Knight, J. (2004). *Subjective well-being poverty versus income poverty and capabilities poverty?* GPRG-WPS-003.

Krueger, A. B., & Schkade, D. A. (2007, January). *The reliability of subjective well-being measures* (CEPS Working Paper, No.138).

McGillivray, M., & Clarke, M. (2006). *Understanding human well-being New York.* United Nations University Press.

National Bureau of Statistics (NBS). (2008). Poverty monitoring report of rural China 2008. China Statistics Press.

National Bureau of Statistics (NBS) (2009). Statistical communique on the 2008 national economic and social development. China Statistics Press.

Ravallion, M., Datt, G., & Van de Walle, D. (1991). Quantifying absolute poverty in the developing world *Review of Income and Wealth*, 37(4),

Rojas, M. (2003). Well-being and the complexity of poverty: a subjective well-being approach. http://unpan1.un.org.

Rojas, M. (2007). Enhancing poverty-abatement programmes: A subjective well-being contribution. ESRC Research Group on Well-being in Developing Countries.

Samman, E. (2007). Psychological and subjective well-being: a proposal for internationally comparable indicators. OPHI Working Papers Series.

Sherraden, M. (2007). Assets and the poor: A new American welfare policy. The Commercial Press.

Sumner, A. (2006). Economic well-being and non-economic well-being. In M. McGillivray & M. Clarke (Eds.), Understanding human well-being United Nations University Press.

Wang, X., & Alkire, S. (2006). Measurement of multidimensional poverty in China: Estimation and policy implication. *China Rural Economy, 12*(X).

Wang, X., & Alkire, S. (2009). Measurement of multidimensional poverty in China: estimation and policy implication. *China Rural Economy, 12.*

World Bank. (2010). *World development report 2000/2001: Attacking poverty.* World Bank.

Chapter 8
The Multidimensional Poverty of Migrant Women in China: A Case Study of Domestic Services in Beijing

8.1 Research Questions

In September 2015, the United Nations Sustainable Development Summit adopted the Sustainable Development Goals (SDGs). Goal 1 was to eradicate all forms of poverty, and Goal 5 was to achieve gender equality and empower all women and girls.[1] These two goals are interlinked because to achieve equal treatment of women, all forms of poverty would have to be eradicated. *The CPC Central Committee and the State Council's Decision on Winning the Battle Against Poverty* ("*the Decision*") clearly stated that "By the year 2020, rural poor populations will have no concerns about food and clothing and will be guaranteed compulsory education, basic medical services, and housing. The per capita disposable income of farmers in impoverished areas will grow at a rate higher than the national average, and the indicators in major areas of basic public services will be close to the national average. We must ensure that all rural residents living below the current poverty line are lifted out of poverty, and poverty is eliminated in all poor counties and regions, thus eradicating overall regional poverty." *The Decision* proposed to lift more than 70 million rural poor people out of poverty by 2020, indicating by extension that all women migrating from the countryside to the cities would be lifted out of poverty.

The proposal in *the Decision* that "rural poor populations will have no concerns about food and clothing and will be guaranteed compulsory education, basic medical services, and housing" essentially underlines that the evaluation criteria for poverty eradication by 2020 are a multidimensional rather than a single indicator of income. This goal goes beyond the income perspective of welfare economics and evaluates and views poverty more from the perspective of micro-development economics, that is, the development of individuals and farmers. However, against a backdrop of population mobility, a huge challenge facing the new round of poverty alleviation is

[1] Sustainable Development Goals: http://www.un.org/sustainabledevelopment/sustainable-development-goals/.

© Social Sciences Academic Press 2022

X. Wang, *Multidimensional Poverty Measurement*,
International Research on Poverty Reduction,
https://doi.org/10.1007/978-981-19-1189-7_8

to accurately identify and evaluate the poverty levels of the poor among the migrant population, especially women. With the industrial transformation and upgrading of China, the value add of the tertiary sector has surpassed that of the secondary sector. As services are the primary sector for employment and income growth, the poverty of women employed in this sector has become a major issue. With an aging population and the accelerating pace of work in big cities, the domestic service industry is becoming increasingly important. Therefore, the research questions in this chapter are as follows: (1) What is the income poverty of migrant women in the domestic service industry? (2) What is the multidimensional poverty of migrant women in the domestic service industry, in which dimensions is it found, and to what extent? (3) What is the multidimensional poverty of migrant women in the domestic service industry if the social inclusion dimension in subjective well-being is factored in? What is the contribution of each dimension or indicator to the multidimensional poverty index (MPI)? This chapter examines these questions through a questionnaire administered to 532 migrant women engaged in the domestic service industry in Beijing.

8.2 Literature Review

The feminization of poverty can generally be attributed to the increase in the number of female-headed poor households and the growing number of women among the poor.[2] The United Nations Development Fund for Women (UNIFEM) describes it as "the burden of poverty on women, especially in developing countries."[3] This suggests that the feminization of poverty is a result of lack of income as well as inadequate empowerment and gender bias in society and government; it is a crucial issue in the urbanization process in developing countries. Both the United Nations Millennium Development Goals (MDGs) and the ongoing post-2015 SDGs have poverty eradication and promotion of gender equality as key development indicators.

Zhang et al. (2011) review of research on "women's poverty" in China since 2000[4] shows that most research on the feminization of poverty in the country only began at the start of the 21st century, around five years after the Fourth World Conference on Women was held in Beijing; it has been interspersed with general poverty studies, with few specific studies. Researchers understand and explain the feminization of poverty in China at different levels. The incidence of poverty is higher among women than among men and in the unpaid economy where female activity is predominant, women are more likely than men to be poor. The new poverty data imply the following with eight principal sources: laid-off and unemployed, low-income workers, migrant women, landless women farmers, female-headed single-parent households, those with HIV, aging elderly groups, and new forms of poverty resulting from climate change.

---

[2] Liu et al. (2004).

[3] Chen et al. (2005).

[4] Zhang et al. (2011).

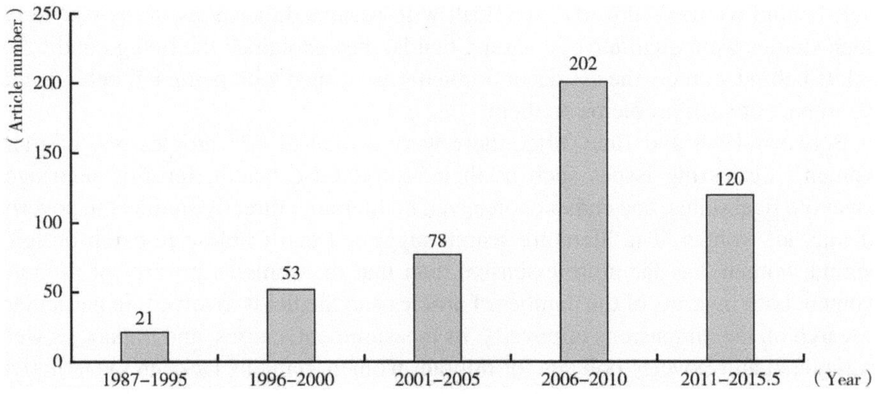

Fig. 8.1 Literature on women's poverty retrieved from CNKI

Poverty among migrant women is a vital component in the feminization of poverty. Duan et al. (2009) argue that in the 1990s, there were evidently more migrant men than migrant women, but recently there has been a gradual "gender balancing."[5] Since 2000, women have accounted for half the migrant population and have even surpassed the number of migrant men in some provinces. According to the Statistical Communique on the 2014 National Economic and Social Development[6] released by the *National Bureau of Statistics (NBS),* China's migrant population that year was 253 million. A migrant population of this size is inevitably accompanied by the emergence of poor groups of migrant women. Therefore, a study of the subdivision of such poor groups is of practical significance to improve the policy of targeted poverty alleviation and relief currently being implemented in China.

A search of Chinese National Knowledge Infrastructure (CNKI) with the keywords "women's poverty," "poor women," and "female poverty" unearthed 474 relevant articles between 1987 and May 2015, with the highest number at 202 between 2006 and 2010 (Fig. 8.1). "Women in poverty" appeared in the title of 25 articles; "women in poor areas" and "rural women's poverty," respectively, in 23 each; "women's poverty" and "poor women" in 4; and "the feminization of poverty" in 6. The research on women's poverty was primarily focused on general research on rural women's poverty and issues such as women's health and microcredit. A small number of studies investigated women's poverty by the subdivision of groups, including six studies on rural elderly women's poverty, four on left-behind women's poverty, and three on minority women's poverty.

Using "left-behind women" as the keyword in a title search revealed that related literature first appeared in 2003, and by June 2015, there were 990 articles on the survival, psychological health, protection of rights and interests, and political participation of left-behind women. Few studies on left-behind women were directly titled

[5] Duan et al. (2009).

[6] National Bureau of Statistics (2015).

"left-behind women's poverty" but dealt with various dimensions of their poverty. Such studies were qualitative in nature, that is, they explained the living conditions of left-behind women, the causes of problems associated with being left behind, and the impact of such problems on them.

Between 1988 and June 2015, there were a total of 427 articles on "migrant women," discussing issues such as their reproductive health, fertility, marriage, psychological status, and career choice; yet, no literature directly studied the poverty of migrant women. The literature search suggested that Chinese research on left-behind women was far more extensive than that on women's poverty or migrant women, both in terms of the number of articles and the fields involved. In particular, research on the dimensions of poverty, its measurement, causes, and impact, as well as targeted anti-poverty policies for migrant women, remains lacking. Quantitative research on the measurement of poverty among migrant women in the domestic service industry, which is one of the major occupations for migrant women, is also scarce.

8.3 Theoretical Framework and Analysis Methods

8.3.1 Theoretical Framework

How poverty is defined is directly related to the dimensions of poverty measurement, indicators, and methods of aggregation and breakdown, as well as the evaluation and perception of poverty and even the impact on anti-poverty strategies and policies. Based on Wang's study (2012), two main types of poverty definitions dominate global poverty measurement[7]: Encyclopedia Britannica defines "poverty" as a state in which a person lacks a certain amount of socially acceptable material wealth or money. Seebohm Rowntree, in his book *Poverty: A Study of Town Life*, calculated the poverty line in the city of York, England, according to the monetary budget required for a "shopping basket" of goods which is "the minimum needed to maintain physical strength." The minimum food budget for a family of six is 15 shillings a week; with some housing, clothing, fuel, and other sundries, a poverty line of 21 shillings a week was measured.[8] The World Bank follows this definition and considers "poverty as a deprivation of well-being."[9] Thus, the definition of poverty depends on how the deprivation of well-being is measured. According to the World Bank, the deprivation of well-being occurs when people lack the means to meet their basic needs. The World Bank (2001) defined and measured poverty using the cost of basic needs approach. Basic needs consist of two parts: one is the amount of food needed to meet adequate nutrition, the calculation of which is recommended to be

[7] Wang (2012).

[8] National Bureau of Statistics (2015).

[9] The World Bank (2001).

based on a daily nutritional intake of 2,100 cal per person; the other is non-food basic needs such as clothing and housing. The two parts are added to derive the poverty line.[10] Following this methodology, the World Bank monitors and compares poverty in countries worldwide, and the most commonly used poverty lines are USD1.25 (purchasing power parity, PPP) and USD2 per day.

Amartya Sen (1985) argued that poverty is not just a lack of income but a phenomenon of capability deprivation.[11] The capability approach is the theoretical basis for the definition and measurement of multidimensional poverty, and Sen emphasizes "immaterial (subjective)," "opportunities," and other key factors contributing to an improved quality of life. On the basis of this epistemology, Alkire and Foster (2007) developed the "AF method" for MPI. This method was adopted by the United Nations Development Programme (UNDP) in the Human Development Report (HDR) in (2010),[12] and it measures multidimensional poverty globally by selecting ten indicators from three dimensions: health, education, and standard of living. Wang and Alkire believe that the greatest contribution of the AF method to poverty measurement is the extension of a single monetary-based poverty measure to more comprehensive dimensions covering well-being and development capacity.[13]

Wang argued that the Chinese notion of "*pinkun*" (literally "poverty") captures the meaning of poverty more accurately than the English word "poverty."[14] The Chinese word "*pinkun*" is composed of "*pin*" (literally "insufficiency") and "*kun*" (literally "hardship"). *Analytical Dictionary of Chinese Characters* defines "*pin*" as "having little wealth." This essentially reflects the economic dimension of poverty (or income/consumption poverty) and, by implication, that fragmentation of property rights ("*pin*" is composed of "*fen*" (literally "allocation") and "*bei*" (literally "money")) is the cause of poverty and affects political rights. Historically, in dynasties where people were more affluent, the "*Jingtian* system" or land system was better implemented. This shows the importance of equitable distribution of land rights, which are the most important property or asset rights to escape poverty. The *Xinhua Dictionary* defines "*kun*" as "trapped in a difficult or painful circumstance from which there is no escape," which is both an objective state and a subjective feeling. It encompasses an individual or family that is trapped in harsh natural conditions and unfavorable social and cultural plights. "*kun*" demonstrates the social, environmental, and cultural dimensions of poverty. The definition of "*kun*" is close to Sen's definition of "capability." Wang et al. (2016) established a multidimensional poverty theoretical framework based on the Chinese notion of "*pinkun*" and examined the relationship between income poverty and multidimensional poverty in China.[15]

---

[10] Haughton and Khandker (2009).

[11] Sen (1985).

[12] Alkire and Foster (2007).

[13] Wang and Alkire (2009).

[14] Wang and Alkire (2009).

[15] Wang et al. (2016).

This study follows the multidimensional poverty theoretical framework developed by Wang et al. and extends it to a multidimensional poverty analysis framework that includes social inclusion in the dimension of subjective well-being poverty. In this way, the measurement of poverty covers three levels: The first is "income/consumption poverty," which implies "insufficiency"; the second is the objective multidimensional poverty that incorporates "income/consumption poverty" as well as education, health, and standard of living; and the third is the broader multidimensional poverty that covers subjective well-being poverty such as social inclusion, which denotes both objective and subjective poverty.

8.3.2 Analysis Methods

With economic and social development, the definition of poverty has changed. In this study, poverty is considered to have many manifestations, at the core of which is extreme poverty, usually measured by income or consumption according to the World Bank's method. Moreover, the ability to access basic services such as education and health, as measured by the MPI, is also important. For migrant women, social inclusion, that is, the subjective sense of well-being, is very important and a necessary component of China's inclusive urban-rural integrated development. Therefore, based on the FGT income poverty measurement and the AF multidimensional poverty methods, this study investigates the poverty of migrant women in the domestic service industry in urban areas at three levels: income poverty, MPI (including income), and MPI (including social inclusion).

8.3.2.1 AF Method

The AF method was adopted by the UNDP to calculate the MPI, which is the most established and widely used method among various multidimensional poverty measures. A detailed discussion of the AF method can be found in Alkire and Foster's (2007) study.[16] The present study summarizes the method as a five-step process: (1) well-being achievement for each dimension, (2) poverty identification for each dimension, (3) poverty aggregation for multiple dimensions, (4) weight setting for aggregation, and (5) decomposition.[17]

---

[16] Alkire and Foster (2007).

[17] Wang and Alkire (2009).

8.3.2.2 Analysis of "Insufficiency"—FGT Method

With regard to the measurement of poverty among migrant women, this study applies the FGT method to measure income poverty. Under the urban-rural household registration system, for the measurement of income poverty of this special group of migrant people, the national rural poverty criterion is clearly on the lower end while the minimum subsistence allowance for urban residents is obviously on the higher end. In this study, income poverty of migrant women is measured according to two principles: first, the national rural poverty criterion, that is, the annual per capita net income, of rural residents is less than RMB2,300 (in constant 2010 prices); second, the monthly per capita income of families with the Beijing minimum subsistence allowance for urban residents in 2012, that is, RMB520, is used as the income poverty line.

8.3.2.3 Measurement of Objective "Insufficiency" and "Hardship"—MPI-I Based on the AF Method

Alkire and Foster (2007) developed the AF method for multidimensional poverty measurement.[18] In (2009), Wang and Alkire used the AF method and data from the *2006 China Health and Nutrition Survey (CHNS)* to measure China's urban and rural multidimensional poverty and determine objective "hardship" in three dimensions: education, health, and standard of living. The *2010 UNDP Human Development Report* first published the global MPI for 104 countries. In 2015, the Oxford Poverty and Human Development Initiative (OPHI) used the *2012 China Family Panel Studies (CFPS)* data to measure Chinese MPI in education, health, and standard of living and included it in the global MPI (which is also a measure of objective "hardship") for publication. Considering the availability of data and the actual situation of the least developed countries, the three dimensions of education, health, and standard of living are usually chosen for comparisons between countries.[19] In essence, the USD1.25 poverty headcount line published by the World Bank measures "insufficiency," while the global MPI published by the UNDP measures "hardship." This chapter establishes the MPI-I covering the four dimensions of income, education, health, and standard of living to measure the objective "insufficiency" and "hardship" of migrant women in the domestic service industry.

8.3.2.4 Measurement of Objective "Insufficiency" and Subjective and Objective "Hardship"—MPI-II Based on the AF Method

The special group of migrant women in the domestic service industry, due to the urban-rural division of household registration, live apart from their families, living

[18] Alkire and Foster (2007).

[19] UNDP (2010).

mostly in the homes of their clients. Here, incorporating "social inclusion" as a dimension to demonstrate the poverty of migrant women is significant if the multidimensional poverty of the 253 million migrant population is to be to eradicated and overall quality of life improved. Therefore, this study uses the dimension of social inclusion to reflect the subjective well-being poverty of migrant women. This chapter establishes the MPI-II covering the five dimensions of income, education, health, standard of living, and social inclusion. Notably, subjective well-being poverty falls into the category of relative poverty.

8.3.3 Dimension Selection and Variable Interpretation

China is in the midst of rapid urbanization and migrant women have gained more employment opportunities in the cities. In the process, they have achieved large-scale income relief from poverty, realized opportunities in mobility, and improved their lives. However, judging from the requirements of building an all-round well-off and a harmonious society, migrant women are beset by the lack of social inclusion. Thus, based on the characteristics of migrant women in China, this study selects variables from five dimensions: income, education, health, standard of living, and social inclusion.

8.3.3.1 Income

China's existing income poverty criterions are divided into rural poverty and urban poverty criterions. The former principle is RMB2,300 (in constant 2010 prices) of annual per capita net income for farmers, while the latter usually consists of the local minimum subsistence allowance for urban residents, which is set by the locality because of the disparity in the standard of living from region to region. This study therefore uses the urban residents' minimum subsistence allowance as the income poverty line for migrant women. As the survey was conducted on 532 domestic service workers in Beijing in 2013, the monthly per capita income of families with the Beijing minimum subsistence allowance for urban residents in 2012, namely RMB520, was chosen as the threshold; thus, migrant women with a per capita monthly disposable income below this threshold are considered to be in income poverty.

8.3.3.2 Education

While years of schooling and school-age children's enrollment are usually considered to be the main indicators of educational poverty when measuring global MPI and country-specific MPI, this study argues that education should also include vocational education and training (VET) opportunities, based on the characteristics of the domestic service industry. Yao and Yu (2006) revealed that VET has a significant impact on the productivity of migrant workers for work in the service sector. Moreover, VET is a vital way to empower poorly educated women, as only with systematic training in vocational skills can migrant women move up the ladder of employment and escape poverty. Therefore, the present study uses the indicators of less than six years of schooling and participation in vocational training as indicators of educational poverty among migrant women.

8.3.3.3 Health

This study uses migrant women's health insurance coverage and self-assessment of their health status to assess health poverty. Participation in health insurance reflects the extent to which migrant women are able to spread the financial burden of disease risk through the social security system. Currently in China, the new rural cooperative health care system has played a positive role in alleviating the contradictions in rural areas that diseases lead to both poverty and a return to poverty. Self-rated health status demonstrates the health of migrant women at the time of the survey; those without any kind of health insurance or who are in poor health are considered to be in health poverty.

8.3.3.4 Standard of Living

Standard of living is measured by housing and bathing and sanitation facilities. Shelter poverty is the most important form of non-income poverty among the migrant population.[20] Housing is a major factor exhibiting the standard of living of the migrant population in the city as well as one of their main expenses. With the constraints of multiple factors such as price, location, transportation, and surrounding environment, the migrant population tends to reside in dilapidated dwellings that provide neither a safe living environment nor qualified sanitation facilities, which affects their ability to survive and develop. Thus, in this study, those who do not live anywhere other than the client's home, or those who live in tube-shaped houses, ordinary cottages in cities and the suburbs, and basements are considered to be in housing poverty. Those without access to bathing or flushing toilets are considered poor in terms of bathing and sanitation facilities.

8.3.3.5 Social Inclusion

Poverty is assessed both from an objective well-being achieved by each individual in society, such as whether or not their net per capita income is above the national

[20] Samanta (2015).

poverty line, and from each individual's subjective assessment of their living conditions. An individual's subjective perception or evaluation of the deprivation of well-being is named "subjective well-being poverty."[21] Social exclusion faced by migrant women is the main problem of subjective well-being deprivation for this group. The social exclusion of migrant women in cities, especially rural migrant women, has psychological effects in addition to medical and educational restrictions; although the migrant population has a strong desire to integrate into local society, there are few channels available for social participation.[22] In this way, this study regards social inclusion as a dimension to measure subjective well-being poverty among migrant women using three indicators: social relations, urban belonging, and job satisfaction (see Table 8.1 for specific evaluation criteria).

Table 8.1 Dimension and indicator settings

	Indicator	Setting of threshold	Weight
Income	Income poverty	An individual with an income below the monthly per capita income of families based on the Beijing minimum subsistence allowance for urban residents in 2012, namely RMB520, is considered poor and assigned a value of 1 and otherwise 0	1/5
Education and training	Years of schooling	An individual with less than 6 years of schooling is considered poor and assigned a value of 1 and otherwise 0	1/10
	Skills training	An individual who has not participated in skills training related to the domestic service industry is considered poor and assigned a value of 1 and otherwise 0	1/10
Health	Health insurance	An individual without any type of health insurance is considered poor and assigned a value of 1 and otherwise 0	1/10
	Self-rated health	An individual who is currently in very poor health is considered poor and assigned a value of 1 and otherwise 0	1/10

(continued)

[21] Wang et al. (2011).

[22] Duan et al. (2009).

Table 8.1 (continued)

	Indicator	Setting of threshold	Weight
Standard of living	Housing	An individual without any housing other than the client's home or who lives in tube-shaped houses, ordinary cottages in cities and the suburbs or basements is considered poor and assigned a value of 1 and otherwise 0	1/15
	Bathing facilities	0 An individual without access to bathing facilities or who heats water for bathing is considered poor and assigned a value of 1 and otherwise 0	1/15
	Sanitation facilities	An individual who has no access to an indoor or outdoor flushing toilet is considered poor and assigned a value of 1 and otherwise 0	1/15
Social inclusion	Social relations	An individual who has no social relations in the local community is considered poor and assigned a value of 1 and otherwise 0	1/15
	Urban belonging	An individual who does not feel they belong in the city is considered poor and assigned a value of 1 and otherwise 0	1/15
	Job satisfaction	An individual who is "dissatisfied" or "very dissatisfied" with their current job is considered poor and assigned a value of 1 and otherwise 0	1/15

Note Refer to http://shbz.beijing.cn/syzx/n21412740.shtml

8.4 Data and Analysis Results

The data for this study were derived from a survey of female domestic workers in Beijing in 2013 conducted by the International Poverty Reduction Center in China (IPPCC). The survey was commissioned by the Beijing FP Domestic Service Center, and 532 nannies, maternity matrons, hourly workers, and caregivers were selected through random sampling to complete self-administered questionnaires; 451 valid questionnaires were obtained. The main analysis results are as follows.

8.4.1 Descriptive Statistics

The participant's age in the survey samples ranged from 18 to 57 years, with a mean of 41 years and 76% of the sample concentrated in the "35–49 years" age group. Agriculturally registered samples accounted for 74%, while those registered non-agriculturally accounted for 26%, of which nearly 3/4th were from western provinces. Han Chinese accounted for 96.03%, while ethnic minorities accounted for only 3.97%. Married subjects made up 78.88% of the total, with the divorced (9.3%) and single (7.75%) making up the balance.

The average monthly disposable income of the survey samples in 2012 was RMB2,978, with a minimum of RMB150 and a maximum of RMB30,000. The average monthly disposable income was concentrated in the range of RMB1,000–2,999, accounting for 53.30%, followed by RMB3,000–4,999, accounting for 42.29%. "High wages" and "easy to find a job" were the main reasons cited by migrant workers for choosing domestic services.

The employment threshold of the domestic service industry is low and suitable for rural women with a low education level. Among the survey samples, 11.39% of women had an education level of primary school or below; 52.56% junior high school; 33.40% high school, technical secondary school, and technical school; and only 2.66% college level or higher. Over 92.66% of domestic helpers had received more than one week of pre-service training.

In the survey samples, health insurance coverage was good: 50% had enrolled in the new rural cooperative health care, 17.7% had enrolled in urban health insurance, and 45.33% had personal accident insurance. Among them, 78.82% rated their health as "very good" or "good," 18.12% as "fair," and only 3.06% as "poor" or "very poor." Among the migrant women who self-rated as "fair," "poor," and "very poor," 67.7% were in the "35–49" age group. Among the migrant women's families, 7.73% had major expenditures on "health care" in 2012, which indicated that disease-caused poverty and return to poverty were not prevalent in households that were able to move away for work.

Generally, the income of migrant women in urban areas was appreciably higher than that in rural areas, with a considerable improvement in living environment and sanitation facilities. In the case of toilets, for example, the proportion of migrant women who had no access to "indoor or outdoor flush toilets" in their hometowns reached 84.75%, but this indicator dropped to 12.03% when they moved to cities. Many migrant women had difficulty obtaining water in their hometowns and were unable to take a bath, while less than 30% had to "use a communal bath or heat hot water to take a bath" in the cities.

The problem of social inclusion of migrant women was more serious, as most, especially the older ones, did not have a sense of belonging and closeness to the city where they usually worked and lived. Among migrant women, 46.21% never interacted with the surrounding residents; of these 13.05% were under 35 years of age, 80.43% between 35 and 50 years, and 6.52% over 50 years. Moreover, 24.69% did not feel they were part of the city, 4.56% were "dissatisfied" or "very dissatisfied"

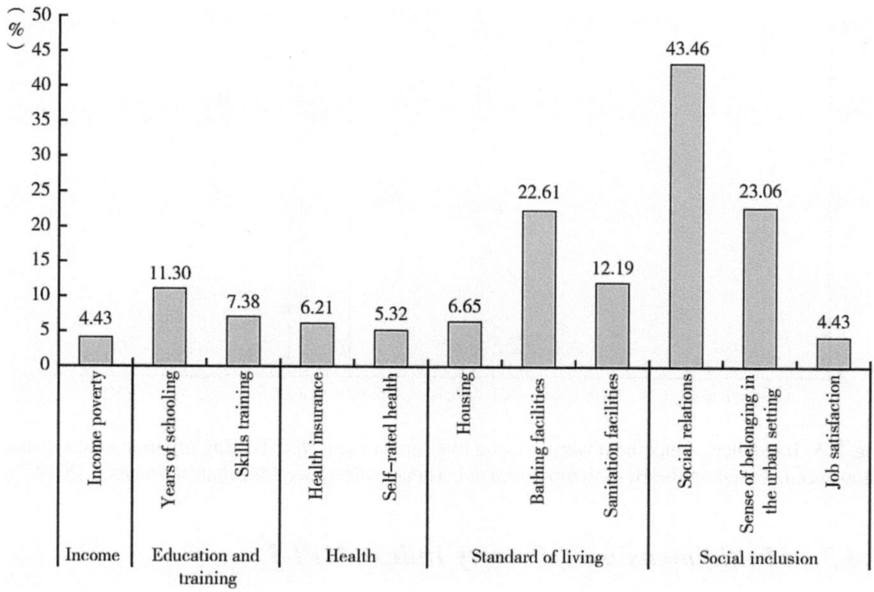

Fig. 8.2 Incidence of poverty by indicator (N = 451)

with their current job, and 12.45% were "dissatisfied" or "very dissatisfied" with their current life.

In terms of the incidence of poverty across the 11 indicators in 5 dimensions (Fig. 8.2), the top 3 indicators of poverty were social relations, urban belonging, and bathing facilities, with incidence rates of 43.46%, 23.06%, and 22.61%, respectively. Income poverty among migrant women in the domestic service industry was not pronounced (4.43%), which suggested that measuring poverty among migrant women based on income alone was one-sided.

8.4.2 Income Poverty

Working in cities provides an important means for migrant women to increase their income. Calculated on the basis of the national rural poverty criterion, that is, the annual per capita income of RMB2,300 (in constant 2010 prices), all migrant women in the domestic service industry in this survey were able to escape income poverty; however, if calculated on the basis of the monthly per capita income of families with the Beijing minimum subsistence allowance for urban residents in 2012, namely RMB520, 0.44% of the migrant women in the sample group were in income poverty. Comparing by occupation type, income was higher for maternity matrons/babysitters and domestic helpers; conversely, income was lower for hourly workers or others, with 7.14% below the urban poverty line of the minimum subsistence allowance (Fig. 8.3).

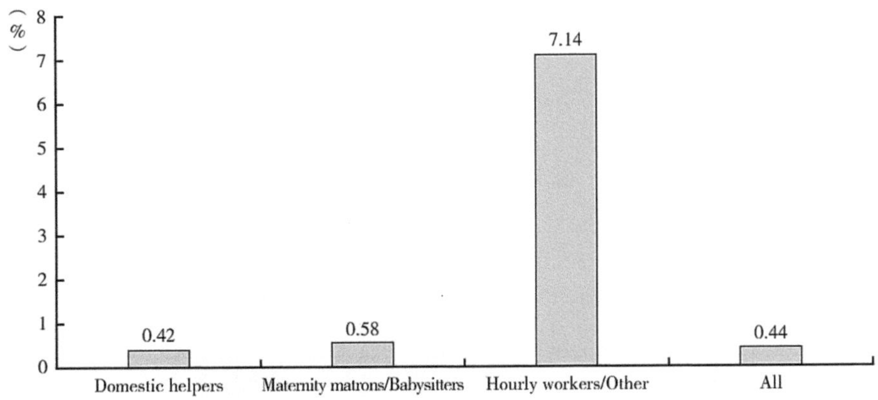

Fig. 8.3 Incidence of income poverty among migrant women. *Note* Beijing minimum subsistence allowance is based on the Beijing minimum subsistence allowance for urban residents in 2012

8.4.3 Multidimensional Poverty Index (MPI-I)

This study sets $k = 30\%$ as the multidimensional poverty threshold, that is, if 1.2 of the four dimensions are deprived, the respondents are considered to be in multidimensional poverty. The measurement of MPI-I showed that 2.44% of the migrant women in the domestic service industry were in multidimensional poverty without allowing for subjective perceptions. Table 8.2 indicates that 2.44% of the women in the samples were in multidimensional poverty (H), with an average deprivation level of 37.12% (A) and an MPI of $M_0 = 0.009$. Judging from the urban-rural breakdown and education level, the prevalence of multidimensional poverty was higher among rural women than among urban women (2.45:0.9%), as well as among women with low education levels than among those with high education levels (13.72:1%).

The contribution of each dimension to the MPI, in descending order, was as follows: standard of living, education and training, health, and income (Table 8.3), with health (29.03%) and education and training (30.28%) contributing almost equally. The contribution of each indicator to the MPI, in descending order, was as follows: health insurance, bathing facilities, skills training, years of schooling, sanitation facilities, self-rated health, income, and housing. Health insurance contributed

Table 8.2 H, A, M_0, and breakdown at the 30% threshold—without social inclusion ($k = 30\%$)

Dimension	Indicator	All	Urban-rural breakdown		Years of schooling	
			Urban registration	Rural registration	6 years or below	7 years or above
MPI	M_0	0.009	0.003	0.009	0.048	0.004
	H (%)	2.44	0.9	2.45	13.72	1
	A (%)	37.12	33.33	37.5	35.12	40.62

Table 8.3 Contribution of each dimension and indicator to MPI-I ($k = 30\%$)

	Indicator	Contribution of indicator to MPI (%)	Contribution of dimension to MPI (%)
Income	Per capita monthly disposable income	6.11	6.11
Education and training	Years of schooling	12.86	30.28
	Skills training	17.42	–
Health	Health insurance	19.06	29.03
	Self-rated health	9.97	–
Standard of living	Housing	5.81	34.58
	Bathing facilities	18.54	–
	Sanitation facilities	10.23	–

significantly to the MPI, largely because although the sample population was fundamentally lifted out of income poverty, it fell into poverty as soon as a family member suffered from a major disease. Among migrant women's households, 7.73% of the major expenditure in 2012 was on health care; furthermore, poor health insurance exacerbated household poverty.

8.4.4 *Multidimensional Poverty Index (MPI-II)*

Social inclusion is a shortcoming of migrant women's poverty. The measurement of MPI-II showed that the incidence of multidimensional poverty increased to 5.54% and the MPI-II increased to 0.019 after adding the subjective well-being indicator of social inclusion for migrant women to the measurement (Table 8.4).

The contribution of each dimension to the MPI (Table 8.5), in descending order, was social inclusion, standard of living, education and training, health, and income. The contribution of each indicator to the MPI, in descending order, was social relations, social security, bathing facilities, skills training, years of schooling, urban belonging, sanitation facilities, self-rated health, job satisfaction, housing, and income. The contribution of social relations was 17.4%; the contributions of social

Table 8.4 H, A, M0, and breakdown at the 30% threshold—with social inclusion ($k = 30\%$)

Dimension	Indicator	All	Urban-rural breakdown		Years of schooling	
			Urban registration	Rural registration	6 years or below	7 years or above
MPI	M_0	0.019	0.006	0.022	0.067	0.013
	H (%)	5.54	1.8	6.44	19.361	3.75
	A (%)	33.87	31.66	33.81	34.33	33.56

Table 8.5 Contribution of each dimension and indicator to MPI-II ($k = 30\%$)

	Indicator	Contribution of indicator to MPI-II (%)	Contribution of dimension to MPI-II (%)
Income	Per capita monthly disposable income	2.32	2.32
Education and training	Years of schooling	10.57	21.14
	Skills training	11.03	–
Health	Health insurance	11.63	18.63
	Self-rated health	7	–
Standard of living	Housing	4.68	23.68
	Bathing facilities	11.22	–
	Sanitation facilities	7.78	–
Social inclusion	Social relations	17.4	33.77
	Urban belonging	10.51	–
	Job satisfaction	5.85	–

security, bathing facilities, skills training, years of schooling, and urban belonging were between 10.51 and 11.63% (around the same level); and the contribution of income was the lowest at 2.32%. This showed that there was much room for improvement for the inclusion of migrant women in cities. Though many domestic workers reported good relationships with their clients, they had a small social radius, a poor sense of belonging, and limited interaction with other social members, as well as little involvement in community activities and minimal leisure time outside of work. More than half of the rural domestic helpers stated that "I work here but I don't belong here."

The survey on "job satisfaction" revealed that the main dissatisfaction of domestic helpers was with regard to long working hours and low pay. With the exception of day laborers and hourly workers, most domestic helpers were at clients' homes 24 h a day, in a state of constant service. Domestic helpers are paid a high monthly salary but a low hourly rate. For babysitters, their monthly salary was RMB3,500, but they worked 26 days a month, at least 12 h a day, for an hourly rate of about RMB11.21, slightly above the minimum hourly rate of RMB9.89 in Beijing.[23]

[23] Beijing Municipal Human Resources and Social Security Bureau (2015).

8.5 Main Conclusions and Policy Recommendations

8.5.1 Main Conclusions

(1) The measurement of poverty among migrant women from the perspective of multidimensional poverty revealed that when using the national rural poverty criterion to measure the income poverty of migrant women, the sample group was completely out of poverty; however, when using the Beijing minimum subsistence allowance for urban residents as the poverty criterion, the incidence of income poverty was 0.44%.

(2) The MPI-I measured by the four dimensions of income, education, health, and standard of living showed that the standard of living dimension among migrant women in the domestic service industry was the lowest, followed by education and training, health, and income. The objective poverty dimension most in need of improvement was the standard of living among migrant women. A breakdown of the MPI by household registration showed that the prevalence of multidimensional poverty was higher among migrant women with rural registration than those with urban registration. A breakdown of the MPI by years of schooling suggested that the incidence of multidimensional poverty was higher among migrant women with low education levels than those with high education levels.

(3) The MPI-II measured by the five dimensions of income, education, health, standard of living, and social inclusion showed that the social inclusion dimension of migrant women in the domestic service industry was the poorest, followed by standard of living, education and training, health, and income. The subjective well-being indicator most in need of improvement was social relations, followed by urban belonging, job satisfaction, and life satisfaction. The results of the study indicate that the social inclusion of migrant women is a priority issue of relative poverty that needs to be addressed as well as the first issue which should be addressed to build an inclusive society. Similarly, the urban-rural breakdown results showed that the MPI, the incidence of multidimensional poverty, and the degree of multidimensional poverty were significantly higher among migrant women with rural registration than those with urban registration. Breakdown by years of schooling also suggested that the incidence of multidimensional poverty, the MPI, and the degree of multidimensional poverty were appreciably higher among migrant women with fewer years of schooling than those with more.

8.5.2 *Policy Recommendations*

1. Improving the urban-rural integration system and mechanism to break the public service system that divides urban and rural areas

A large number of migrant women is a problem that has arisen from the division of urban and rural households and the rapid urbanization process. Migrant women have found jobs in cities, solved their employment problems, and increased their incomes; however, the division of urban and rural households has made it difficult for them to obtain public services on an equal footing with urban residents in terms of housing, children's education, health, and social security. This is the root cause of the widespread feeling of exclusion and lack of a sense of belonging among migrant women who, in their own words, stated "I work here but I don't belong here." Thus, efforts should go toward the problems of the household registration system that divides urban and rural areas, as well as the related education, medical and health, employment, and social security systems, so that migrant inclusion into the population in cities can be fairly guaranteed. For instance, efforts should be at the earliest to resolve the problem of one-card settlement for cooperative health care and pension insurance across provinces and regions.

2. Promoting the multidimensional urbanization of the migrant population to truly embrace them in the urban fabric

The current government has proposed that, in the coming period, emphasis will be placed on solving the existing "three 100 million people" strategy, that is, promoting the settlement of some 100 million agricultural migrants in cities, transforming urban shantytowns and villages where roughly 100 million people live, and guiding around 100 million people to urbanization in the central and western regions near their homes. Under this development strategy, we cannot simply settle down and build houses; the multidimensional development needs of the migrant population, such as social inclusion, standard of living, and health, must be considered so that the migrant population, especially migrant women, can integrate into cities in every respect.

3. Establishing a sound and effective poverty identification mechanism to cover poor migrant women

As indicated by the income poverty measurement among migrant women in this chapter, according to the national rural poverty criterion, migrant women are not considered to be in income poverty. Thus, from 2014 onward, when rural poor populations were documented nationwide and targeted poverty alleviation was implemented, most migrant women were not covered. Existing policies undoubtedly target the absolute poor; however, with economic and social development, there is a greater need to focus on multidimensional poverty and alleviate relative poverty. In the future, it will be necessary to establish an effective poverty identification mechanism to cover migrant poor women and alleviate comprehensive multidimensional poverty. In particular, in order to build a harmonious society, the subjective well-being of migrant women should also be highlighted.

4. Mobilizing enterprises and social forces to strengthen capacity building for migrant women

The grassroots nature of social organizations makes them more conducive to promoting changes in the attitudes and habits of the migrant population, and they can easily play a role in promoting the re-socialization of the migrant population. Intermediary organizations (e.g., labor service and domestic service companies), social organizations, communities, and volunteers have a wealth of experience in mobilizing migrant populations for capacity building and can compensate for the lack of human resources at the "last mile" of government public services. It is therefore possible to help migrant women through training and various activities, especially to enable them to understand and adapt to working and living in cities and to reduce their sense of unfamiliarity and alienation. Communication barriers are common among migrant women, which affects their quality of life in cities and their communication with clients. Thus, intermediaries and social organizations should reinforce communication skills training.

5. Refining the legal system to safeguard women's rights and interests

At present, domestic workers in cities seek jobs mainly through domestic service companies and referrals from friends. Many domestic workers do not sign employment contracts with employers and are informally employed, making it difficult for them to enforce their rights. Even for those who have signed service contracts, there are obstacles to their ability to enforce their rights as they lack legal awareness of these rights. The government should strengthen the building of industry associations and join with them to regulate the domestic service market, intensify legal training and legal aid for employees, and tighten the supervision of intermediaries, thereby helping to safeguard the rights and interests of both employers and employees.

References

Alkire, S., & Foster, J. (2007). *Counting and multidimensional poverty measurement*. (OPHI Working Paper Series, No. 07). Oxford University Press.

Beijing Municipal Human Resources and Social Security Bureau. (2015). *Notice on the adjustment of Beijing's 2015 minimum wage standard*. http://zhengwu.beijing.gov.cn/gzdt/gggs/t1381895.htm. (Visited on August 30, 2015).

Chen, M., Joann, V., Francie, L., James, H., Renana, J., & Christine, B. (2005). *Progress of the world's women 2005: Women, work and poverty*. United Nations Development Fund for Women Report. http://Www.unwomen.org/en/digital-library/publications/2005/1/progress-of-the-world-s-women-2005-women-work-and-poverty.

Duan, C., Zhang, F., & Lu, X. (2009). A study on the female migrant population in China. *Collection of Women's Studies*, (4).

Haughton, J., & Khandker, S. (2009). *Handbook on poverty and inequality* (pp. 67–81). The World Bank.

Liu, X., Li, X., & Ye, J. (2004). Poverty from a gender perspective. *Agricultural Economic Issues*, (10).

National Bureau of Statistics. (2015). *Statistical communique on the 2014 National Economic and Social Development*. http://www.stats.gov.cn/tjsj/zxfb/201502/t20150226_685799.html.

Samanta, D. (2015). Urban poverty in developing Asia—Dichotomy between the income and non-income dimensions: Are we not grossly underestimating its incidence? In A. Heshmati, E. Maasoumi, & G. Wan (Eds.), *Manila poverty reduction policies and practices in developing Asia, economic studies in inequality, social exclusion and well-being* (pp. 80–105). Asian Development Bank and Springer Open.

Sen, A. (1985). *Commodities and capabilities* (pp. 26–33). Oxford University Press.

The World Bank. (2001). *World Development Report 2000/2001: Attacking poverty* (pp. 7–8). Washington: The World Bank. http://www-wds.worldbank.org/external/default/WDSContentServer/WDSP/IB/2000/12/13/000094946_00092605361978/Rendered/PDF/multi_page.pdf.

UNDP. (2010). Human Development Report (2010). *The real wealth of nation: Pathways to human development* (pp. 11–22). New York: United Nations Development Programme.

Wang, X., & Alkire, S. (2009). Multidimensional poverty measurement in China: estimation and policy implications. *Chinese Rural Economy*, 12.

Wang, X. (2012). *Poverty measurement: Theories and methods*. Social Sciences Academic Press.

Wang, X., Feng, H., Xia, Q., & Alkire, S. (2016). *On relationship between income poverty and multidimensional poverty in China*. OPHI Working Paper Series No. 101. Oxford University Press.

Wang, X., Shang, X., & Xu, L. (2011). Subjective well-being poverty of the elderly population in China. *Social Policy and Administration, 6*(45), 714–731.

Yao, X., & Yu, L. (2006). Migrant workers' occupational stratification and human capital constraints. *Journal of Zhejiang University* (Humanities and Social Sciences Edition), (5).

Zhang, X., Li, J., & Li, X. (2011). Women's poverty: From rural to urban-rural, from income poverty to multidimensional poverty: A review and prospect of research on 'women's poverty' in China since 2000. *Collection of women's studies*, (5).

Chapter 9
Analysis of Multidimensional Child Poverty in China

9.1 Introduction

Children are the future if the development of human society is to progress, and their development has thus become a major indicator of social equity and progress. The *United Nations Convention on the Rights of the Child* (UNCRC) clearly stipulates that children should enjoy all the rights of a person. However, as children are immature both physically and mentally, they need special protection and care, including appropriate legal protection, both before and after birth. *The Law of the People's Republic of China on the Protection of Minors* clearly stipulates that "minors enjoy such rights as the right to survival, the right to development, the right to protection, and the right to participation, and the State provides special and priority protection to minors in accordance with the characteristics of their physical and mental development, so as to ensure that their legal rights and interests are not infringed upon." The guiding philosophy of China's *National Program for Child Development (2011–2020)* is holding high the great banner of socialism with its Chinese characteristics. The program uses Deng Xiaoping's theory and the important concept of the Three Represents as a guide to thoroughly implement the Scientific Outlook on Development, while adhering to the principle of Children First, in order to safeguard children's rights to survival, development, protection, and participation; reduce disparities between urban and rural areas in child development; raise the level of child welfare; improve the overall quality of life for children; and promote their healthy, all-round development.

The *UNCRC* clearly states that contracting states should ensure that every child enjoys a safe, nutritious, and happy childhood and that a sound environment is created for child development. Governments have taken various measures to ensure that children can enjoy their rights, but more than two decades after *the Convention*

This chapter is based on the results of a data analysis of child welfare demonstration zones in China conducted by the author, Prof. X. Shang and Dr. S. Wang.

© Social Sciences Academic Press 2022

X. Wang, *Multidimensional Poverty Measurement*,
International Research on Poverty Reduction,
https://doi.org/10.1007/978-981-19-1189-7_9

came into force, there remain major problems in improving the environments in which children live, grow, and develop. According to a study by the United Nations Children's Fund (UNICEF), over half of the children in developing countries live in poverty (UNICEF, 2004). Poverty affects the lives of millions of children worldwide, and it is a problem persisting in both developing and developed countries. Overall, there have been some global successes in the fight against poverty and many people have been lifted out of poverty; however, the problem of child deprivation remains insurmountable. Depriving children in poverty of their rights will have an extremely important impact on future society's well-being and freedom (Sen, 2009).

Eradicating child poverty requires special studies and policies. This is because poverty has a different impact on children than on adults. Children have few means to lift themselves out of poverty and have to rely more on the equitable provision of public services and the fair distribution of resources within the household. Traditional poverty reduction strategies, which eradicate poverty by promoting economic growth, do not recognize the specific and particular needs of children and therefore cannot fully address child poverty. Eradicating poverty means reducing inequalities and narrowing the gap between the rich and poor so that all children can thrive. In the meantime, the eradication of child poverty is a key link in breaking the chain of intergenerational transmission of poverty and a major component of achieving fair and just social development.

Public policy interventions on child poverty are based on poverty measurement. The widely accepted income- or consumption-based monetary approach has encountered significant challenges because, while it is simple and easy to measure poverty with per capita net income, this approach does not adequately reflect children's multiple rights to survival, development, protection, and participation as defined by the UNCRC.

Taking Amartya Sen's (2009) capability approach as the basic theory, this chapter constructs multidimensional indicators for the measurement of child poverty in accordance with the multidimensional framework of the UNCRC and the Law of the People's Republic of China on the Protection of Minors. The aim is to measure the dimension and degree of poverty of poor children in child welfare demonstration zones and investigate the main causes of child poverty.

9.2 Literature Review

9.2.1 On the Meaning of Child Poverty

No uniform approach has been adopted so far to define, identify, and measure child poverty (UNICEF, 2006). Different research institutions have assigned different meanings to child poverty according to their own research objectives.

9.2.1.1 Definition of UNICEF

The UNICEF defines child poverty as the most basic "Deprivation of Social Services" (UNICEF, 2006). The most fundamental set of goods and social services on which children depend for survival are food, safe drinking water, sanitation facilities, health services, shelter, education, and information services (Gordon et al., 2003a, 2003b). In *The State of the World's Children 2005*, UNICEF states that poor children are those who are deprived of the material, mental, and emotional resources that are necessary for human survival, development, and reproduction. Without these resources, children cannot enjoy equal rights with other members of society and reach their full potential.

The psychological, physical, emotional, and mental development of children is affected if they are trapped in poverty. Therefore, it is particularly important to go beyond income or consumption poverty in the traditional sense and instead define poverty from a multidimensional perspective (UNICEF, 2011). In fact, deprivation in a single dimension, even in the short term, can have long-term adverse effects on child development, and these adverse effects interact with each other (Abello & Harding, 2006). Deprivation of material resources often leads to malnutrition, which in turn affects children's health and education, thereby further affecting their long-term development. In addition, children from poor families often face interruption in their schooling to join the workforce and reduce their family's debt burden, which impacts on their cognitive ability and physical development.

9.2.1.2 Definition of the Childhood Poverty Research and Policy Centre, UK

The Childhood Poverty Research and Policy Centre (CHIP) defines child poverty as the inability of children and youth to access and use various types of resources that are essential to their well-being and potential as they grow. Broadly, these resources are economic, social, cultural, physical, environmental, and political. Specifically, poor children face the following issues in their development.

(1) Insufficient economic, material, and environmental resources: Lack of adequate means of subsistence and access to the financial resources and nutritional substances necessary for survival and development.
(2) Insufficient social, cultural, and material resources: Lack of opportunities necessary for human development, that is, opportunities to live life to the fullest potential, such as equitable access to education, life skills, health, drinking water, and sanitation facilities.
(3) Inadequate social and material resources, that is, not being nurtured and protected by family or community organizations: Parents or guardians who do not have the time, ability, or willingness to raise a child; no foster family or community that can take over the responsibility of raising a child in place of

the parents or guardians when they are unable to do so or are not present; or no group or community to care for and protect the child.

(4) Inadequate social resources: Lack of voice, which often aggravates other aspects of poverty, both for adults and children.

9.2.1.3 Definition of the Christian Children's Fund

The Christian Children's Fund (CCF) conducted a study on children's experiences of poverty and its impact in 2002 to understand how children suffer from poverty by directly contacting poor children and their families (Feeny & Boyden, 2003). Poverty, in its usual sense, is the condition in which a person lacks a certain amount of money or material things that are necessary for survival or social recognition. According to the CCF, two issues need to be considered when identifying or measuring child poverty: First, poverty is relative and is understood differently in different times and societies and, second, poverty can be expressed as the ability to purchase goods or services or the ownership of physical assets (Feeny & Boyden, 2003). In this way, it is inappropriate to adopt a poverty line to identify and measure child poverty because children do not have the ability to earn or dispose of income. Similarly, it is incorrect to estimate child welfare based on household consumption, as it mistakenly assumes that children have the same income distribution ratio or consumption ratio as other household members (Boyden, Feeny, & Scott, 2003). Furthermore, Arjun Appadurai suggests that the monetary measure highlights material aspects but ignores the intangible aspects of poverty, such as sense of security, freedom from harassment and sexual abuse, and social exclusion (Boyden et al., 2003). Therefore, the CCF argues that child poverty is a multidimensional phenomenon that encompasses both tangible and intangible poverty.

Child poverty, as defined by the CCF, covers three interrelated areas. First is deprivation, that is, the lack of material conditions and services that are usually considered essential for the development of a child's full potential. Second is the injustice suffered as a result of the denial of children's dignity, voice, and other rights, or when their survival is threatened. Third is vulnerability, that is, the possibility that a society is incapable of coping with existing or future threats that may affect child growth and development.

9.2.2 *Key Measures of Child Poverty*

The most common approach to measuring child poverty is the monetary approach, which emphasizes the importance of income. A sufficient income is crucial for a person's well-being and future development (Howe & Pidwell, 2004). However, recently, with the advancement of poverty research, in particular, the emergence of the concept of multidimensional poverty, academics have realized the limitations of the monetary approach and have shifted from a unidimensional approach that emphasizes income alone to the measurement of multidimensional poverty.

Currently, there are four main approaches to child poverty measurement: monetary, deprivation, social exclusion, and well-being.

9.2.2.1 Monetary Approach

The monetary approach considers children in poverty as those living in low-income families, as low family income is strongly associated with child welfare and children's development opportunities. A child in a family is poor if the income of that family is below the set poverty line.

The monetary approach uses two methods to identify and measure poverty: the absolute poverty line and the relative poverty line. The absolute poverty line is set based on the ability to purchase a certain amount of goods and services, while the relative poverty line is related to the standard of living in a specific country (UNICEF, 2005). A person is identified as poor or not based on their ability to purchase a "basket" of food and services necessary for survival (Corak, 2006a, b). Low- and middle-income countries usually have two poverty lines: an official national poverty line and an internationally accepted poverty line, such as the "USD1/day" poverty line. The former cannot be used for cross-country comparisons as the basis for setting it varies across countries. The most widely used is the internationally accepted absolute poverty line, as used in the Millennium Development Goals.

Relative poverty lines are more commonly used in developed countries to measure poverty. The setting of this line needs to consider specific time and place as well as country-specific standards of living (Save the Children UK, 2000) and is constantly adjusted to changes in national welfare levels. The European Union, for example, employs Laeken indicators to set a relative poverty line at 50–60% of the median income (UN, 2007).

UNICEF, in its report *Child Poverty in Rich Countries 2005*, measures child poverty in OECD countries by setting a relative poverty line at 50% of the median income. It shows that child poverty rates only decline when children from low-income families benefit more from economic growth than those from wealthy families (UNICEF-IRC, 2005). The report indicates that child poverty rates remain high in OECD countries, even in countries such as the UK, Italy, the US, and Mexico. Among the 14 countries cited, only 5 had performed well in the reduction of child poverty, while performance had worsened in others (UNICEF, 2006).

9.2.2.2 Deprivation Approach

The "Bristol Study" and the Young Lives' Project are the most influential studies to use the deprivation approach as a measure of child poverty. The former was an empirical study conducted by a research team established by the University of Bristol and the London School of Economics, with the aim of understanding the deprivation or poverty experienced by poor children in developing countries with regard to the seven basic needs: food, drinking water, sanitation facilities, health care, housing, education, and information. This study was the first ever to use scientific methods to measure the extent and depth of poverty among poor children in all developing countries (Gordon et al., 2003a). The Bristol Study revealed that there were over 1.8 billion poor children in developing countries. Among them, 15% of the children under 5 years old were severely food-deprived; 376 million (20%) lacked safe drinking water or had to walk more than 15 min to get water; over 500 million (31%) did not have access to sanitation facilities; 265 million (15%) had no health care; over 500 million (34%) lacked safe housing; nearly 134 million (13%) among those aged 7–18 years had never attended school; and nearly 500 million (25%) had no access to information (Gordon et al., 2003b).

The Young Lives' Project was an international collaborative research project funded by the British Department for International Development (DFID). The project used the deprivation approach to study the causes and consequences of child poverty (UNDP, 2004). Different from the Bristol Study, the Young Lives' Project aimed to understand changes in child well-being over time. It was a long-term project that tracked the poverty experiences of around 12,000 children and their families in 4 countries (Ethiopia, Peru, Vietnam, and India) for more than 15 years to examine changes in child welfare. The project's indicators covered all aspects of children's lives: (1) access to basic services including electricity, safe drinking water, and sanitation facilities; (2) access to both primary and child health care, such as vaccines, prevalence and control of childhood diseases, and distance to health centers; (3) child care and child rearing; (4) child malnutrition; (5) literacy and numeracy; (6) child labor; and (7) social capital in the community.

The findings of the Young Lives' Project are similar to those of the Bristol Study: poor children are severely deprived of basic needs such as clean drinking water, quality education, electricity, and safe housing, especially in rural areas where children, especially girls, are the most vulnerable group to child poverty (Attawell, 2003).

9.2.2.3 Social Exclusion Approach

Social exclusion is a complex and multidimensional process that encompasses the lack of resources, rights, goods, and services as well as the inability to participate in economic, social, cultural, or political activities and to establish normal social relations with people, a right to which all in society are entitled. From a child's point of view, social exclusion includes both restrictions on the child's participation in social activities (e.g., hobbies, celebrations, school-organized camping trips, family gatherings, and inviting friends to the house) and the influence that parents, families, and neighbors may have on the child (e.g., parents' mental health, employment, and the character of neighbors). In judging whether a child is socially excluded, the following need to be considered: his/her relationships with friends and family, whether there is pocket money, school performance, future aspirations, and emotional development

(Adelman & Middleton, 2003). Thus, social exclusion affects the quality of human life as well as the fairness and cohesion of society.

Social exclusion affects children in two principal aspects: relationships with peers and participation in formal and informal activities. Poor children are under much pressure from their peers and society and often feel ashamed of their poverty. Some children feel embarrassed and uneasy about their current situation, especially when they want to participate in certain social activities but are limited by the low income of their families. Poor children experience tremendous pressure from both societies at large and their peers. Although they may want to participate in certain activities, fear and sadness can arise from their inability to pay for them. In addition, children trapped in poverty have a very low sense of belonging to school and very little participation in school activities. To avoid being excluded by peers and friends, children from poor families have to struggle hard to change the status quo and are under too much psychological pressure.

9.2.2.4 Well-Being Approach

Measures of child well-being are the EU Child Well-Being Index and the US Child and Youth Well-being Index (USCWI). The former is a child well-being index constructed by Bradshaw et al. (2006) with 8 indicators, which was used for comparisons among 25 EU member states. The eight indicators were adopted because they were considered to have a significant influence on children's lives and health (Keetie & Franziska, 2008), and they were material means of subsistence, housing, health care, subjective well-being, education, children's social relations, civic engagement, and risk and safety.

The greatest advantage of the EU Child Well-Being Index is that it combines those indicators that affect child survival and development into one easily comparable index. However, the index is only suitable for comparisons between countries or regions within a given area, as the index score itself does not provide much relevant information, such as the achievements of individual indicators and the overall well-being of children in an absolute sense. In addition, upward or downward movements in complementary indicators are not demonstrated in the index (Micklewright, 2001).

The USCWI was constructed by Land et al. (2001) to measure changes in the well-being of children and youth in the US over time, focusing on specific demographic characteristics and changes in their well-being in different geographic areas. This index is based on an assessment of quality of life and measures both subjective and objective well-being. The child well-being described here is based on Cummins' (1996, 1997) study and covers seven different aspects of a child's life: material well-being, health care, safety, productive activities, location in the community, sexuality, and emotional well-being.

While the greatest strength of the USCWI is that it describes the dynamic changes in child and youth well-being over time, the index has certain limitations: the large amount of data required and its limited applicability (limited to the US). To be applied to measure child well-being in other countries, the index should be adapted to the context of different countries and the availability of data.

9.3 Analysis Framework and Data Illustration

9.3.1 Analysis Framework

To a certain extent, deprivation of capacities is essentially a denial of rights. According to the UNCRC, children have the right to survival (the right to life and health), protection (the right to be protected from discrimination, exploitation, abuse, or neglect, and basic guarantees for children deprived of their families and refugee children), development (the right to formal and non-formal education and the right to living conditions that promote their physical, psychological, mental, moral, and social development), and participation (the right to participate in family, cultural, and social life). This system of children's basic rights is central to the construction of an analysis framework for multidimensional child poverty and of a framework for an inclusive child well-being system.

Based on the set of basic rights stipulated in the *UNCRC* and *the Law of the People's Republic of China on the Protection of Minors* as well as the availability of data from the research questionnaire for child welfare demonstration zones, this chapter investigates multidimensional child poverty in the following five dimensions shown in Fig. 9.1.

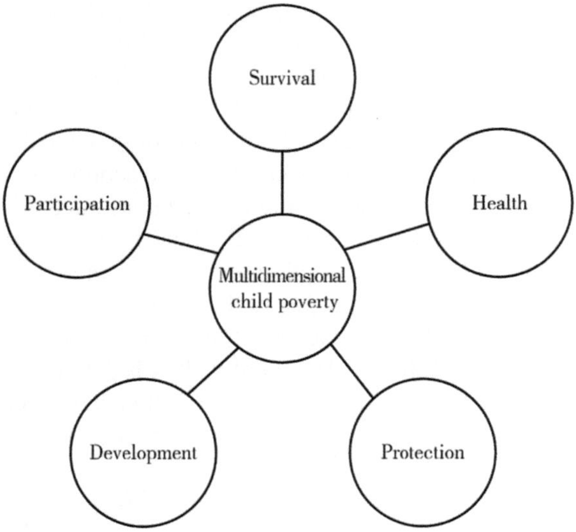

Fig. 9.1 Dimension analysis framework of multidimensional child poverty

After the above five dimensions have been identified, the analytical indicators under each dimension need to be determined. Analytical indicators are highly dependent on the availability of data. In the present study, the analytical indicators are set according to the household questionnaire of the Child Welfare Demonstration Project. Notably, some important indicators of child deprivation are not covered in the questionnaire, resulting in a data gap in the analysis of child poverty.

(1) Survival: basic livelihood security
(2) Health: including health and health care, drinking water, sanitation facilities, and energy security
(3) Protection: including protection of children from domestic violence or corporal punishment by parents, school violence, and violence against children in society
(4) Development: safeguarding the right to education
(5) Participation: children's participation in social activities and other types of social participation.

9.3.2 Data Illustration

The Department of Social Welfare and Charity Promotion of the Ministry of Civil Affairs and UNICEF have jointly launched the 6-year Child Welfare Demonstration Project (2010–2015) to establish a child welfare system with Chinese characteristics. This system targets all children and covers rural communities, providing empirical experience and enabling China to establish a comprehensive child welfare system. The project covered 120 villages in 12 counties in 5 provinces (regions) in China, directly benefiting around 80,000 children. The data analyzed in this chapter come from the household questionnaire of Child Welfare Demonstration Project (2010–2015) conducted in 2010. The survey was conducted in villages in 20 townships (offices) on households with children aged 0–18 years as the population. An equidistant sampling method was used to select respondents, and data at a community and individual level within the sample were obtained by interviewing participants via a questionnaire survey. A total of 120 community questionnaires and 4549 household questionnaires were collected, totaling 4669 questionnaires, among which 4462 were valid (Table 9.1).

The purpose of the household questionnaire was to learn about the basic conditions of the local children and their families. The basic information of the respondents includes gender, age, education level, ethnicity, and family status. The basic information about the family includes family size, housing, utilities, consumption, and whether there are special types of children in the family, such as those with disabilities or AIDS, orphans, left-behind children, and those with serious illnesses. The basic information of children under 18 years of age includes the name, gender, year of birth, education level, ethnicity, physical condition, daily life, family relations,

Table 9.1 Total number of questionnaires in five project provinces (regions)

Project provinces (regions)	Community questionnaires	Household questionnaires	Total
Shanxi	20	745	765
Henan	20	830	850
Yunnan	30	1222	1252
Sichuan	30	982	1012
Xinjiang	20	770	790
Total	120	4549	4669

and social relations. Further, supplementary surveys which included the right to self-determination, study or work status, sense of security, and interpersonal relationships were conducted on children aged 12–18 years.

With respect to demographic characteristics, 18 of the 4462 households in the valid sample were empty nesters, with 41.91% of the households having one child, 41.55% two children, and 12.33% three children (Table 9.2). Minority families made up 55.65% of the families surveyed (Table 9.3). For the sake of reliability of the analysis, this chapter does not follow the sample data to extrapolate the population

Table 9.2 Distribution of children in the sample households in the project areas

Number of children in the families	Frequency	Percentage	Cumulative percentage
0	18	0.40	0.40
1	1870	41.91	42.31
2	1854	41.55	83.86
3	550	12.33	96.19
4	145	3.25	99.44
5	23	0.52	99.96
6	1	0.02	99.98
7	1	0.02	100
Total	4462	100	–

Table 9.3 Ethnicity distribution of the sample household heads in the project areas

Ethnicity	Frequency	Percentage	Cumulative percentage
Han	1979	44.35	44.35
Hui	107	2.40	46.75
Uighur	459	10.29	57.04
Yi	980	21.96	79.00
Tibetan	1	0.02	79.02
Other	936	20.98	100
Total	4462	100	–

based on sample data, and the conclusions apply only to the 12 counties in the Child Welfare Demonstration Project. Although we refer to the five provinces (regions) in our descriptions, they represent only the project's counties and are not representative of the status of the entire province (region).

The ratio of male to female respondents was 47.71:52.29. In terms of age, 3.07% were under 18 years, 53.65% between 19 and 40 years, 35.01% between 41 and 60 years, and 8.27% over 60 years (Table 9.4).

In terms of education, 23.40% were illiterate; 37.88% had studied in primary school; 30.88% junior high school; and 6.99% high school, technical secondary school, and technical school (Table 9.5). The ratio of agricultural to non-agricultural households was 97:3, 44.35% of the respondents were Han Chinese and the remainder ethnic minorities, and 89% were married.

Among the children surveyed, 1.26% were disabled, 1.06% were orphans, 2.09% were affected by AIDS, 1% were de facto unsupported, and 1.15% had serious illnesses (e.g., heart disease, kidney disease, hematological disease, and intracranial tumors). There were no street children among the survey participants.

9.4 Multidimensional Poverty Analysis of Children

9.4.1 Survival

Survival is a fundamental right of children. The China National Program for Child Development (2011–2020) clearly states that the Scientific Outlook on Development should be thoroughly implemented and the principle of Children First adhered to; children's rights to survival, development, protection, and participation should be safeguarded and the gap between urban and rural areas in child development should be narrowed; the level of child welfare should be raised and the overall quality of children improved, promoting their healthy, all-round development.

Assessing children's survival covers several dimensions and indicators, and experts and scholars have different views. This chapter investigates survival from the perspective of poverty, limiting it to basic survival. Basic survival suggests five categories of "basic needs" of human beings. In his 1942 book *The Beveridge Report: Social Insurance and Allied Services*, William Beveridge proposed a social welfare system to overcome the "Five Giants" that stood in the way of post-war reconstruction: want, disease, ignorance, squalor, and idleness. This is Beveridge's perspective of basic needs. This chapter examines children's material deprivation in meeting their survival needs with objective material conditions (hunger and shelter) and analyzes their own perceptions of basic survival from the viewpoint of subjective well-being.

Table 9.4 Age distribution of the respondents in the sample households in the project areas

Project provinces (regions)	0–18 years		19–40 years		41–60 years		> 60 years	
	Frequency	Percentage	Frequency	Percentage	Frequency	Percentage	Frequency	Percentage
Shanxi	29	3.89	273	36.64	335	44.97	108	14.50
Henan	28	3.77	308	41.51	303	40.84	103	13.88
Yunnan	20	1.64	792	64.81	359	29.38	51	4.17
Sichuan	60	6.11	516	52.55	328	33.40	78	7.94
Xinjiang	0	0	505	65.50	237	30.74	29	3.76
Overall	137	3.07	2394	53.65	1562	35.01	369	8.27

Table 9.5 Distribution of the education level of the respondents in the sample households in the project areas (Unit: %)

Project provinces (regions)	Illiteracy	Primary school	Junior high school	High school, technical secondary school, and technical school	Junior college	University	Other	Total
Shanxi	4.56	30.2	52.48	11.41	0.94	0.4	0	100
Henan	11.32	32.48	47.17	8.63	0.27	0	0.13	100
Yunnan	19.97	51.06	24.06	4.17	0.49	0	0.25	100
Sichuan	62.93	31.67	4.38	1.02	0	0	0	100
Xinjiang	8.30	37.48	38.91	13.23	1.56	0.39	0.13	100
Overall	23.40	37.88	30.88	6.99	0.61	0.13	0.11	100

9.4.1.1 Food

Data from the sample of 5 provinces (regions) show that out of 7936 children who gave valid responses from the 4462 surveyed households, 24 children ate one meal a day and 1974 children ate two meals a day, accounting for 0.30% and 24.87%, respectively (Tables 9.6 and 9.7). Children who ate one meal a day should be considered

Table 9.6 Daily meals of the children in the project sample (frequency) (Unit: person)

Project provinces (regions)	1 meal	2 meals	3 meals and above	Total
Henan	5	9	1321	1335
Shanxi	4	83	1008	1095
Sichuan	7	1856	508	2371
Xinjiang	4	12	1288	1304
Yunnan	4	14	1813	1831
Total	24	1974	5938	7936

Table 9.7 Daily meals of the children in the project sample (Unit: %)

Project provinces (regions)	1 meal	2 meals	3 meals and above	Total
Henan	0.37	0.37	98.95	100
Shanxi	0.37	7.58	92.05	100
Sichuan	0.30	78.28	21.43	100
Xinjiang	0.31	0.92	98.77	100
Yunnan	0.22	0.76	99.02	100
Overall	0.30	24.87	74.82	100

extremely hungry; a higher proportion of children who ate two meals a day may be malnourished and were estimated to be primarily skipping breakfast.

By region, children who did not have three meals a day were mainly found in three sample counties in Sichuan Province (Butuo, Jinyang, and Zhaojue), with the proportion of children who ate two meals reaching 78.28% (Table 9.7). By ethnicity, the proportion of children eating two meals (78.23%) was highest among the Yi children in Sichuan (Table 9.8).

From a gender perspective, the proportion of boys eating two meals was significantly higher than the proportion of girls (Table 9.9).

In terms of standard of living, Fig. 9.2 shows the results for the self-reported

Table 9.8 Daily meals of the children in the project sample by ethnicity (Unit: %)

Ethnicity	One meal	Two meals	Three meals and above	total
Han	0.32	3.26	96.42	100
Hui	0	0	100	100
Uighur	0.49	0.73	98.78	100
Yi	0.30	78.23	21.47	100
Other	0.21	1.04	98.75	100
Overall	0.30	24.87	74.82	100

Table 9.9 Daily meals of the sample children by gender (Unit: %)

Gender	One meal	Two meals	Three meals and above	Total
Boy	0.26	30.22	69.51	100
Girl	0.36	17.63	82.02	100
Overall	0.30	24.87	74.82	100

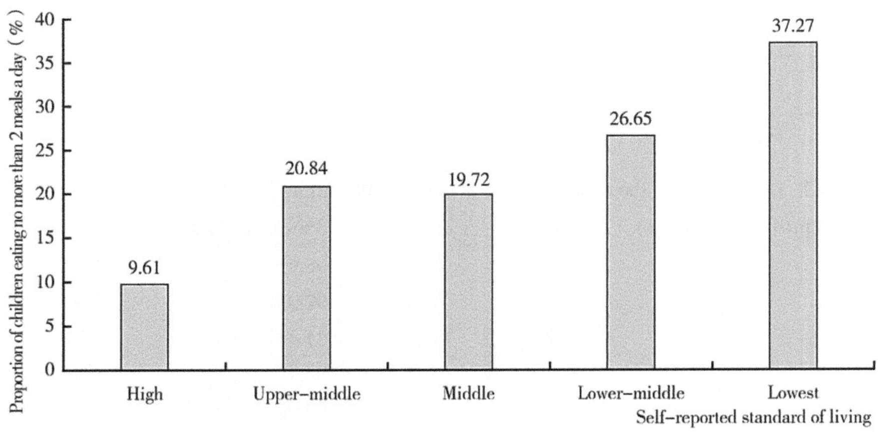

Fig. 9.2 Daily meals of the children by the standard of living

Table 9.10 Whether the sample children had enough to eat every day (Unit: %)

Project provinces (regions)	Have enough to eat or not			Total
	Yes	No	Unknown	
Henan	99.25	0.45	0.30	100
Shanxi	97.90	0.64	1.46	100
Sichuan	90.68	7.04	2.28	100
Xinjiang	98.82	0.31	0.84	100
Yunnan	99.24	0.44	0.33	100
Overall	96.43	2.42	1.15	100

"Compared to those around you, your standard of living is estimated to be...?" In households with the lowest standard of living, 37.27% of the children had two or fewer meals a day, followed by 26.65% in households with a lower middle standard of living. Thus, children eating less than three meals a day is related to a family's standard of living.

Regarding the question "Do you have enough to eat every day?" of the 7,936 children who responded, 192 (2.42%) answered "No." In other words, 2.42% of the children felt hungry, and these were mainly distributed in the three Yi-dominated counties in Sichuan (Table 9.10). The proportion of boys who answered "No" was 3.2% and that of girls was 1.36%.

9.4.1.2 Housing

With respect to living conditions, 96.66% of the households owned their houses, while 3.34% were living on rent or borrowed other people's houses. The per capita living area of the surveyed households in the 12 project counties in the 5 provinces (regions) was 24.81 square meters, with the lowest per capita living area of only 15.45 square meters in Sichuan (Table 9.11).

The quality of the children's housing cannot be judged based on the questionnaire, as it did not address the structure, floors, or roofs of the house.

Table 9.11 Per capita housing area (Unit: %)

Project provinces (regions)	Mean (m^2)	Standard deviation	Frequency
Henan	25.88	17.76	736
Shanxi	33.55	24.14	736
Sichuan	15.45	10.62	968
Xinjiang	23.00	20.31	771
Yunnan	27.49	23.99	1215
Overall	24.81	20.93	4426

9.4.1.3 Subjective Poverty

The assessment of poverty in this chapter is not based on income or consumption but on the respondents' answers to the question "Is your household classified as poor or low-income in the local area?".

Of the 12 project counties in the five project provinces (regions), 8.56% of the households surveyed were poor and 16.49% had minimum subsistence. The three project counties in Sichuan had the highest proportion of poor households and households with minimum subsistence, 20.16% and 22.5%, respectively (Table 9.12).

Satisfaction of basic needs has always been a measure of poverty, regardless of whether the perspective is objective or subjective. The subjective poverty rate of the households surveyed was high. From the respondents' self-evaluation on the question, "How would you rate your household's total income compared to your household's basic needs? (unsatisfied, basically satisfied, relatively well off)," 61.32% of the households felt that their basic needs could not be met, 36.06% had their basic needs met on the whole, and less than 3% were relatively well off (Table 9.13).

The Yi ethnic group had the highest percentage of households failing to meet basic needs, at 77.96% (Fig. 9.3).

Table 9.12 Poverty status (Unit: %)

Project provinces (regions)	Poor	Minimum subsistence	Both	Neither	Total
Henan	6.74	14.29	2.83	76.15	100
Shanxi	3.76	5.50	0.67	90.07	100
Sichuan	20.16	22.51	5.91	51.43	100
Xinjiang	8.04	9.08	1.56	81.32	100
Yunnan	3.60	24.39	2.13	69.89	100
Overall	8.56	16.49	2.73	72.21	100

Table 9.13 Satisfaction of the basic needs of the households (Unit: %)

Project provinces (regions)	Unsatisfied	Basically satisfied	Relatively well off	Total
Henan	43.67	3.77	3.77	100
Shanxi	51.28	44.70	4.03	100
Sichuan	77.80	21.69	0.51	100
Xinjiang	57.59	39.43	2.98	100
Yunnan	67.27	30.20	2.54	100
Overall	61.32	36.06	2.62	100

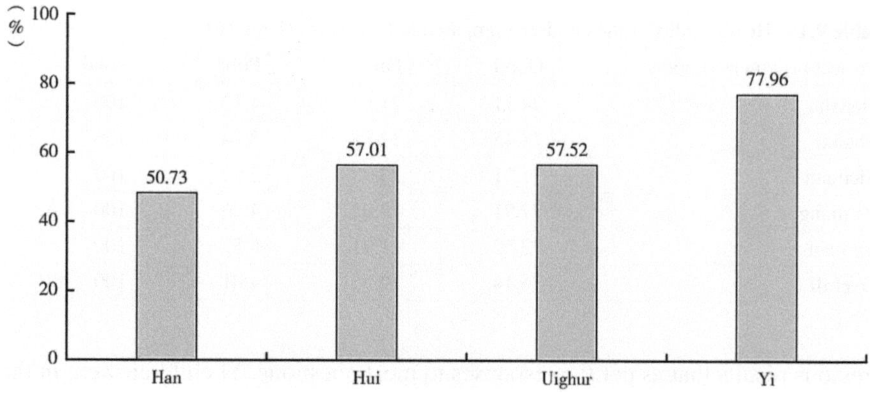

Fig. 9.3 Percentage of households that could not meet basic needs by ethnic group

9.4.1.4 Vulnerability

Household savings are a major safeguard against risk. There is a growing consensus that the traditional definition and measurement of poverty from an income perspective has led to a long history of anti-poverty policies that intervene only from income support. Households are economically more vulnerable if they have no assets or a low proportion of assets in their "safety net." This is because assets are the only thing that can prevent households from falling into poverty if alternative sources of income, such as that from labor and family business as well as government transfers, are in jeopardy.

Savings are a crucial liquid asset to cope with risk. Of the 4,462 households surveyed, 90.81% had no savings and 63.43% had debt, with an average household debt of RMB10,985. Xinjiang had the highest average household debt at RMB14,400 and Sichuan the lowest at RMB4,903. Therefore, such household savings and debt indicate general vulnerability and the majority of children lived in vulnerable households.

9.4.2 Health

9.4.2.1 Health Status and Health Behaviors

Health status. Health and health care are among the basic development rights of children. This survey found that compared to their peers, 76.44% of the children considered themselves to be in good health, 19.55% in fair health, and only 4.01% in poor health (Table 9.14).

However, the descriptive statistics by ethnicity showed that the Hui children had the highest proportion of perception of poor health (10.53%), which differs from the

Table 9.14 Health status of the children compared to their peers (Unit: %)

Project provinces (regions)	Good	Fair	Poor	Total
Henan	74.31	21.57	4.12	100
Shanxi	78.45	17.81	3.74	100
Sichuan	71.21	25.98	2.82	100
Xinjiang	77.91	18.02	4.06	100
Yunnan	82.52	11.91	5.57	100
Overall	76.44	19.55	4.01	100

previous results that as per the responses to most questions, Yi children were in the worst situation (Table 9.15).

Health behaviors. Among the sample children, 3.54% smoke, with the highest percentage in Sichuan (5.42%) and the lowest in Xinjiang (1.69%) and Shanxi (1.69%) (Table 9.16).

Only 84.66% of the children brush their teeth daily. In the three counties in the Sichuan project area, this figure dropped to 54.55%, suggesting that 45.45% of the children were not in the habit of brushing their teeth (Table 9.17).

Table 9.15 Health status of the respondents (by ethnicity) (Unit: %)

Ethnicity	Good	Fair	Poor	Total
Han	77.59	18.48	3.93	100
Hui	60.82	28.65	10.53	100
Uighur	85.57	11.84	2.90	100
Yi	71.17	26.00	2.83	100
Other	79.41	14.54	6.05	100
Overall	76.44	19.55	4.01	100

Table 9.16 Do you smoke? (Unit: %)

Project provinces (regions)	Yes	No	Total
Henan	4.76	95.24	100
Shanxi	1.69	98.31	100
Sichuan	5.42	94.58	100
Xinjiang	1.69	98.31	100
Yunnan	3.41	96.59	100
Overall	3.54	96.46	100

Table 9.17 Do you brush your teeth everyday? (Unit: %)

Project provinces (regions)	Yes	No	Total
Henan	93.84	6.16	100
Shanxi	93.24	6.76	100
Sichuan	54.55	45.45	100
Xinjiang	92.29	7.71	100
Yunnan	99.83	0.17	100
Overall	84.66	15.34	100

9.4.2.2 Access to Health Services

Judging from the survey results, access to health services was not a problem in most areas. All villages in the project counties in Shanxi and Henan provinces as well as the vast majority of villages in the project counties in Yunnan Province had either public or private village clinics or health stations. In Xinjiang, only 3% of the children lived more than 5 km from the nearest health service facility, with the majority being less than 1 km away. In Sichuan, the situation was much worse, with health rooms in only 4 out of 30 villages in the 3 project counties.

9.4.2.3 Drinking Water

The *Human Development Report 2011* suggests that lack of access to clean water and proper sanitation facilities affects the lives of many people, particularly in poor countries. In countries with a medium human development index (HDI), more than half of the population lacks access to improved sanitation facilities and one-eighth lacks access to acceptable water sources. In contrast, in countries with a low HDI, 65% of the population lack access to water, while 38% lack access to appropriate sanitation facilities. Globally, almost 40% of the population lack access to sanitary latrines, and among the multidimensional poor, the proportion doubles to 80%. In addition, there is a wide urban-rural divide: in 2008, less than half of the rural population had access to improved sanitation facilities, compared to nearly three-quarters of the urban population. For children under 5 years of age, environmental factors account for over one-third of the global burden of disease. Approximately 2 million children under this age die from diarrhea each year, and recent projections suggest that improved sanitation facilities and drinking water could save 2.2 million children's lives each year, around 5500 per day (UNDP, 2011).

(1) Access to piped water is poor and unevenly developed. Table 9.18 shows that the penetration rate of tap water in the three project counties in Sichuan was only 10.08%, and 87.17% of the household drinking water was accessed from rainwater harvesting, surface water, and unprotected springs and shallow wells, which is a hidden danger to drinking water safety.

Table 9.18 Types of drinking water (by region) (Unit: %)

Project provinces (regions)	Tap water	Well water at a depth of more than 5 m	Protected springs	Other water sources (rainwater harvesting, surface water, and unprotected springs and shallow wells)	Other	Total
Shanxi	89.40	8.72	0.13	0.94	0.81	100
Henan	41.64	57.41	0.13	0.54	0.27	100
Yunnan	55.48	41.49	1.06	1.23	0.74	100
Sichuan	10.08	2.55	0.10	87.17	0.10	100
Xinjiang	58.75	40.21	0	0.26	0.78	100
Overall	49.42	29.87	0.36	19.81	0.54	100

(2) Difficulties in access to safe drinking water for children from Yi households and poor households. Table 9.19 shows that children from Yi households had difficulty obtaining safe drinking water. In the survey, of the 980 Yi households (21.96% of the total), 87.04% had unsafe water sources. The proportion of poor households with access to safe drinking water was much lower than that of non-poor households. The proportion of poor households using other water sources (rainwater harvesting, surface water, and unprotected springs and shallow wells) was 33.47%, while that of non-poor households was 14.56% (Table 9.20).

Table 9.19 Types of drinking water (by ethnicity) (Unit: %)

Ethnicity	Tap water	Well water at a depth of more than 5 m	Protected springs	Other water sources (rainwater harvesting, surface water, and unprotected springs and shallow wells)	Other	Total
Han	61.70	36.69	0.20	0.71	0.71	100
Hui	27.10	71.03	0	0.93	0.93	100
Uighur	77.12	22.00	0	0.44	0.44	100
Yi	10.20	2.55	0.10	87.04	0.10	100
Other	53.53	43.27	1.18	1.39	0.64	100
Overall	49.42	29.87	0.36	19.81	0.54	100

Table 9.20 Type of drinking water (by poor household) (Unit: %)

Poor household	Tap water	Well water at a depth of more than 5 m	Protected springs	Other water sources (rainwater harvesting, surface water, and unprotected springs and shallow wells)	Other	Total
No	52.58	32.00	0.40	14.56	0.47	100
Yes	41.21	24.35	0.24	33.47	0.73	100

9.4.2.4 Sanitation Facilities

Access to basic sanitation facilities is generally poor and requires high priority. In this chapter, children's access to basic sanitation facilities is judged by the type of latrine: children using indoor flush latrines, outdoor flush latrines, and dry sanitary latrines are considered as having access to basic sanitation facilities, while the converse applies to those using honey buckets, dry latrines, no facilities, and other types. The statistics in Table 9.21 show that children in the sample households in Sichuan had the least access to basic sanitation facilities (97.97%). Among them, 86.66% had no sanitation facilities and 10.49% used dry latrines. The situation was also dire in Henan, Shanxi, and Xinjiang, where 96–98% of the children had no access to basic sanitation facilities; this was only slightly better than in Sichuan, where the majority of children had no access to sanitation facilities and mainly used dry latrines. There were no significant differences in sanitation facilities among households of different ethnicity (Table 9.22).

Table 9.21 Types of latrines (by region) (Unit: percent)

Project provinces (regions)	Indoor flush latrines	Outdoor flush latrines	Dry sanitary latrines	Honey buckets	Dry latrines	No facilities/ bushes/fields	Other	Total
Shanxi	0.94	1.21	0.67	0.94	95.84	0.13	0.27	100
Henan	1.35	1.62	1.08	0.94	94.61	0.40	0	100
Yunnan	4.83	14.16	1.39	1.80	61.37	13.01	3.44	100
Sichuan	0.61	0.20	1.22	0	10.49	86.66	0.82	100
Xinjiang	1.04	0.26	0.91	0.13	97.28	0.13	0.26	100
Overall	2.02	4.44	1.10	0.83	67.66	22.75	1.21	100

Table 9.22 Types of latrines (by ethnicity) (Unit: percent)

Ethnicity	Indoor flush latrines	Outdoor flush latrines	Dry sanitary latrines	Honey buckets	Dry latrines	No facilities/ bushes/fields	Other	Total
Han	2.02	2.68	0.81	0.81	89.84	2.58	1.26	100
Hui	1.87	0	0	0.93	96.26	0.93	0	100
Uighur	0.44	0.44	1.53	0	97.39	0.22	0	100
Yi	0.61	0.20	1.22	0	10.61	86.53	0.82	100
Tibetan	0	0	0	0	100	0	0	100
Other	4.27	15.06	1.50	2.14	62.61	12.18	2.24	100
Overall	2.02	4.44	1.10	0.83	67.66	22.75	1.21	100

9.4.2.5 Energy and Environment

The UN Secretary-General Ban Ki-moon announced the "Sustainable Energy for All" initiative at the UN General Assembly, aiming to achieve three major goals by 2030: ensure universal access to modern energy services, double the rate of improvement in energy efficiency, and double the proportion of renewable energy in the global energy mix. In accordance with the UN statistics, one out of every five people worldwide does not have access to modern energy, with approximately 3 billion people relying on firewood, coal, charcoal, or animal dung for cooking and heating, living in "energy poverty" that is hard to escape. Moreover, to prevent further global warming, the world urgently needs to shift to a clean energy economy. The Asian Development Bank (ADB) announced plans to invest USD370 million over the next decade to build renewable energy infrastructure in Asia. Energy and environmental issues are becoming major concerns in the development arena.

Household fuels dominated by firewood and coal threaten children's health. Data from the household survey of the Child Welfare Demonstration Project in five provinces (regions) provided a valid sample of 4,462 households to observe the type of fuel used at home: 67.79% used firewood as their main fuel. In Sichuan, 99.08% of the sample households used firewood for cooking and only 0.51% had access to electricity for cooking. In Yunnan, 87.15% of the households used firewood for cooking (Table 9.23). The proportion of poor households using firewood for cooking was 81.48% and that of non-poor households was 62.91%.

Table 9.24 shows that up to 12.93% of the households in the sample counties in Sichuan (Zhaojue, Jinyang, and Butuo) had no access to electricity. In Yunnan and Henan, even though up to 99.75% and 99.73% of the households, respectively, had electricity only 5.16% and 4.72% of the households used electricity for cooking. None of the 771 households surveyed in Xinjiang used electricity for cooking, with most using coal and firewood. Farmers' use of electricity is affected by two issues: availability and affordability when it is available. In all five provinces (regions) surveyed, although the proportion of access to electricity was high, that of using

Table 9.23 Main types of fuel used in the households (Unit: %)

Project provinces (regions)	Natural gas	Biogas	Coal	Firewood	Electricity	Other	Total
Shanxi	8.32	0.81	11.01	34.90	44.97	0	100
Henan	5.12	6.20	27.22	56.47	4.72	0.27	100
Yunnan	1.39	4.58	0.16	87.15	5.16	1.55	100
Sichuan	0	0	0.31	99.08	0.51	0.10	100
Xinjiang	0.65	0.26	58.88	39.95	0	0.26	100
Overall	2.73	2.47	16.65	67.79	9.82	0.54	100

Table 9.24 Availability of electricity (Unit: %)

Project provinces (regions)	Yes	No	Total
Shanxi	99.73	0.27	100
Henan	99.73	0.27	100
Yunnan	99.75	0.25	100
Sichuan	87.07	12.93	100
Xinjiang	99.61	0.39	100
Overall	96.93	3.07	100

electricity for cooking was low, indicating that the high cost of using electricity for cooking limited its use among farmers to some extent.

9.4.3 Protection

Security is an important aspect of child welfare. The survey mapped child safety issues in the family, society, and at school. The main finding was that corporal punishment and verbal abuse of children were very common in the families. As many as 19.16% of the children had been subjected to corporeal punishment or verbally abused by teachers, and that number reached 34.82% in Shanxi.

9.4.3.1 Domestic Violence or Corporal Punishment of Children by Parents

In China, corporal punishment of children is quite common, and parents and society often use it as a means of educating children. The *Three Character Classic*, an enlightenment text from the Southern Song Dynasty (1127–1279), says that "the father should be blamed if the child is better fed than taught" and that "jade requires chiseling, as a man needs training and education." *The Rules for Students*, an enlightenment text from the Qing dynasty (1636–1912), reads that "beatings are borne

Table 9.25 Whether parents (primary caregivers) beat their children (Unit: %)

Project provinces (regions)	Often	Occasionally	Never	Total
Henan	1.35	51.24	47.42	100
Shanxi	1.00	34.34	64.66	100
Sichuan	0.63	41.18	58.19	100
Xinjiang	1.07	33.44	65.49	100
Yunnan	0.33	53.96	45.71	100
Overall	0.81	43.60	55.59	100

without complaint," which means that children are taught not to hold grudges if their elders beat them.

This is reflected in the behavior of parents in the demonstration zones, where only 55.59% of the children were never beaten and around 45% suffering beatings from their parents (Table 9.25). At school, 19.16% of the children were beaten by teachers and 13.79% by classmates; 2.49% were subjected to violence outside of school. Further, 1% of the parents were aware of sexual violence against their children.

The existence of such a situation is related to our beliefs about children's education: 65% of the parents believed that "beating represents care and scolding represents love" and "a stick makes a filial child" were justified and 51% believed that it was not a crime to beat their children.

Severe corporal punishment, such as parents (primary caregivers) beating children with hard objects including straps, sticks, and hairbrushes, also occurred occasionally. Approximately 11% of the parents did so often or occasionally (Table 9.26). In Butuo, Sichuan, 19.5% of the parents often beat their children with hard objects (straps, sticks, and hairbrushes), 18.0% did so occasionally, and 62.5% never did it. The percentage of parents beating and scolding their children was quite high. Most parents said they beat and scolded only when the children were disobedient or when they themselves were angry. The Sichuan survey team argued that some respondents may conceal the fact that they beat and scolded their children to save face or for other reasons. Therefore, the actual situation was more serious than indicated by the survey.

Table 9.26 Whether parents (primary caregivers) beat their children with hard objects (straps, sticks, or hairbrushes) (Unit: %)

Project provinces (regions)	Often	Occasionally	Never	Total
Shanxi	0.37	4.75	94.89	100
Henan	0.37	6.59	93.03	100
Yunnan	0.33	8.85	90.82	100
Sichuan	0.17	18.06	81.77	100
Xinjiang	0.15	7.75	92.10	100
Overall	0.26	10.47	89.26	100

Table 9.27 Whether children have been subjected to corporeal punishment or verbally abused by teachers (Unit: %)

Project provinces (regions)	Yes	No	Unknown	Total
Shanxi	34.82	55.36	9.82	100
Henan	11.55	82.34	6.11	100
Yunnan	14.73	78.29	6.97	100
Sichuan	12.90	79.44	7.66	100
Xinjiang	23.10	71.83	5.07	100
Overall	19.16	73.49	7.35	100

Table 9.28 Whether children have been beaten or verbally abused by classmates (Unit: %)

Project provinces (regions)	Yes	No	Unknown	Total
Shanxi	22.87	66.70	10.43	100
Henan	15.08	80.16	4.76	100
Yunnan	14.15	76.62	9.23	100
Sichuan	5.79	87.96	6.25	100
Xinjiang	13.71	81.37	4.92	100
Overall	13.79	78.86	7.35	100

9.4.3.2 School Violence

In addition to violence at home, children may also be physically punished by teachers at school. The survey showed that as many as 19.16% of the children were beaten and scolded by teachers. In Shanxi, the proportion was as high as 34.82% (Table 9.27).

The existence of such phenomenon in public educational institutions is not only related to the teachers' concept of education but also to the parents' understanding of educational methods. As many as 78% of the parents had no objection to teachers beating their children if it was good for them. This proportion was 95% in Sichuan. Other parents believed that it was irresponsible toward children if teachers did not strictly discipline them (including corporal punishment).

School violence includes abuse and conflict among children. The survey revealed that 13.79% of the children had the experience of being beaten and scolded by classmates (Table 9.28). Parents thought that "beating and scolding" between children and classmates was normal and not worth making a fuss about.

9.4.3.3 Violence Against Children in Society

In the 12 counties surveyed, there was relatively little violence against children in society. When asked if they had been robbed outside of school (e.g., money, school bags, bicycles, food, clothing, toys, and books), only 2.49% of children answered

Table 9.29 Whether children have been robbed outside of school (Unit: %)

Project provinces (regions)	Yes	No	Unknown	Total
Shanxi	3.04	89.57	7.39	100
Henan	3.53	93.61	2.85	100
Yunnan	1.18	95.19	3.63	100
Sichuan	1.33	93.98	4.69	100
Xinjiang	4.77	93.14	2.09	100
Overall	2.49	93.14	4.37	100

"Yes." However, the situation was worse in Xinjiang, where the proportion was 4.77% (Table 9.29).

9.4.3.4 Other Insecurities

Traffic accidents and drowning were the two major causes of death by unintentional injury among Chinese children. This survey found that the potential problems of these two types of accidents were very obvious. In the process of economic development, environmental pollution is also becoming a vital aspect that threatens the healthy growth of children.

In Luoning County, Henan, concerning personal safety, there were large canals in some villages without any safety precautions, endangering the safety of children and adults and causing a number of incidents of children drowning. Thus, there is an urgent need to take protective measures to safeguard the personal safety of children and adults. In terms of environmental pollution, some villages did not use water from the county waterworks, and surface well water was being polluted, threatening the safety of villagers' drinking water. Crematoriums and poultry enterprises were more severely polluted, which was not conducive to children's growth.

In Sichuan, children played and walked to school on the highway. Vehicles passing by at high speed led to a higher incidence of traffic accidents.

9.4.4 Development

Access to education is one of the fundamental rights for child development. This survey mapped the situation of children's access to education. While the majority of children had access to education, there were some serious problems in the three counties in Sichuan, such as low enrollment rate of school-age children. Overall, 17.43% felt that school was "very far" from home and 8.50% "disliked" going to school. In terms of learning conditions, 22.47% of all the children "did not have" a dictionary at home, the proportion rising to 58.53% in the three counties of Sichuan.

9.4.4.1 Enrollment Rate of School-Age Children

Table 9.30 shows that the enrollment rate of children aged 6–15 years was 82.8% and children aged 7–15 years 86.5%, with the difference of 3.7 percentage points resulting from the low enrollment rate of 6-year olds. This indicates that the enrollment rate in pre-school education is very low in rural areas, as pre-school education is not part of the compulsory education and some villages in the surveyed counties did not have pre-school education. Furthermore, although some villages had private kindergartens, there was no government subsidy and all costs had to be managed by parents.

Figure 9.4 shows, by province, that in the three counties in Sichuan, less than 60% of children aged under 9 years were enrolled in school. The educational status of Yi children was far from meeting the national compulsory education requirements, but the situation had improved in Shanxi and Henan. The three areas with more ethnic minorities (Sichuan, Yunnan, and Xinjiang) had poorer enrollment status for school-age children, indicating large differences in educational attainment between regions and ethnic groups.

Table 9.30 Enrollment of school-age children by province (region)

Project provinces (regions)	6–15 years (%)	7–15 years (%)
Henan	98.4	99.0
Shanxi	98.3	98.6
Sichuan	58.4	64.8
Xinjiang	93.6	95.6
Yunnan	86.8	91.9
Overall	82.8	86.5

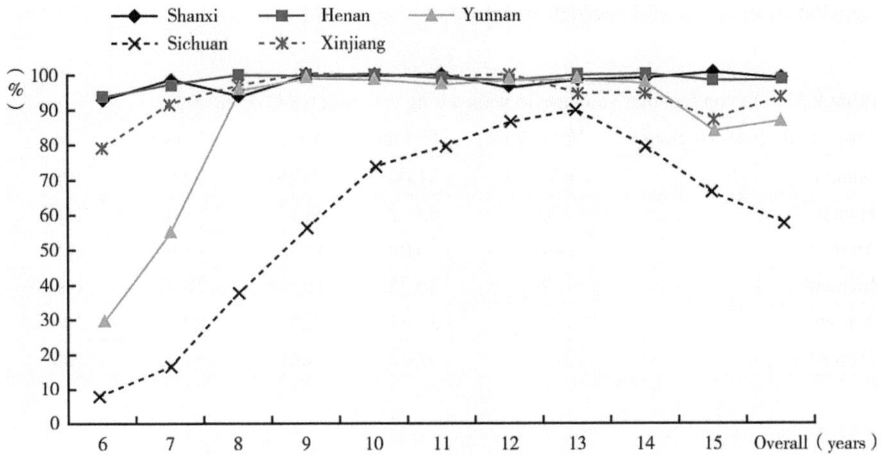

Fig. 9.4 Enrollment of school-age children aged 6–15 years in project areas

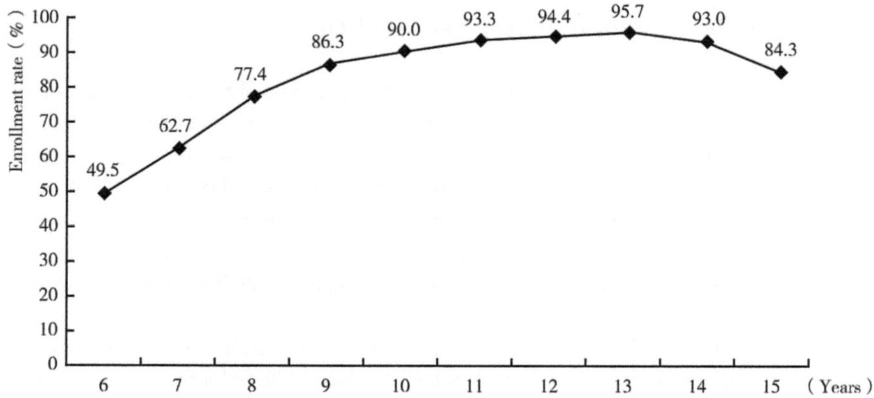

Fig. 9.5 Overall enrollment rate of children aged 6–15 years in project areas

Among children aged 6–15 years, enrollment rates increased from age 6 and decreased after reaching a peak at age 13 (Fig. 9.5).

9.4.4.2 Some Children Felt School Was "Very Far"

Distance may be one of the most important reasons for the low enrollment rate of children in school. In general, when children were asked "Do you feel like you have to walk a long way to school?" 51.91% answered "a bit far" or "very far" (Table 9.31).

The survey of the 381 children between the ages of 13 and 18 in Yunnan who received education found that 61.53% felt that the distance to school was "a bit far" or "very far," indicating that the majority of children in this age group traveled a long distance to school. This is attributed to the educational facilities and the geographic location of primary and secondary schools.

Table 9.31 Do you feel that you have to walk a long way to school? (Unit: %)

Project provinces (regions)	Very Close	Not far	A bit far	Very far	Total
Shanxi	6.75	31.00	40.25	22.00	100
Henan	14.33	53.92	28.33	3.41	100
Yunnan	8.46	30.00	42.56	18.97	100
Sichuan	11.98	38.25	31.34	18.43	100
Xinjiang	13.51	37.64	27.87	20.98	100
Overall	10.78	37.32	34.48	17.43	100

9.4.4.3 Lack of Physical and esthetic Education

In addition to the facilities and distance, there were some problems with schooling itself: 8.5% of children said they "did not like" going to school. However, in the three counties in Sichuan with the lowest enrollment rates, the percentages of children who "liked" and "liked very much" going to school were the highest (Table 9.32).

9.4.4.4 Lack of Family and Community Education

Children's education is not just a school issue; the family and community are also important places for education. The survey attempted to determine whether the family provided a basic educational environment for children by examining the prevalence of dictionaries, a basic tool for children's learning. It was found that 22.47% of the children did not have a dictionary at home, with the percentage more than doubling to 58.53% in Sichuan (Table 9.33).

9.4.4.5 Children's Aspirations for Community Sports Facilities

A survey in Wenxi County, Shanxi, found that children were eager to have community sports and recreational facilities. As a result of the combination of the sports welfare lottery and the new rural construction initiative, villages have been equipped with sports resources, and they generally have level concrete basketball courts and a full

Table 9.32 Do you like going to school? (Unit: %)

Project provinces (regions)	Like very much	Like	Neither like nor dislike	Dislike	Total
Shanxi	22.71	47.10	20.53	9.66	100
Henan	8.96	62.18	18.21	10.64	100
Yunnan	19.11	50.85	18.60	11.43	100
Sichuan	29.19	60.13	6.70	3.99	100
Xinjiang	47.23	37.11	7.47	8.19	100
Overall	25.72	51.94	13.84	8.50	100

Table 9.33 Do you have a dictionary at home? (Unit: %)

Project provinces (regions)	No	Yes	Total
Shanxi	4.59	95.41	100
Henan	7.28	92.72	100
Yunnan	10.92	89.08	100
Sichuan	58.53	41.47	100
Xinjiang	15.18	84.82	100
Overall	22.47	77.53	100

set of sports equipment. In 18 of the 20 villages, the courts and sports equipment were in good condition; in one village, the basketball hoop was not in place; and in another, the basketball court was severely damaged. According to our observations, children had the highest probability of using these venues and facilities for sports, playing, gathering, or communicating. During four workshops, the children expressed their love for the sports venues and equipment as well as their common wish for future "children's homes" or "children's centers" to be located close to the sports grounds, so that they could have easy access to the existing sports resources. Older people also enjoyed gathering here to take a little exercise and talk to each other. The children in the interviews expressed a desire for more child-friendly playgrounds and facilities. Of the existing facilities, the basketball court was the only favorite of the children, who felt that all the other facilities were built for the elderly.

9.4.4.6 Children Without Household Registration

A considerable number of children in the surveyed areas were not registered (Table 9.34). There were also some adult villagers who had not been registered. The Sichuan survey team were of the opinion that villagers were not sufficiently aware of the importance of household registration. There were several reasons why villagers were not registered: first, they thought it did not matter; second, their families lived far away from the village police station and they did not want to travel; third, newborns were not registered; and fourth, they were afraid of being punished if they had extra births. However, one of the main reasons given by the respondents for children not being registered was an extremely high cost (Fig. 9.6).

9.4.5 Participation

The right to participation is defined as children's right to take part in family, cultural, and social life. In this study, questions were designed to allow the children to assess for themselves their right to participate in some affairs.

Table 9.34 Whether a child is registered (Unit: %)

Project provinces (regions)	Yes	No	Total
Shanxi	97.72	2.28	100
Henan	97.08	2.92	100
Yunnan	97.76	2.24	100
Sichuan	89.28	10.72	100
Xinjiang	94.40	5.60	100
Overall	94.56	5.44	100

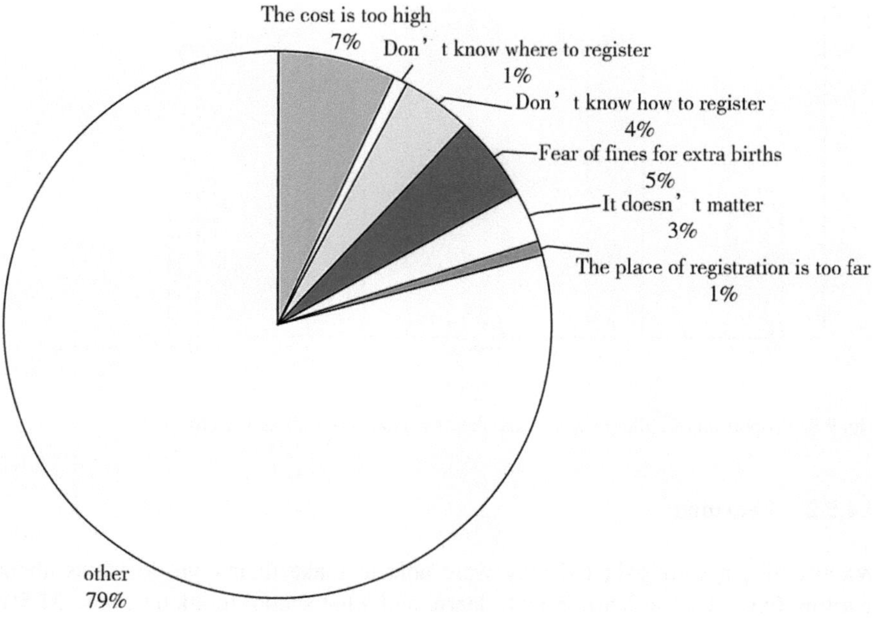

Fig. 9.6 Reasons for children not being registered

9.4.5.1 Daily Life

Figure 9.7 shows that two minority project counties in Sichuan and Xinjiang had the lowest proportion of children making their own decisions about daily life (e.g., what to eat, what clothes to buy, and where to play), at 60.1% and 62.9%, respectively, while Shanxi and Henan had higher proportions, at over 70%.

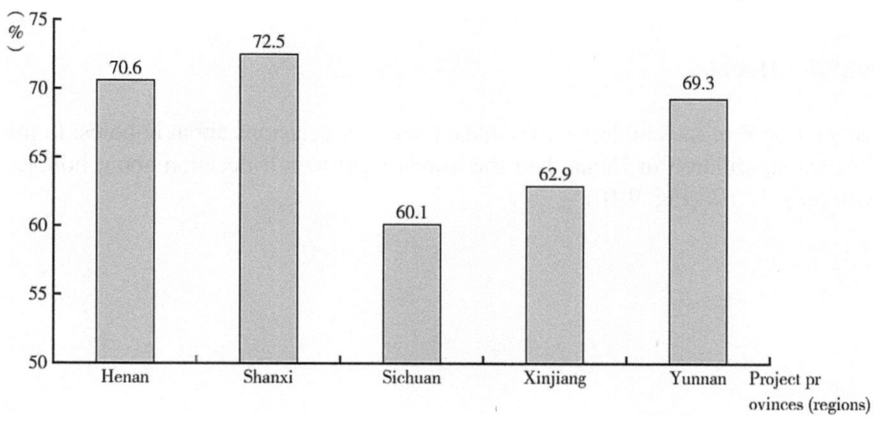

Fig. 9.7 Proportion of children making their own decisions about daily life

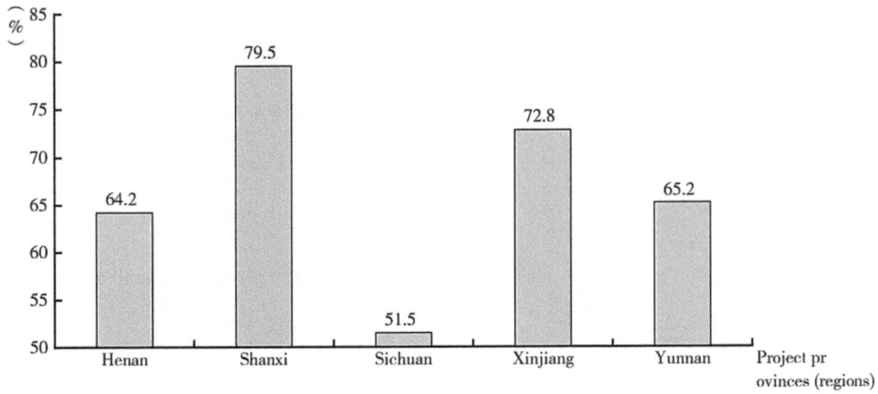

Fig. 9.8 Proportion of children who make their own decisions about learning

9.4.5.2 Learning

When children were asked if they were able to make their own decisions about learning (e.g., what to learn, how to learn, and what school to attend), only 51.5% in Sichuan responded positively, with the proportion in Shanxi being the highest at 79.5% (Fig. 9.8).

9.4.5.3 Making Friends

When children were asked if they were able to make friends on their own, 73.28% answered "Yes," while 26.72% were subject to parental intervention while making friends. Sichuan still had the lowest proportion, whereas Xinjiang had the highest proportion at 81.5% (Fig. 9.9).

9.4.5.4 Hobbies

Only 64.36% of the children could make their own decisions about hobbies. In this dimension, children in Henan had the lowest right to self-decision about hobbies, with only 47.1% (Fig. 9.10).

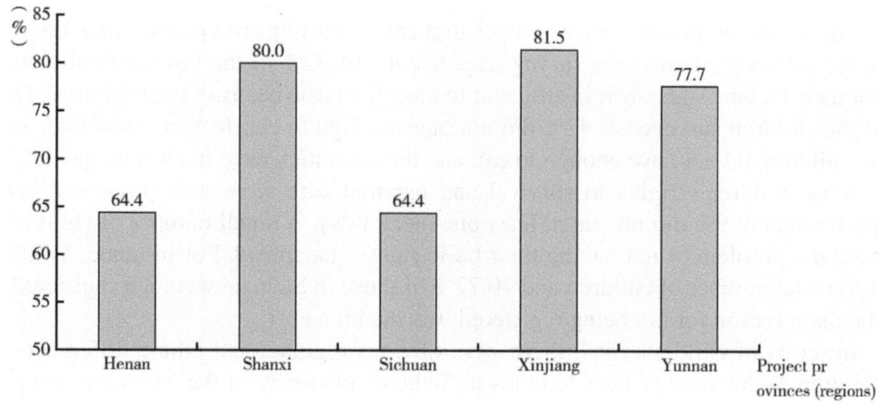

Fig. 9.9 Proportion of children deciding to make friends on their own

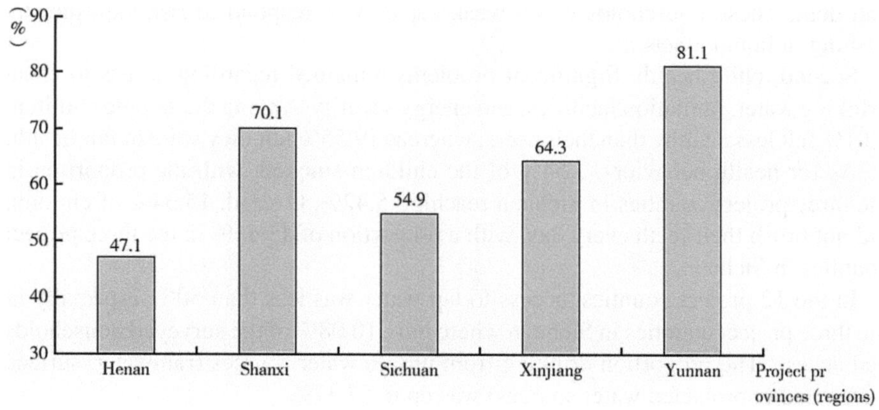

Fig. 9.10 Proportion of children making their own decisions about hobbies

9.5 Main Conclusions and Policy Recommendations

9.5.1 Main Conclusions

The study used the theoretical framework of multidimensional child poverty and designed the dimensions of child survival, health, protection, development, and participation based on various dimensions of children's rights. The survey obtained data from 7936 children and the main findings were as follows.

First, child survival. From the perspective of income poverty, this survey investigated child poverty in terms of both objective and subjective poverty. From the perspective of objective poverty, around 28% of the children in the demonstration zones lived in poor families based on the official definition of poverty or low income.

The subjective poverty rate was much higher than the objective poverty rate. Based on the self-evaluation of the survey respondents, 61.32% of the villagers indicated that their income status was insufficient to meet the basic needs of their families. Of all the children surveyed, 2.42% did not have enough to eat. In Sichuan, 7.04% of the children did not have enough to eat, and their families were in absolute poverty.

Most children's rights to survival and parental care were well protected, but approximately 9% did not eat at least one meal a day. A small number of children faced the problem of not having their basic rights guaranteed. For instance, 5.44% of the total number of children and 10.72% of those in Sichuan were not registered. The main reason for not being registered was the high cost.

In terms of child survival, there were obvious regional and ethnic differences. Children in the three project counties in Sichuan, primarily of the Yi ethnic group, were the worst off in terms of housing, food, and subjective feelings.

Most children lived in extremely vulnerable families that were vulnerable to poverty at the slightest risk: 90.81% of the families had no savings and 63.43% had debt. These households had a weak capacity to respond to risk exposure by cashing in liquid assets.

Second, child health. Significant problems remained regarding access to clean drinking water, sanitation facilities, and energy security. Among the sample children, 4.01% felt less healthy than their peers, whereas 19.55% felt they were in fair health.

As for health behaviors, 3.54% of the children smoked, with the proportion in the three project counties in Sichuan reaching 5.42%. Overall, 15.34% of children did not brush their teeth every day, with a proportion of 45.45% in the three project counties in Sichuan.

In the 12 project counties, access to tap water was less than 50%, especially in the three project counties in Sichuan where only 10.08% of the surveyed households had access. The proportion drinking from unsafe water sources (rainwater, surface water, and unprotected water sources) was up to 87.17%.

Children in the sample households in Sichuan had the least access to basic sanitation facilities, at 97.97%, of which 86.66% had no sanitation facilities and 10.49% used dry latrines. In Henan, Shanxi, and Xinjiang, where 95–98% of the children had no access to basic sanitation facilities, the situation was only slightly better than in Sichuan.

The use of clean energy was very low, with only 5.2% using natural gas and biogas. In the Sichuan project area, the use of firewood for cooking reached 99.08 and 12.93% of the households had no access to electricity.

Third, child protection. The survey mapped child safety issues from the aspects of family, society, and school. The main finding was that corporal punishment and verbal abuse of children in the family was very common. This was reflected in the behavior of parents: only 55.59% of the children were never beaten, with around 43.60% occasionally being beaten by their parents; especially alarming was the 10.47% who were beaten occasionally with hard objects such as straps, sticks, and hairbrushes. Overall, 19.16% of the children were beaten and scolded by their teachers at school, with the highest percentage in Shanxi at 34.82%; 13.79% were beaten and scolded by their classmates, 2.49% were subjected to violence outside of school, and 1% of the parents were aware of sexual violence against their children.

The existence of such a situation is related to Chinese views on children's education: 65% of parents believed that "beating represents care and scolding represents love" and "a stick makes a filial child" were justified and 51% of parents believed that it was not a crime to beat their children. As many as 78% of the parents had no objection to teachers beating their children if it was good for them. The highest proportion was 95% in Sichuan. Some parents even believed that teachers who did not discipline children strictly (including corporal punishment) were irresponsible.

The survey also revealed that children's safety hazards existed everywhere, mainly in the form of drowning and road traffic. Environmental pollution was found to be another major threat to children's safety.

Fourth, child development. While the majority of children had access to education, there existed some serious problems, including the low enrollment rate of school-age children in the three counties in Sichuan. Among all children, 17.43% felt that school was "very far" from home and 8.50% "disliked" going to school. In terms of learning conditions, 22.47% "did not have" a dictionary at home, of which 58.53% were in the three counties of Sichuan. Children had a strong demand for cultural life and sports facilities.

Fifth, child participation. Only 60.1% and 62.9% of the children in the project counties of Sichuan and Xinjiang, respectively, were able to make their own decisions about daily life (e.g., what to eat, what clothes to buy, and where to play). Only 51.5% of the children in the project counties in Sichuan could make their own decisions about learning (e.g., what to learn, how to learn, and what school to attend). In the five project provinces (regions), 26.72% of the children could not make their own decisions about making friends. In Henan, only 47.1% of the children could make their own decisions about hobbies.

9.5.2 Policy Recommendations

First, the quality of child survival should be improved. In key counties in China's national development-oriented poverty alleviation work, improving the quality of child survival remains a public policy priority to (1) eradicate absolute child poverty and address the problem of hunger among a small number of children, (2) promote the good habit of eating breakfast and effectively control potential child malnutrition, (3) implement asset-building policies in poor areas to promote the accumulation of household assets and reduce vulnerability, and (4) develop specific development-oriented poverty alleviation and welfare intervention strategies and implement targeted public policy interventions in special types of Yi-dominated poor areas in Sichuan.

Second, equity in the right to development should be promoted to (1) universalize access to tap water in ethnic minority and remote mountainous areas, solve the problem of drinking water safety, and ensure that children have access to clean drinking water; (2) popularize sanitary latrines according to local conditions, especially in ethnic minority areas, and raise awareness among cadres and the public of their importance; and (3) implement the policy of "sustainable energy for all" in rural areas, change the use of firewood and animal dung for cooking and heating in ethnic minority areas as well as poor and backward areas, and thus lift the majority of children out of "energy poverty."

Third, children's physical and mental health should be comprehensively protected by (1) applying public media such as radio and television to disseminate correct communication between parents and children so as to reduce corporal punishment and even domestic violence by parents against children, (2) facilitating publicity and education for teachers and children to reduce school violence, and (3) advancing government supervision and services to reduce traffic accidents and other accidental deaths and disabilities among children.

Fourth, an environment conducive to the all-round development of children should be created to (1) reflect on the phenomenon of young children dropping out of school as a result of the consolidation of educational resources in remote rural areas, adverse social consequences of parents accompanying the students during schooling, and school buses as a safety hazard; (2) call upon enterprises, volunteers, and other non-governmental organizations to cope with vulnerable populations with particular needs as well as specific areas with issues such as the lack of dictionaries and resources for physical and esthetic education; and (3) address the psychological toll that household registration difficulties can take on children.

Fifth, children should be encouraged to participate in social life by (1) publicizing the idea that children, under the supervision of their parents and guardians, can participate in decision-making in family, cultural, and social life; (2) cultivating the good habit of children making their own decisions and being responsible for their own actions; and (3) researching, promoting, and guiding children on how to properly participate in activities and decision-making in family, cultural, and social life.

Sixth, building an inclusive child welfare system. Beginning with the livelihood security of orphans, a breakthrough in China's child welfare system has already started by addressing the poverty of special groups through public financial transfers from the government. However, while the basic livelihood of orphans and even all disadvantaged children is guaranteed, the need for social welfare services for the multifaceted development of children, that is, the establishment of an inclusive child welfare system, is inevitably on the agenda.

References

Abello, A., & Harding, A. (2006). Income mobility and financial disadvantage: Australian children. *Agenda, 13*(1).

Adelman, L., & Middleton, S. (2003). *Social exclusion in childhood: Why and how it should be measured. Some thoughts from Britain.* Paper presented at the Australian Social Policy Conference, University of New South Wales, Sydney, Australia. July.

Attawell, K. (2003). *International longitudinal research on childhood poverty: Practical guidelines and lessons learned from young lives*. Young Lives.
Boyden, J., Feeny, T., & Scott. (2003). Voices of children: Experiences and perceptions from Belarus, Bolivia, India, Kenya and Sierra Leone. *Children and Poverty Series*, Part II, Christian Children's Fund, Richmond. http://www.christianchildrensfund.org/uploadedFiles/Publications/7660_Poverty%20Pt%02.pdf (2-27-05).
Bradshaw, J., Hoelscher, P., et al. (2006). An index of child well-being in the European Union. *Social Indicators Research, 80*(1).
Corak, M. (2006a). *Do poor children become poor adults? Lessons from a cross country comparison of generational earnings mobility*. Institute for the Study of Labor (IZA).
Corak, M. (2006b). Principles and practicalities for measuring child poverty. *International Social Security Review, 29*(2).
Feeny, T., & Boyden, J. (2003). *Children and poverty, a review of contemporary literature and thought on children and poverty: Rethinking the causes, experiences and effects*. Children and Poverty Series, Part I. Christian Children's Fund.
Gordon, D., Nandy, S., Pantazis, C., Pemberton, S., & Townsend, P. (2003a). *The distribution of child poverty in the developing world*. Centre for International Poverty Research.
Gordon, D., Nandy, S., Pantazis, C., Pemberton, S., & Townsend, P. (2003b). *Child poverty in the developing world*. Policy Press.
Howe, B., & Pidwell, R. (2004). Single parents and paid work. *Australian Journal of Social Issues, 39*(2).
Land, K., Lamb, V., et al. (2001). Child and youth well-being in the United States, 1975–1998: Some findings from a new index. *Social Indicators Research, 56*, 00–00.
Micklewright, J. (2001). *Should the UK government measure poverty and social exclusion with a composite index?* UNICEF Innocenti Research Centre.
Sen, A. (2009). *Expanding the field of child development research to address child poverty*. Speech at the International Symposium on "Anti-Poverty and Early Childhood Development." October 29–30, 2009.
UNDP. (2004). *Human development report*. Oxford University Press.
UNDP. (2011). *Human Development Report*. Oxford University Press.
UNICEF. (2004). *The state of the world's children.*
UNICEF. (2005). *Child poverty in rich countries 2005*. UNICEF Innocenti Research Centre.
UNICEF. (2006). *Children living in poverty: Overview of definitions. Measurements and policy.*
UNICEF. (2011). *A multidimensional approach to measuring child poverty*. Social and Economic Policy Working Briefs.
UNICEF-IRC. (2005). *Child poverty in rich countries*. UNICEF Innocenti Research Centre.

Chapter 10
Child Poverty in Rural China: Multidimensional Perspective

This paper describes a pilot study on child multidimensional poverty in rural China by introducing the Alkire–Foster method based on survey data collected from five provinces/autonomous regions. Results showed that the head-count ratio of child multidimensional poverty was 14.29%. On average, multidimensionally poor children were deprived in 37.62% of all the dimensions, and their adjusted headcount ratio (multidimensional poverty) index was 0.054. Health was the most deprived dimension, followed by the subsistence and participation dimensions. Disabled children, children influenced by HIV/AIDS, and ethnic minority children were severely deprived. This study not only adds to the current literature on child poverty in China, but also provides policy suggestions for future action plans.

10.1 Introduction

Since the economic reform and opening-up policy, China has witnessed remarkable achievements in poverty alleviation as a result of three decades of continuous, rapid economic development and effective development-oriented poverty reduction programs. Since 1981, the number of Chinese people living below the poverty line (USD 1.25 daily) has dropped by 660 million (Wang et al., 2012). However, according to a study by Wang et al. (2012), the incidence of child poverty exceeds that of adults and the elderly. Children are one of the most vulnerable groups in rural China. Currently, child poverty is becoming an issue of great concern. From a policy perspective, children have been identified as a key target group in the national poverty alleviation strategy. The National Programme of Action for Child Development in China (2011–2020) has formulated the development agenda for promoting general child development as well as children's rights protection.

© Social Sciences Academic Press 2022

X. Wang, *Multidimensional Poverty Measurement*,
International Research on Poverty Reduction,
https://doi.org/10.1007/978-981-19-1189-7_10

It is generally acknowledged that child poverty cannot be understood simply from an income and consumption perspective; rather, it needs to be addressed from multidimensional perspectives covering basic human rights and social services (Minujin & Delamonica, 2005; Roelen & Gassman, 2008). The theoretical framework in this paper is based upon Sen's "Capability Approach", and it applies Alkire–Foster's multidimensional poverty measurement approach. It attempts to establish a multidimensional poverty index for rural Chinese children and, by decomposition, to explore the interconnection among dimensions and compare the divergence among subgroups.

10.2 Literature Review

Reducing child poverty has been recognized as the greatest policy challenge, and there is a growing number of studies on child poverty or well-being internationally (Fernandes et al., 2010; Gordon & Nandy, 2012; Minujin et al., 2006). Regarding child poverty or deprivation, the review of Minujin et al. (2006) provides a good guide for the current discussion. In their review, they discuss and compare the definitions of child poverty and its measurements. It is concluded that there is not a uniform approach to define or identify child poverty even though current definitions incorporate human rights precepts and notions, and try to go beyond the monetary approach. Material deprivation, children's social participation, and voice are examples of shared dimensions in identifying child poverty.

In terms of a monetary approach, although it is sometimes judged as inadequate and inappropriate for identifying and measuring child poverty (Gordon & Nandy, 2012), Minujin et al. (2006) emphasize the fact that the core meaning of poverty, which is linked to material deprivation, should not be diluted during the discussion.

From a multidimensional perspective, Gordon et al. (2003) use a variant of the basic needs approach to measure poverty by evaluating the deprivation of at least one of seven dimensions (Gordon et al., 2003; Minujin & Delamonica, 2005). They set thresholds for each indicator to measure deprivation and distinguished children living in conditions where at least one deprivation is assessed as poor ("severe deprivation"), and where at least two deprivations are assessed as "absolute poverty". Equal importance is implicitly given to each dimension. In addition to poverty incidence, they also measure poverty depth and severity by the average number of deprivations and adjust deprivation by standard deviation. This is one of the first efforts to incorporate a multidimensional perspective into a study on child poverty. Alkire and Roche (2011) examine multidimensional poverty among children under the age of five by applying the Alkire–Foster method (AF method) (Alkire & Foster, 2007, 2009; Wang & Alkire, 2009). Advantages of their approach is that it not only presents indicators of multiple dimensions with a single summary index, but it also has desirable axiomatic properties and can be broken down among the dimensions and different groups.

The measure of child well-being is another highly relevant issue. Fernandes et al. (2010) also contribute to the existing literature by an elaborate review of the measurement of child well-being. The authors point out that, in recent years, multidimensionality and composite index have commonly be applied in studies into child well-being. The American child and youth well-being index (CWI), the index of child well-being in Europe, and the microdata child well-being index (NSAF) are some of the first efforts used to build a single composite index for child well-being.

The abovementioned multidimensional studies on child poverty or child well-being share some common choices of dimension, cluster, and domain (Bradshaw et al., 2007; Land et al., 2001, 2007; UNICEF, 2007), which include:

- living conditions—material well-being, food/nutrition, housing/shelter, drinking water, sanitation, health, basic social services
- protection—risks, safety, peer and family relationships
- development—education, information
- participation—participation in society
- subjective well-being/emotional well-being.

In regards to the weight of these dimensions, most of the indexes apply equal weights implicitly or explicitly (Alkire & Roche, 2011; Bradshaw et al., 2007; Fernandes et al., 2010; Gordon et al., 2003; Land et al., 2001). It is argued that, "given the indivisibility of rights, children ought to be considered poor if they suffer from any rights violation" (Minujin & Delamonica, 2005). To simplify interpretation, Alkire and Roche (2011) argue that equal weight is plausible and commonly adopted.

In China, most research focuses on the poverty target of the poor population as a whole, or on a particular region. It is not until recently that vulnerable groups, such as children, have become the focus of research (Qin & Qiao, 2012). Compared with the extensive international literature, evaluating child poverty or well-being in China is relatively limited (Qin & Qiao, 2012; Song & Zhang, 2014).

Similarly to their international counterparts, Chinese researchers have not been able to agree on a definition of child poverty. In Chen's empirical work in 2009 on child poverty determinant analysis, child poverty was defined by household income. In Zhang and Tang's (2009) estimation of the population of poor children in China, they identify poor children as the sum of six categorized groups: children from families depending on subsistence allowance, orphans, children from "five guarantees family",[1] orphans adopted by urban welfare agencies, waifs in the care of aid agencies, and children affected by HIV/AIDS. Based on international frontier studies, the multidimensional poverty analysis approach is often proposed, but few empirical studies have been conducted using this approach. Shang and Wang's (2012) pilot study builds a normative rights-based child multidimensional poverty framework according to Convention on the Rights of the Child (CRC) and the Law for

[1] A five guarantees family is a family with difficulties (the aged, the infirm, old widows, and orphans) that can be taken care of by the community in five ways: food, clothing, medical care, housing, and burial expenses.

Protection of Minors of China, with dimensions which included subsistence, health, protection, development, and participation.

This paper is based upon Shang and Wang's theoretical framework, but it takes a further step by building a multidimensional poverty index and applying it to evaluate multidimensional poverty among rural Chinese children. Given its appealing properties, the AF method is a suitable approach for our index building, as the purpose of this research is not only to report on the general poverty status of rural Chinese children, but also to understand the reasons behind their deprivation and identify the most deprived.

10.3 Methodology

10.3.1 Theoretical Framework

The capability approach is the theoretical framework of the AF method. Sen et al. abandoned the concepts of "income", "consumer spending", and "utility" commonly referred to in traditional economics and welfare economics, and instead resorted to individual "capability" as a metric for levels of human well-being and social development. Sen's capability approach is a moral framework which defines poverty as a deprivation of capabilities, and as a lack of multiple freedoms people value and have reason to value. It proposes that social arrangements should be primarily evaluated according to the extent of freedom people have to promote or achieve functionings they value (Alkire, 2007).

In terms of how to select the dimension of capability, Robeyns (2003) and Alkire (2007) point out that the capabilities valued (or that should be valued) by the study subjects should be considered while also taking into account the policy and project objectives. When applying the capability approach to children, Sen states that the freedom of children should be considered not only at present, but also in the future (Saito, 2003). The Convention on the Rights of the Child stipulates some basic capabilities, e.g. able to be nourished, able to acquire safe drinking water, and able to be free from disease. If a child does not have the freedom to realize these basic functionings, this means his/her capability is deprived and the child is in capability poverty. In this paper, child poverty in rural China is defined by this notion. The dimension framework proposed by Shang and Wang (2012) is a reflection of the abovementioned basic functionings which children should have.

The AF method can be broken down into several steps (Alkire, 2007). It identifies a "poverty line" for each indicator to define deprivation and assesses the poverty status of each individual on each indicator. The weights are applied to each indicator, followed by the calculation of a weighted sum of deprivations for each person. A second poverty cut-off (k) is defined for censoring multidimensional poor. If 1/3 is the k for measuring multidimensional poverty, a person is believed to be multidimensional poor when they fall under 1/3 of the weighted dimensions. Censoring is followed by a focus on the multidimensional population. "Multidimensional poverty headcount ratio" (H) can be estimated as the percentage of those who have a weighted deprivation score of at least 1/3. "Intensity of multidimensional poverty deprivation" (A) can also be obtained, and this represents the average percentage deprivation of people in multidimensional poverty. By multiplying these two figures, the multidimensional poverty index (M_0, also called adjusted headcount ratio) can be calculated as the percentage of people in multidimensional poverty adjusted for poverty intensity (Alkire & Foster, 2007).

10.3.2 Data Sources

Results in this paper were based on data from the China Child Welfare Demonstration Area Baseline Survey (2010), which covered 12 counties in five provinces/autonomous regions, namely: Sichuan, Yunnan, Henan, Xinjiang Uygur autonomous region, and Shanxi. Twenty townships/towns were selected from 12 counties, and 120 villages were further selected.

Two types of surveys were conducted: one at a community and one at a household level. Community surveys were conducted with the head of the village, in order to obtain collective information such as locations of schools, the demographics of children attending school, and locations of clinics. The household surveys were targeted at households with children aged 0–18 years. A systematic sampling approach was adopted for the household surveys, which was subsequently followed by face-to-face interviews by enumerators. The household survey questionnaires were divided into two parts: one targeting the parents and one targeting the children. The parent part focused on demographic information, including the family's financial situation. It also tried to reflect the parents' attitude and philosophy regarding, for example, child education and child protection. The child part focused on child information such as physical data and daily routines. If a household had more than one child, then information for each child was gathered separately. When possible, children were encouraged to respond to the interviewer's questions. For a child over the age of 12, supplementary questions were designed to evaluate information on school participation, safety, relationship with their parents, and health behavior.

In total, information on 7936 children was collected. Among them, there were 4182 boys and 3754 girls, and 39.42% of children over the age of 6 responded by themselves. The sample distribution across different regions and ethnic groups can be found in Tables 10.1 and 10.2.

Table 10.1 Sample distribution across regions

Province/Autonomous region	Frequency	Percent of sample (%)	Cumulative percentage (%)
Sichuan	2372	29.89	29.89
Yunnan	1831	23.07	52.96
Henan	1334	16.81	69.77
Xinjiang	1304	16.43	86.2
Shanxi	1095	13.8	100.00
Total	7936	100.00	–

Table 10.2 Sample distribution among ethnics

Ethnic group	Frequency	Percent of sample (%)	Cumulative percentage (%)
Han	3128	39.43	39.43
Hui	171	2.16	41.58
Uyghur	823	10.37	51.95
Yi	2370	29.87	81.83
Other	1442	18.17	100.00
Total	7934	100.00	–

10.3.3 Analysis Method

This paper established the child multidimensional poverty index in China based on five dimensions: subsistence, health, protection, development, and participation. The selection of indicators aimed to reflect the current policy focus and public debates in order to provide more practical and feasible policy options (see Table 10.3).

The first dimension was subsistence. It focused on whether the child could obtain basic identification after birth, and if the parents could provide their children with essential protection and care. More specifically, the latter included whether a child had enough food and was in their biological parents' care. The subsistence dimension also included poverty level and vulnerability, as household income has a direct impact on the provision of basic goods and care. In order to evaluate if a child received basic care from their parents, children were separated into different age groups. The reason for this was that parents' approach to caring for their children may vary according to age.[2]

The second dimension, health, examined children's basic health and sanitation situations, and the external conditions that influenced their health status. On an individual level, the basic health status of children was assessed from both subjective and objective perspectives. A parent's report on a child's heath status was more subjective, while a proxy provided a more objective evaluation of a child's health-related behavior. On a household level, access to drinking water, sanitation facilities, and

[2] http://www.unicef.org/crc/index_understanding.html.

Table 10.3 Dimensions and indicators

Dimension	Indicator
1. Subsistence	1.1 Identification
	1.2 Food and nutrition
	1.3 Accompanying and caring
	1.4 Income poverty
	1.5 Financial vulnerability
2. Health	2.1 Health status
	2.2 Health behavior
	2.3 Drinking water
	2.4 Sanitation facilities
	2.5 Cooking fuel
	2.6 Accessibility of health services
3. Protection	3.1 Domestic violence
	3.2 Campus violence
	3.3 Social violence
4. Development	4.1 School enrolment
	4.2 Satisfaction of needs in learning
	4.3 Possession of learning tools
	4.4 Distance from school
5. Participation	5.1 Decision making on daily life
	5.2 Decision making on learning
	5.3 Decision making on hobbies

cooking fuels were indicators which assessed the deprivation of a household's provision of basic facilities. Accessibility of health clinics assessed the status of the right of children to access health from a community perspective. Based on consultations with experts in child health care, it was decided that a distance of 5 km would be used as a threshold for accessibility. These six indicators generally provided a comprehensive coverage of the health dimension of rural children.

The third dimension, protection, examined the deprivation of a child being free from violence, including domestic violence, violence at school, and violence against children by the public.

The fourth dimension, development, focused on the deprivation of children in education and development-related issues. If a school-age child dropped out of school, they were considered to be deprived. For children aged 12 years or above, an additional indicator, satisfaction of needs in learning, was also introduced, in an attempt to evaluate deprivation from a child's perspective. The development dimension was also addressed from the household and community perspectives. Possessing a dictionary was considered as a proxy to evaluate if a child has basic learning tools which a family could provide. Distance to school addressed the deprivation on a community level. China's current policy of rural education, which recommends a reduction in the number of village elementary schools and encourages primary level students to attend township schools, is under debate. As some rural school bus systems did not exist in some areas and in others functioned very poorly, it left some students with no choice but to walk to school. Long daily commutes were physically exhausting and also a safety risk. Therefore, distance to school was introduced as an indicator in the development dimension. According to a report, a sampling survey among rural elementary and high school children in ten provinces estimated that the average distance between home and school was 5.4 km.[3] It was difficult to judge what distance should be considered as deprivation, so this finding was used as a reference, and the critical value was defined as 5 km.

With regard to the fifth dimension, participation, Article 12 of CRC states that "State parties shall assure to the child who is capable of forming his or her own views the right to express those views freely in all matters affecting the child, the views of the child being given due weight in accordance with the age and maturity of the child." In the survey questionnaire, it was assumed that children aged 12 years or above, i.e. children who had completed elementary school, possessed this ability, and therefore should have the right to express their views in their daily lives, study, and hobbies.

This paper assigned equal weight to all five dimensions as well as the indicators within each dimension. One advantage was that this made it easier to interpret the index. Another advantage was that all dimensions were closely linked to the welfare and basic rights defined in CRC. It was also a commonly adopted scheme in CWI, index of child well-being, and international MPI. Table 10.4 provides a definition of deprivation for each indicator as well as the weight application.

The second poverty cut-off (k) set the sum of weighted dimensions in which a child must be deprived in order to be identified as living in multidimensional poverty. After censoring, exclusive focus was placed on children who lived in multidimensional poverty. Multidimensional poverty headcount ratio (H) varied according to k (Fig. 10.1).

We set $k = 30\%$ (Fig. 10.2) (Table 10.5). At this k, 14.29% of the children were in multidimensional poverty. From a policymaking perspective, it would be practical and target-oriented to focus on the poorest 14% of rural children. In our case, A was 37.62%, which meant that poor children were deprived in around 1.88 dimensions, and the multidimensional poverty index (M_0) was 0.054.

[3] *Yanzhao Metropolis Daily*, 2012.

Table 10.4 Indicators: deprivation cut-offs

No	Indicator	Deprivation cut-off of indicator	Weight	
1.1	Identification	1: The child is deprived if he/she is NOT registered in the census register and doesn't have an ID; 0: The child is not deprived	1/5	1/25
1.2	Food and nutrition	1: The child is deprived if he/she only dines only twice per day (or less) or "cannot eat his/her fill (or does not know clearly)" every day; 0: The child is not deprived		1/25
1.3	Accompanying and caring	1: The child is deprived if a 0–2-year-old child does not receive care from his/her mother for over 1 month; or a 3–5-year-old child does not receive care from his/her mother for over 3 months; or a 6–11-year-old child does not receive care from his/her mother for over 5 months; or a 12–15-year-old child does not receive care from his/her mother for over 7 months; or a 16–18-year-old child does not receive care from his/her mother for over 9 months; 0: The child is not deprived		1/25
1.4	Income poverty	1: The child is deprived in income poverty if he/she comes from a household that depends on subsistence allowance or is identified as a "poverty-stricken household"; 0: The child is not deprived		1/25
1.5	Financial vulnerability	1: The child is deprived in financial vulnerability if he/she comes from a household which is in debt; 0: The child is not deprived if the household has no debt		1/25
2.1	Health status	1: The child is deprived if his/her parents rate the child's health status as "average" or "poor"; 0: The child is not deprived if the rating is "good"	1/5	1/30
2.2	Health behavior	1: The child is deprived if he/she is aged 12 years or above and does not brush their teeth; 0: The child is aged 12 years or above and brushes their teeth daily, or the child is under 12 years of age[a]		1/30

(continued)

Table 10.4 (continued)

No	Indicator	Deprivation cut-off of indicator	Weight	
2.3	Drinking water	1: The child is deprived if he/she comes from a household where the water source is a lake or pond; 0: The child is not deprived if the household uses tap water, a well with a depth of five or more metres, or protected spring water		1/30
2.4	Sanitation facilities	1: The child is deprived if the household uses a pail latrine, latrine pit, or other type of latrine; 0: The child is not deprived if the household uses an indoor/outdoor toilet or dry hygienic toilet		1/30
2.5	Cooking fuel	1: The child is deprived if the household uses firewood or coal as cooking fuel; 0: The child is not deprived if the household uses natural gas, biogas or electricity to cook		1/30
2.6	Accessibility of health services	1: The child is deprived if his/her home is more than 5 km away from the nearest clinic; 0: The child is not deprived if the home is within 5 km of the nearest clinic		1/30
3.1	Domestic violence	1: The child is deprived if his/her parents "frequently" beat or scold him/her or "occasionally" (including "frequently") hit the child with a hard object; 0: The child is not deprived	1/5	1/15
3.2	Campus violence	1: The child is deprived if he/she is 6–18 years old and was once beaten or scolded by teachers or classmates; 0: The child is not deprived if he/she is 6–18 years old and was never beaten or scolded by teachers or classmates, or the child is 0–6 years old		1/15
3.3	Social violence	1: The child is deprived if he/she was once robbed; 0: The child is not deprived if he/she has never been robbed		1/15
4.1	School enrolment	1: The child is deprived if he/she is 6–15 years old and is not attending school or never attended school, or is 16–18 years old and has never attended school; 0: The child is not deprived if he/she is 0–5 years old, or he/she is 6–15 or 16–18 years old and is attending school or has graduated from school	1/5	1/20

(continued)

Table 10.4 (continued)

No	Indicator	Deprivation cut-off of indicator	Weight	
4.2	Satisfaction of needs in learning	1: The child is deprived if he/she is aged 12 years or above and "is unwilling to work or do the manual work assigned by parents, but to attend school"; 0: The child is younger than 12 years old, or the child is older than 12 years but satisfied with current status		1/20
4.3	Possession of learning tools	1: The child is deprived if he/she is 6 years or older, and does not have a dictionary at home; 0: The child is not deprived if he/she is 6 years or older and has one or more dictionaries at home, or the child is younger than 6		1/20
4.4	Distance from school	1: The child is deprived if he/she is older than 12 and his/her home is more than 5 km away from school, or he/she considers it takes a "very long time" to get to school; 0: The child is not deprived if he/she is younger than 12 years old and his/her home is within 5 km of school, and does not consider it takes a "very long time" to go to school		1/20
5.1	Decision making on daily life	1: The child is deprived if he/she is older than 12 and cannot decide his/ her own daily life activities (dining, buying clothes, going out to play); 0: The child is not deprived is he/she is older than 12 can decide his/her own daily life activities, or the child is younger than 12	1/5	1/15
5.2	Decision making on learning	1: The child is deprived if he/she is older than 12 and doesn't have right to make his/her own decisions about studying; 0: The child is not deprived if he/she is older than 12 and can decide on his/her own studying, or the child is younger than 12		1/15
5.3	Decision making on hobbies	1: The child is deprived if he/she is older than 12 and cannot decide on his/her own hobby; 0: The child is not deprived if he/she is older than 12 can decide his/her own hobby, or the child is younger than 12		1/15

[a] The questionnaire survey was conducted in 2010. "Child aged 12 years or above" refers to children born in 1998 or earlier. Part of the survey was done with children older than 12 years old. Therefore, for some indicators limited by data resources, only children older than 12 responded

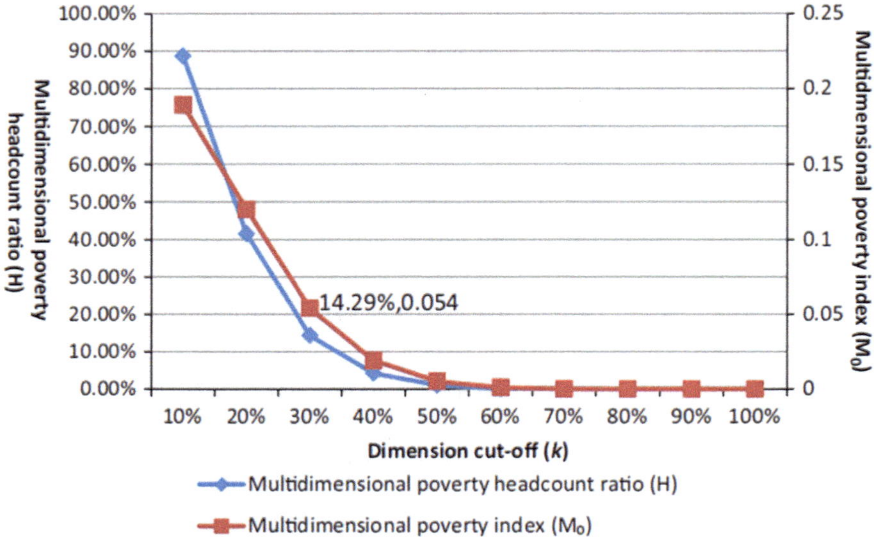

Fig. 10.1 Multidimensional poverty headcount ratio (H) and multidimensional poverty index (M_0)

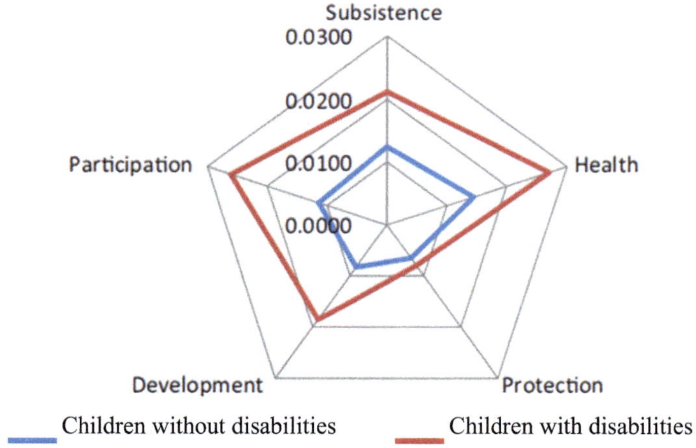

Fig. 10.2 Dimensional breakdown of M_0: children with disabilities versus children without disabilities

Table 10.5 H, A, and M_0 with different k

k (%)	Multidimensional poverty headcount ratio (H) (%)	Average poverty dimension (A) (%)	Multidimensional poverty index (M_0)
10	88.66	21.31	0.189
20	41.47	29.05	0.120
30	14.29	37.62	0.054
40	4.16	46.63	0.019
50	0.98	55.06	0.005
60	0.11	63.11	0.001
70	0.00	–	0.000
80	0.00	–	0.000
90	0.00	–	0.000
100	0.00	–	0.000

10.4 Key Findings

10.4.1 Surveyed Children were Severely Deprived in the Health and Subsistence Dimensions

By breaking down M_0, Table 10.6 provides a comparison among different dimensions. The health dimension had the highest rate of contribution to M_0, which meant that health caused children the most serious deprivation. This was followed by the dimensions of subsistence and participation.

On an indicator level, children in multidimensional poverty were most deprived in financial vulnerability, sanitation facilities, and cooking fuel indicators. Results showed that children were more vulnerable to multidimensional poverty when their households were in debt. In fact, 81.7% of children in multidimensional poverty came from families with debts. In addition, 39.9% of their families lacked living assets (TV, telephone, etc.), which was three times more than other children. Households without an effective financial buffer generally had a weak capacity to respond to unexpected financial difficulties, and were at a greater risk of falling into chronic poverty. While facing capital constraint and shocks, families with debt were usually forced to reduce their expenditure on their children (Guarcello et al., 2002). These factors all left children at serious risk of falling into multidimensional poverty.

The contribution of sanitation facilities was also high as 28.89% of children came from families without any sanitation facilities, and 62.49% of these used latrine pits. Lack of access to satisfactory sanitation facilities may lead to the spread of diarrhoea and other diseases which children are vulnerable to.

The relative contribution of cooking fuel was 8.5%. Although the government encouraged rural households to update their energy resources, access to clean and

Table 10.6 Relative contribution of dimensions and indicators to the multidimensional poverty index ($k = 30\%$)

Dimension	Indicator	Contribution of indicator to multidimensional poverty index (%)	Contribution of dimension (%)
Subsistence	Identification	0.42	23.30
	Food and nutrition	6.82	–
	Accompanying and caring	1.47	–
	Income poverty	5.90	–
	Financial vulnerability	8.69	–
Health	Health status	0.63	27.22
	Health behavior	2.05	–
	Drinking water	5.69	–
	Sanitation facilities	8.63	–
	Cooking fuel	8.50	–
	Accessibility of health services	1.71	–
Protection	Domestic violence	6.41	12.20
	Campus violence	4.89	–
	Social violence	0.91	–
Development	School enrolment	3.89	15.73
	Satisfaction of needs in learning	1.51	–
	Possession of learning tools	8.05	–
	Distance from school	2.27	–
Participation	Decision making on daily life	6.83	21.55
	Decision making on learning	7.67	–
	Decision making on hobbies	7.05	–

safe energy (natural gas, liquefied petroleum gas, and biogas) was still limited. Of the households surveyed, 70.69% used firewood to cook and 16.14% used coal. With the use of solid fuel for cooking, indoor air pollution was a major health risk factor. According to The World Bank (2011), children and women are especially vulnerable to this exposure.

10.4.2 Children with Disabilities Suffered More Severe Multidimensional Poverty, Particularly in Participation and Health

UNICEF pointed out that, in China, children with disabilities remained one of the most marginalized groups whose rights were the least protected. Among 5 million children with disability, 80% dwell in rural areas.[4] In our study, out of 1739 children, 100 suffered from some kind of disability. In poverty-stricken families, 1.83% had children with disabilities, compared with 1% of other families.

Of the children with disabilities, 26% were considered to be in multidimensional poverty. They were on average deprived in 38.73% dimensions, and their multidimensional poverty index was 0.1007 (Table 10.7). The differences in M_0 and H were both significant, which highlighted that more care and attention should be given to disabled children.

Children with disabilities were most deprived in the dimensions of health and participation, with a comparative contribution to M_0 of 26.8% and 25.2%, respectively. Apart from the indicator health status, which reflected the challenges generally faced by disabled children, deprivation in the participation dimension showed that disabled children may have had fewer opportunities to express their ideas, and were less likely to be encouraged to take their own initiative. Furthermore, children with a disability were more deprived of indicators such as school enrolment and possession of learning tools. This indicated that they may not have been treated in the same way in terms of education as children without a disability and that their opportunity for future development was therefore somehow neglected.

Although, there were good indications of these children not being ignored by the community, as the identification indicator was satisfactory, a significant effort was needed to improve their education and opportunity to express their voices. Identification provided these children with the possibility to further develop and become independent while education and participation provided them the actual capacity to do so (Table 10.8).

Table 10.7 H, A, and M_0 of children with disabilities versus children without disabilities (k = 30%)

H***		A (%)	M_0***	M_0 (95% CI)	
Children without disabilities	14.14%	37.60	0.0532	0.0502	0.0561
Children with disabilities	26.00%	38.73	0.1007	0.0667	0.1347

*** Significant difference at 1% by adjusted Wald test

[4] http://www.unicefchina.org/campaign/DC1011C/.

Table 10.8 Absolute contribution of indicators to M_0 among different groups ($k = 30\%$)

	Children without disabilities	Children with disabilities	Children not affected by HIV/AIDS	Children affected by HIV/AIDS	Han children	Children of ethnic minorities
Identification	0.0002	0***	0.0002	0.0013**	0	0.0004***
Food and nutrition	0.0036	0.0048	0.0035	0.0105***	0.0002	0.0059***
Accompanying and caring	0.0008	0.0008	0.0007	0.0038***	0.0005	0.001***
Income poverty	0.0031	0.008***	0.003	0.0098***	0.0009	0.0047***
Financial vulnerability	0.0046	0.0076*	0.0045	0.0118***	0.0021	0.0064***
Health status	0.0003	0.0047*	0.0003	0.0018***	0.0002	0.0004***
Health behavior	0.0011	0.0017	0.001	0.0034***	0.0003	0.0017***
Drinking water	0.0031	0.0033	0.0029	0.0097***	0.0001	0.005***
Sanitation facilities	0.0046	0.008	0.0044	0.0122***	0.0021	0.0063***
Cooking fuel	0.0045	0.008	0.0043	0.0121***	0.0018	0.0064***
Accessibility of health services	0.0009	0.0013	0.0009	0.0022***	0.0001	0.0015***
Domestic violence	0.0034	0.004	0.0034	0.0054	0.0021	0.0043***
Campus violence	0.0026	0.0033	0.0025	0.0068***	0.0027	0.0026
Social violence	0.0005	0.0007	0.0004	0.0018*	0.0006	0.0004*
School enrolment	0.002	0.0055***	0.0019	0.0074***	0.0002	0.0033***
Satisfaction of needs in learning	0.0008	0.001	0.0008	0.0018	0.0004	0.0011***
Possession of learning tools	0.0043	0.0095***	0.004	0.0138***	0.0009	0.0066***
Distance from school	0.0012	0.0025	0.0012	0.0027***	0.0006	0.0016***
Decision making	0.0036	0.0087***	0.0035	0.008***	0.0027	0.0043***
on daily life						

(continued)

Table 10.8 (continued)

	Children without disabilities	Children with disabilities	Children not affected by HIV/AIDS	Children affected by HIV/AIDS	Han children	Children of ethnic minorities
Decision making on learning	0.004	0.01***	0.004	0.0086***	0.0027	0.005***
Decision making on hobby	0.0037	0.0073*	0.0037	0.008***	0.0026	0.0045***
Total	0.0532	0.1007	0.0511	0.1429	0.0237	0.0733

***, **, *Indicate significant difference at 1%, 5%, and 10%, respectively, by adjusted Wald test

10.4.3 Children Affected by HIV/AIDS were the Most Severely Deprived Group

Of the children surveyed, 224 were from families affected by HIV/AIDS: that is, families in which one or more members were living with or had died of HIV/AIDS. Of these children, 36.61% lived in multidimensional poverty and were deprived in 39.03% of the dimensions. Their M_0 was 0.1429, which was even higher than children with disabilities.

HIV/AIDS is not only a major public health issue, but also a social issue. In the survey, 96% of the children affected by HIV/AIDS were from Sichuan and Henan provinces, and predominantly from the Butuo and Zhaojue counties of the Sichuan province, and the Shangcai county of the Henan province. Butuo and Zhaojue are situated in Liangshan Yi autonomous prefecture, which is one of the most seriously HIV/ AIDS-affected areas in China,[5] the result of HIV/AIDS transmission via drug use. Shangcai is also an area seriously affected by HIV/AIDS, which has been spread through contaminated blood transfusions. Many of these HIV/AIDS-affected families had limited employment opportunities, and suffered from social discrimination, and were therefore often subject to serious poverty.

These children who were affected by HIV/AIDS faced disproportionally higher rates of multidimensional poverty (Fig. 10.3), with significant differences in almost all the indicators (Table 10.9). Deprivation in "food and nutrition" and "accompanying and caring" reflected the difficulties these children faced at home; deprivation at school and social violence showed the discrimination that they suffered from society. Consequently, this was one of the most deprived groups.

[5] http://www.gov.cn/gzdt/2011-11/17/content_1996531.htm.

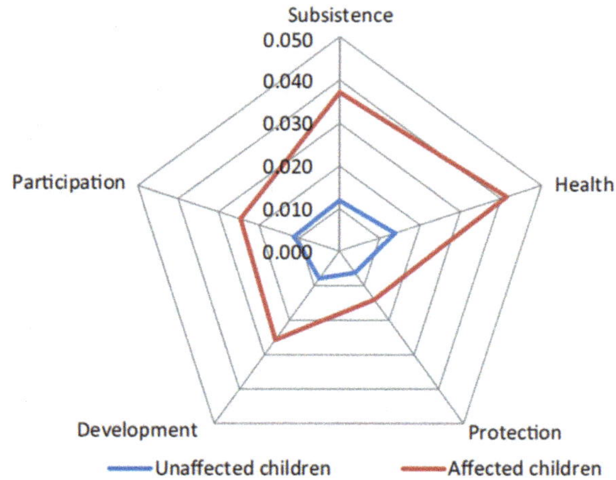

Fig. 10.3 Dimensional breakdown of M_0: children affected by HIV/AIDS versus children not affected by HIV/AIDS

Table 10.9 H, A, and M_0 of children affected by HIV/AIDS versus children not affected by HIV/AIDS ($k = 30\%$)

H*** (%)		A (%)	M_0***	M_0 (95% CI)	
Unaffected children	13.63	37.52	0.0511	0.0482	0.0541
Affected children	36.61	39.03	0.1429	0.1174	0.1683

*** Indicates significant difference at 1% by adjusted Wald test

10.4.4 Children of Ethnic Minorities Faced Serious Multidimensional Poverty

This survey included children from Han, Hui, Uyghur, Yi, and other ethnic groups (Table 10.10). Han represents the largest ethnic group, accounting for over 90% of the total population in 2005. There were significant differences in H, A, and M_0 between children of ethnic minorities and Han (Table 10.10 and Fig. 10.4). Of the ethnic minority children, 19.2% were in multidimensional poverty; on average they were deprived in 38.20% of the dimensions, and M_0 was 0.0733. Among the children of ethnic minorities surveyed, Uyghur children had the lowest M_0, while Yi children had the highest M_0.

Table 10.10 H, A, and M_0 of children of different ethnic groups ($k = 30\%$)

H*** (%)		A*** (%)	M_0*** (%)	M_0 (95% CI)	
Han children	6.75	35.10	0.0237	0.0196	0.0256
Children of ethnic minorities	19.20	38.20	0.0733	0.0546	0.0624

*** Indicates significant difference at 1% by adjusted Wald test

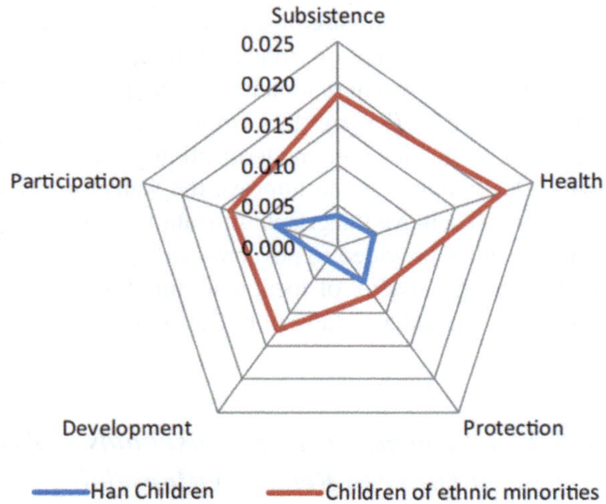

Fig. 10.4 Dimensional breakdown of M_0: Han children versus children of ethnic minorities

Poverty was more serious among children of ethnic minorities than Han children on all dimensions, particularly the health dimension. There were significant differences between the two groups in the majority of indicators (Table 10.10).

10.5 Conclusion and Policy Recommendations

The above analysis attempts to provide a pilot study on child multidimensional poverty in China by introducing the AF method based on survey data. The purpose of this research is not only to add to the existing literature on child poverty in China, but also to provide guidance for future action plans. By decomposition, deprivation can be explored explicitly on the dimensional and indicator levels. This assists in prioritizing the objectives and guiding public resources. The subgroup comparison shows which groups are the most vulnerable ones and therefore need urgent intervention. The combination of two decompositions can lead to a more accurate and effective plan design.

10.5.1 Proactively Promote Improvement of Sanitation Facilities and Use of Clean Energy in Rural Areas

Surveyed children are severely deprived in the health dimension, particularly in the sanitation facilities and cooking fuel indicators. Compared with education and clinics, which have been prioritized in child-related policies, sanitation facilities and cooking fuel have somehow been neglected. International experience shows that improved sanitation facilities and use of safe energy sources can assist in breaking the vicious cycle of unclean sanitation, spread of disease, and poverty.

Complying with international practice, the updated Chinese poverty alleviation policy *Outline of Poverty Alleviation and Development in Rural Areas in China (2011–2020)* includes the modernization of basic household facilities as one of its goals. One example is "to improve the water supply, kitchen, sanitation facilities, pig pens and achieve integrated utilization of crop residues". In addition to government subsidies provided to poverty-stricken households, efforts should be made to strengthen the capacity of local communities, promote technology innovation and dissemination, and also raise public awareness.

10.5.2 Encourage Rural Households to Accumulate Assets in Order to Reduce Vulnerability

Most of the households with children in multidimensional poverty suffer from debt and a shortage of assets. With the lack of coping strategies, the household, and children in particular, is fragile when faced with unexpected financial difficulties. In this sense, the endeavor to reduce child multidimensional poverty is in line with the effort to reduce financial vulnerability. The current policies for subsidizing asset accumulation, such as "subsidy for the procurement of large agricultural implements" and "subsidy for household living assets in rural areas", have mainly benefited rich rural households. Policies to improve the financial capacity of poor households, and encourage their accumulation of assets are therefore called for. The scope of the current community level "poverty alleviation mutual fund" can also be expanded to help poverty-stricken households to accumulate assets.

10.5.3 Strengthen Relief and Support for Disabled Children, Children Affected by HIV/AIDS, Children of Ethnic Minorities, and Other Vulnerable Groups

No vulnerable child should ever be neglected in any aspects. Based on this study, disabled children in particular should have full access to treatment and rehabilitation services. The number of specialized schools for children with disabilities needs to be increased in rural areas, so that every child's right to education can be guaranteed. This allows the disabled child to be both physically and mentally prepared to participate in society in the future. For HIV/AIDS-affected children, a joint effort from government departments as well as society is needed. Joint efforts from both government and civil society are called for. In addition to in-kind support, these children need social identification and care. Ethnic minority children are also highly deprived and, in line with the current poverty alleviation strategies, ethnic minorities have been identified as a general target group. It is believed that ethnic minority children will also benefit from this as community infrastructure and household facilities will be updated overall. However, their deprivation in other areas such as development and participation also need attention.

Furthermore, preventative measures should be emphasized to reduce the risk of disabilities among children due to, for example, traffic accidents, and natural disasters, and to prevent children from becoming infected with HIV/AIDS.

10.5.4 Further Protect and Promote the Rights of Children to Protection, Development and Participation

Each and every child should have the right to be protected, and to fully develop and express their voice. Social awareness and consensus should be raised to promote the understanding of children's rights to protection, development, and participation. A child welfare mechanism has been suggested to be created at a rural community level in order to boost child protection and participation (Shang & Wang, 2012). In doing so, child welfare workers need to be trained, for better coordination, guidance, and service delivery.

References

Alkire, S. (2007). *Choosing dimensions: The capability approach and multidimensional poverty*. Chronic Poverty Research Centre Working Paper 88.

Alkire, S., & Foster, J. E. (2007). *Counting and multidimensional poverty measurement*. OPHI Working Paper 7.

Alkire, S., & Foster, J. E. (2009). *Counting and multidimensional poverty measurement*. OPHI Working Paper 32.

Alkire, S., & Roche, J. (2011). *Beyond headcount: Measures that reflect the breadth and components of child poverty*. OPHI Working Paper 45.

Bradshaw, J., Hoelscher, P., & Richardson, D. (2007). An index of child well-being in the European Union. *Social Indicators Research, 80*, 133–177.

Chen, Y. (2009). Determinant analysis on the juveniles poverty in China. *Chinese Journal of Population Science, 4*, 71–80.

Fernandes, L., Mendes, A., & Taixeira, A. (2010). *A review essay on child well-being measurement: Uncovering the paths for future research*. Universidade Cato´lica Portuguesa Economics Working Papers 2.

Gordon, D., & Nandy, S. (2012). Measurement and methodologies measuring child poverty and deprivation. In A. Minujin & S. Nandy (Eds.), *Global child poverty and well-being measurement, concepts, policy and action* (pp. 57–101). The Policy Press.

Gordon, D., Nandy, S., Pantazis, C., Pemberton, S., & Townsend, P. (2003). *Child poverty in the developing world*. Policy Press.

Guarcello, L., Mealli, F., & Rosati, F. (2002). Household Vulnerability and child labor: The effect of shocks, credit rationing and insurance. Understanding Children's Work Project Working Paper Series.

Land, K., Lamb, V., & Mustillo, S. (2001). Child and youth well-being in the United States, 1975–1998: Some findings from a new index. *Social Indicators Research, 56*, 241–320.

Land, K., Lamb, V., Meadows, S., & Taylor, A. (2007). Measuring trends in child well-being: An evidence-based approach. *Social Indicators Research, 80*, 105–132.

Minujin, A., & Delamonica, E. (2005). *Incidence, depth and severity of children in poverty*. UNICEF Division of Policy and Planning, Working paper.

Minujin, A., Delamonica, E., Davidziuk, A., & Gonzalez, E. D. (2006). The definition of child poverty: A discussion of concepts and measurements. *Environment and Urbanization, 18*, 481–500.

Qin, R., & Qiao, D. (2012). Literature review on child poverty research. *Journal of China Youth College for Political Sciences, 4*, 41–46.

Robeyns, I. (2003). Sen's capability approach and gender inequality: Selecting relevant capabilities. *Feminist Economics, 9*(2/3), 61–92.

Roelen, K., & Gassman, F. (2008). *Measuring child poverty and well-being: A literature review*. Maastricht, The Netherlands: Maastricht Graduate School of Governance Working Paper, Series No. WP001.

Saito, M. (2003). Amartya Sen's capability approach to education: A critical exploration. *Journal of Philosophy of Education, 37*, 17–33.

Shang, X., & Wang, X. (2012). *Update on Welfare for Chinese Children (2012)*. Social Sciences Academic Press.

Song, Y., & Zhang, K. (2014). Research view on definition and measurement of child poverty. *Beijing Youth Research, 2*, 71–78.

The World Bank. (2011). *One goal, two paths: Achieving universal access to modern energy in East Asia and Pacific*. The World Bank.

UNICEF (2007). *Child poverty in perspective: An overview of child well-being in rich countries*. Innocent Report Card 7. Wang, X. (2012). *The measurement of poverty—Theories and methods*. Beijing: Social Sciences Academic Press.

Wang, X., & Alkire, S. (2009). Chinese multidimensional poverty measurement: Estimation and policy implications. *China Rural Economy, 12*, 4–23.

Wang, X., Wang, L., & Wang, Y. (2012). *The quality of growth and poverty reduction in China*. Social Sciences Academic Press.

Zhang, S., & Tang, J. (2009). Poor children in China: Conception and scale. *Journal of Hohai University (philosophy and Social Sciences), 11*(4), 42–46.

Chapter 11
Pro-Poor Measurement of China's Economic Growth

11.1 Introduction

As a country moves from a low-income to a middle-income economy, very often, the income gap widens, making it difficult for the poor to benefit from economic growth; this leads to a rise in relative poverty and social conflicts. The consumption flexibility of the poor is greater than that of the rich, and if the poor do not experience income growth, the domestic demand of the country as a whole will not rise, resulting in a lack of internal impetus for sustained economic growth and the country falling into a "middle-income trap."

Since many middle-income countries, such as those in Latin America, have fallen into this trap and have not joined the ranks of high-income countries, the issue of whether growth is pro-poor has received increasing attention. Since China entered the 21st century, the gap in income distribution has continued to widen, the pressure on employment continues to increase, and economic growth is moving in a direction that is not pro-poor. For this reason, the *11th Five-Year Plan (2006–2010) for China's National Economic and Social Development* clearly addresses pro-poor policies for economic growth and income distribution, explicitly stating that "efforts will be made to raise the income level of low-income earners, gradually increase the proportion of middle-income earners, effectively regulate excessive income, and standardize the order of personal income distribution, thus narrowing the gap in income distribution between regions and among some members of society. Emphasis will be placed on social equity, particularly fairness in employment opportunities and the distribution process."

The "*Outline for Development-oriented Poverty Reduction for China's Rural Areas (2011–2020)*" unequivocally states that "by the year 2020, rural poor populations will have no concerns about food and clothing and will be guaranteed compulsory education, basic medical services, and housing. The per capita disposable income of farmers in impoverished areas will grow at a rate higher than the national average, and the indicators in major areas of basic public services will be close to the

© Social Sciences Academic Press 2022

X. Wang, *Multidimensional Poverty Measurement*,
International Research on Poverty Reduction,
https://doi.org/10.1007/978-981-19-1189-7_11

national average, reversing the trend of widening development gaps." That "the per capita disposable income of farmers in impoverished areas will grow at a rate higher than the national average" essentially suggests that growth should be pro-poor.

Judging whether growth is pro-poor requires first defining pro-poor growth, followed by determining a measurement method based on such definition, and finally, measuring the data to provide well-defined policy implications. The second section of this chapter discusses the existing definitions and measurement methods of pro-poor growth, while the third takes a different approach to the measurement of growth in China, clarifying whether it is pro-poor.

11.2 Definition of Pro-Poor Growth and Measurement Methods

According to the literature review, there are three clear definitions and measurement methods used for pro-poor growth: they are the pro-poor growth indices of Kakwani and Pernia (2000), Ravallion and Chen (2003), and Kakwani, Khandker, and Son, respectively.

11.2.1 Kakwani and Pernia's Pro-Poor Growth Index (PPGI)

Kakwani and Pernia (2000) proposed the pro-poor growth index (PPGI) in *What is pro-poor growth?* to measure the extent to which growth is pro-poor.[1] They argued that the theory of pro-poor growth stemmed from the "trickle-down effect" that dominated development theory in the 1950s and 1960s. The trickle-down effect indicates that economic growth benefits the rich first and the poor only when the rich begin to consume the benefits they derive from economic growth. Thus, the poor only benefit indirectly through the vertical flow of wealth from the rich to the poor and, by extension, will always benefit less from growth. In fact, when inequality in income distribution increases, economic growth can lead to an increase in poverty.

Sen (1993) discusses well-being in terms of functionings and capability. Functionings are defined as the condition wherein an individual has access to adequate nutrition, basic education, and housing, while a person's capabilities reflect various combinations of functionings to which the person has access. In layman's terms, a person's combination of functionings, such as education, health, and housing, constitutes that person's capabilities. Well-being, however, is the state realized by a person's capabilities composed of various functionings. According to Sen, basic capabilities aim to isolate the ability that satisfies certain particularly important functionings to a sufficient level. The identification of a minimum acceptable level of such basic capabilities (below which one can be regarded as shamefully deprived)

[1] Kakwani and Pernia (2000).

provides a possible approach to poverty analysis.[2] Therefore, identifying a minimum combination of basic capabilities is a suitable approach to poverty analysis and its measurement. Based on Sen's theory, pro-poor growth can be defined as growth in which the poor benefit markedly from their active participation in economic activities. In this way, there is a clear distinction between pro-poor growth theory and the "trickle-down effect."

The reason the poor tend to be less well off than the wealthy is a lack of resources to meet their minimum subsistence needs. With an inherent advantage (e.g., human capital and physical capital), the market-driven growth process is more beneficial to the rich. In many countries, governments have, intentionally or unintentionally, adopted policies that benefit the rich. As a result, the well-being gap between the rich and the poor has persisted, if not widened, over time. To promote the overall well-being of society, governments need to take measures to narrow the gap (Kakwani & Pernia, 2000). Pro-poor growth requires governments to develop policies that are specifically pro-poor, so that they benefit more than the rich from growth, rapidly bridging the gap. Pro-poor growth strategies include the elimination of prejudice against the poor in systems and policies, as well as the adoption of policies that directly benefit them.

To understand the impact of growth on poverty, it is imperative to measure the effects of income changes as well as distributional changes on poverty. In other words, poverty incidence needs to be decomposed in two ways: (1) the effect of growth on poverty incidence given a constant income distribution and (2) the effect of income distribution on poverty given a constant income.

Assuming that O is the corresponding change in poverty when the growth rate is 1%, O can be decomposed into O_g and O_I, that is,

$$O = O_g + O_I$$

where O_g is the effect of growth on poverty reduction and O_I is the effect of inequality. O_g is the percentage change in poverty that would result from growth if the income distribution is held constant and O_I is the percentage change in poverty when inequality changes in the absence of growth.

Assuming that θ represents poverty measurement based on the income poverty line,

$$\theta = \theta(z, \mu, L(p))$$

where z is the poverty line, μ is the mean social income, and *L(p)* is the Lorenz curve that represents the income share of *p percent* of the population and implies the degree of inequality. The change in poverty between the base period (1) and the reporting period (2) can be defined as follows:

[2] Sen (1993).

$$P_{12} = \text{Ln}[\theta(z, \mu_2, L_2(p))] - \text{Ln}[\theta(z, \mu_1, L_1(p))]$$

where μ_1 and μ_2 are the mean income for the base and reporting periods and $L_1(p)$ and $L_2(p)$ are the Lorenz curves for the two periods, respectively. Notably, μ_1 and μ_2 are data after price index adjustment, whereas the poverty line z is fixed every year.

The effect of net growth on poverty reduction is the corresponding change in poverty brought about by changes in mean income, provided that the relative income distribution measured by the Lorenz curve remains constant. Similarly, the net inequality effect is the change in poverty brought about by a change in the curve, provided the mean income measured at constant prices remains constant.

Let G_{12} represent the growth effect in the base and reporting periods and I_{12} represent the inequality effect in the two periods. The change in poverty can then be expressed as

$$P_{12} = f(G_{12}, I_{12})$$

Assuming that there is a positive change in growth rate g_{12} between these two periods, the poverty flexibility can be defined as

$$\eta = \frac{P_{12}}{g_{12}}$$

This equation shows the change in poverty as the growth rate increases by 1%. Similarly, it can be defined as

$$\eta_g = \frac{G_{12}}{g_{12}}$$

$$\eta_I = \frac{I_{12}}{g_{12}}$$

where η_g is the change in poverty—the net growth effect of poverty—when relative inequality is held constant and the growth rate increases by 1% and η_I is the change in poverty—the net distributional effect of poverty—when the real mean income is held constant and inequality changes. Thus,

$$\eta = \eta_g + n_I$$

The above equation shows that when the growth rate increases by 1%, the change in poverty consists of the sum of two factors: η_g (the income effect of growth on poverty) and η_I (the effect of inequality on poverty).

The income effect on poverty η_g is always negative, which indicates that income growth always reduces poverty when relative inequality is constant. The inequality effect η_I can be either positive or negative. A negative η_I implies that growth has led to a pro-poor income distribution and thus a reduction in poverty, which can be regarded as pro-poor; a positive η_I implies that the change in income distribution is pro-rich. Thus, we can define the PPGI as

$$\varphi = \frac{\eta_I}{\eta_g}$$

$\eta_I < 0$, $\varphi > 1$ implies that growth is strictly pro-poor. Conversely, $0 < \varphi < 1$ implies that $\eta_I > 0$; however, poverty is still reduced by growth, which may be commonly referred to as the "trickle-down effect." When $\varphi < 0$, growth is detrimental to the poor, leading to an increase in poverty.

The drawback of this approach is that while it considers whether the poor benefit from changes in income distribution, it does not consider the real growth rate or the monotonicity axiom.

11.2.2 Ravallion and Chen's Pro-Poor Growth Index

Ravallion and Chen (2003), in *Measuring pro-poor growth,* define a growth rate curve and a PPGI based on the Watts poverty index, which ranks per capita income by quartiles and calculates the mean growth rate of the poorest one-fifth of the population.[3]

11.2.2.1 Growth Incidence Curve (GIC)

One way to examine whether growth has been pro-poor is to directly observe the poor's growth rate. It is common practice to calculate the growth rate of different quintiles of the population in different periods according to income distribution in ascending order, that is, the Pen cohort. Thus, to assess whether growth is pro-poor, it is natural to calculate the growth rate of the lowest-income one-fifth (the poor) in the Pen cohort.

Assuming that the proportion of the population with income in period t is less than y, let $F_t\ (y)$ denote the cumulative distribution function of income. The inverse of the cumulative distribution function of income for the p-th quantile is

$$y_t(P) = F_t^{-1}(P) = L_t^{'}(p)\mu_1(p)\mu_1(Y_t^{'}(p)) > 0) \tag{11.1}$$

where $L_t\ (p)$ is a Lorenz curve with slope $L'_t\ (p)$ and mean μ_t. Change p from 0 to 1 to produce a Pen cohort, that is, a fractional function.

---

[3] Ravallion and Chen (2003).

Comparing periods $t-1$ and t, the income growth rate of the p-th quantile is $g_t(p) = [y_t(p)/y_{t-1}(p)] - 1$. By varying p from 0 to 1, $g_t(p)$ depicts the "growth incidence curve (GIC)" as

$$g_t(p) = \frac{L_t^{'}(p)}{L_{t-1}^{'}(p)}(\gamma_t + 1) - 1 \tag{11.2}$$

where $\gamma_t = (\mu_t/\mu_{t-1}) - 1$ is the growth rate at μ_t. The above equation shows that if the Lorenz curve does not change, then $g_t(p) = \gamma_t$ for any p, and $g_t(p) > \gamma_t$ if and only if $y_t(p)/\mu_t$ increases with time. For all p, if $g_t(p)$ is a decreasing (increasing) function, inequality decreases (increases) and the Pigou-Dalton principle is satisfied for the measurement of inequality.

11.2.2.2 Pro-Poor Growth Measurement

It is assumed that the pro-poor growth rate measurement satisfies the following conditions.

Axiom 1: The measurement should be consistent with the change in direction of poverty, that is, a positive (negative) pro-poor growth rate implies a decrease (increase) in poverty.

Axiom 2: Poverty measurement implies that the measurement of pro-poor growth should satisfy the standard axiom of poverty measurement.

Sen (1976) proposed three axioms of poverty measurement: (1) Focus Axiom: Changes in the income of people who are not poor do not affect poverty measurement, that is, poverty measurement focuses only on the poor. (2) Monotonicity Axiom: Any decline in the poor's income will increase poverty. (3) Transfer Axiom: Any decline in inequality among the poor will reduce poverty. Subsequently, Sen supplemented the axioms with Additive Decomposability, which states that the sum of poverty can be expressed as a poverty measure weighted by population weights averaged across subgroups, that is, poverty can be decomposed by group. Foster and Shorrocks (1991) called this subgroup coherence.

The most popular measure of poverty incidence is the poverty headcount index, that is, $H_t = F_t(z)$, where z is the poverty line. However, this measurement method does not satisfy the monotonicity or transfer axioms. Atkinson (1987) conducted a literature review and found many studies that satisfied the focus, monotonicity, transfer, and decomposability axioms of poverty measurement. The index that satisfies the four axioms is the Watts poverty index. According to the quantile function, this index can be formulated as

$$W_t = \int_0^{H_t} \log[z/y_t(p)]dp \tag{11.3}$$

Ravallion and Chen (2003) define the pro-poor growth rate as the change in the Watts poverty index divided by the index of the poor. Thus, the pro-poor growth rate can be expressed as

$$Index = \frac{W_1(z) - W_2(z)}{F_1(z)} \tag{11.4}$$

where $W_D(z)$ is the Watts poverty index in $D \in [1, 2]$, $F_1(z)$ is the poverty headcount index of the first distribution (base period), and z is the poverty line.

While the Watts poverty index in the numerator part satisfies the monotonicity axiom, in the denominator part, poverty incidence in the reporting period is not considered, and only poverty incidence in the base period is used, thus circumventing the monotonicity axiom.

11.2.3 Kakwani, Khandker, and Son's Poverty Equivalent Growth Rate (PEGR)

Pro-poor growth focuses on the relationship among growth, poverty, and inequality. Kakwani, Khandker, and Son measure pro-poor growth using the Poverty Equivalent Growth Rate (PEGR), an index that accounts for not only the amount of growth but also how much the poor benefit from it. The poverty reduction rate is a monotonically increasing function of the PEGR, that is, a larger PEGR indicates a larger poverty reduction rate. Thus, maximizing the PEGR implies maximum poverty reduction.

Poverty depends on two factors: one is the number of economic growth rates, that is, a higher economic growth rate results in greater poverty reduction; the other is the change in inequality, that is, an increase in inequality leads to an increase in poverty. To measure these two effects, the definition is

$$\frac{d\theta}{\theta} = \frac{1}{\theta} \int_0^z \frac{\partial P}{\partial x} d(x) f(x) dx \tag{11.5}$$

where, assuming $P(z, z) = 0$, if an individual's income is equal to the poverty line, the individual is not poor.

Assuming that $x(p)$ is the income level of the population at the p-th quantile, Eq. (11.5) can be expressed as

$$d\text{Ln}(\theta) = \frac{1}{\theta} \int_0^H \frac{\partial P}{\partial x} x(p) g(p) dp \tag{11.6}$$

where $g(p) = d\text{Ln}\ (x(p))$ is the income growth rate of the population at the p-th quantile.

If $L(p)$ is the Lorenz function, it is defined as the share of total income for the bottom p percent of the population when individuals are ranked in the ascending order of income. This can be expressed as

$$x(p) = \mu L'(\text{p}) \tag{11.7}$$

where μ is the mean social income and $L'(p)$ is the first-order derivative of the Lorenz function. Taking the logarithm of Eq. (11.7) and differentiating its yield,

$$d\text{Ln}(xp) = d\text{Ln}(\mu) + d\text{Ln}(L'(\text{p}))$$

Then,

$$g(p) = \gamma + d\text{Ln}(L^{'}(p)) \tag{11.8}$$

where $\gamma = d\text{Ln}\ (\mu)$ is the growth rate of the mean income. Inserting Eq. (11.8) into Eq. (11.6) yields

$$d\text{Ln}(\theta) = \gamma\eta + \frac{1}{\theta}\int \frac{\partial P}{\partial x} x(p) d\text{Ln}\Big(L^{'}(p)\Big) dp \tag{11.9}$$

Where

$$\eta = \frac{1}{\theta}\int_{0}^{H} \frac{\partial P}{\partial x} x(p) dp \tag{11.10}$$

η is the growth flexibility of poverty, which is the percentage change in poverty when inequality is held constant and when the mean social income increases by 1% point.

Equation (11.9) divided by γ gives

$$\delta = \eta + \xi \tag{11.11}$$

where $\delta = d\text{Ln}(\theta)/\gamma$ is the total poverty flexibility and

$$\zeta = \frac{1}{\theta y}\int_{0}^{H} \frac{\partial P}{\partial x} x(p) d\text{Ln}(L'(p)) dp \tag{11.12}$$

ζ is used to measure the inequitable effect of poverty, that is, to show how poverty changes in response to an inequitable change in the growth process.

A growth rate $\gamma*$ indicates that if there is no unfair change in the growth process (that is, everyone in society benefits from the growth in the same proportion), poverty decreases at the same level. The real poverty reduction rate is $\delta\gamma$, where δ is the total flexibility of poverty. If growth is distribution-neutral (that is, inequality does not change), a growth rate $\gamma*$ will lead to the same proportional reduction in poverty, that is, $\eta\gamma*$, and should be equal to $\delta\gamma$. Thus, the PEGR represented by $\gamma*$ can be expressed as

$$y^* = (\delta/\eta)\gamma = \varphi\gamma \tag{11.13}$$

where $\varphi = \delta/\eta$ is the pro-poor index given by Kakwani and Pernia (2000). The equation shows that growth is pro-poor (anti-poor) if $\gamma*$ is greater than (less than) γ. If $\gamma*$ is between 0 and γ, growth is accompanied by an increase in inequality but poverty remains reduced, that is, the "trickle-down effect" of poverty.

According to Eqs. (11.6) and (11.10), Eq. (11.13) can be expressed as

$$y^* = \frac{\int_0^H \frac{\partial P}{\partial x} x(p)g(p)dp}{\int_0^H \frac{\partial P}{\partial x} x(p)dp} \tag{11.14}$$

The PEGR is shown to be a weighted average of the income growth rate at each quantile, with the weights depending on the poverty measurement methods used. Thus, $\gamma*$ can be calculated based on any poverty measurement method. For the classical poverty measurement method of FGT, $\gamma*$ can be expressed as

$$\gamma_\alpha^* = \frac{\int_0^H \left(\frac{z-x(p)}{z}\right)^{\alpha-1} x(p)g(p)dp}{\int_0^H \left(\frac{z-x(p)}{z}\right)^{\alpha-1} x(p)dp} \tag{11.15}$$

where $\alpha \geq 1$. When $\alpha = 1$, the PEGR of the poverty gap index is

$$\gamma_1^* = \frac{\int_0^H x(p)g(p)dp}{\int_0^H x(p)dp}$$

Subtracting $P(z, x) = Ln(z) - Ln(x)$ from Eq. (11.14) yields a PEGR based on the Watts poverty index:

$$\gamma_W^* = \frac{1}{H}\int_0^H g(p)dp$$

11.3 Pro-Poor Growth in China

This chapter uses data from the *China Health and Nutrition Survey (CHNS)* between 1989 and 2009 for the measurement of pro-poor economic growth. The dataset included data for eight years: 1989, 1991, 1993, 1997, 2000, 2004, 2006, and 2009. Nine provinces and autonomous regions were surveyed: Liaoning, Heilongjiang, Jiangsu, Shandong, Henan, Hubei, Hunan, Guangxi, and Guizhou.

11.3.1 Pro-Poor Growth Measurement Results

11.3.1.1 Kakwani and Pernia's PPGI Measurement Results

According to the previous definition, $\eta_I < 0$, $\varphi > 1$ implies that growth is strictly pro-poor. However, $0 < \varphi < 1$ implies that $\eta_I > 0$ and poverty remains reduced, that is, the "trickle-down effect" of poverty. When $\varphi < 0$, growth is detrimental to the poor, leading to an increase in poverty.

Figure 11.1 presents Kakwani and Pernia's PPGI measurement results. Evidently, in the six different growth periods between 1989 and 2006, the PPGI was between 0 and 1. That is, economic growth still led to poverty reduction, but it was not strictly

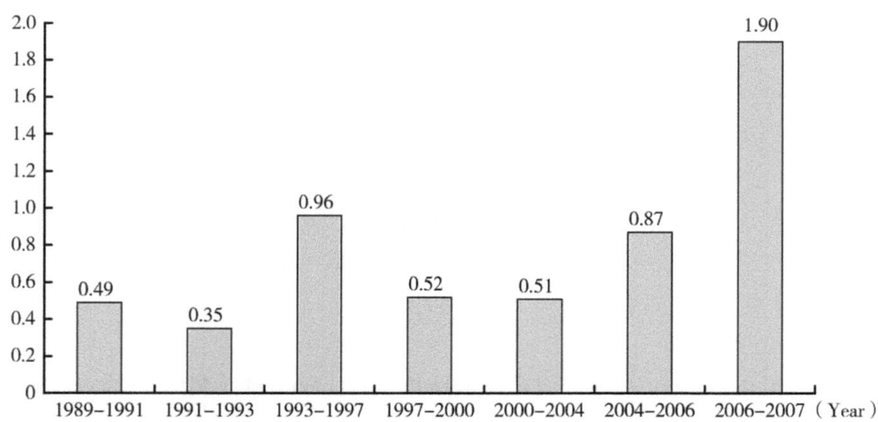

Fig. 11.1 Kakwani and Pernia's PPGI measurement results

pro-poor, as poverty reduction was mainly attributed to the aforementioned "trickle-down effect." The result for 2006–2009 was 1.90, greater than 1, suggesting that economic growth during this period was strictly pro-poor. Furthermore, the relative poverty measurement in Chapter Three shows that the incidence of both urban and rural relative poverty in China increased from 1989 to 2006 but decreased from 2006 to 2009.

11.3.1.2 Ravallion and Chen's PPGI Measurement Results

Ravallion and Chen (2003) define pro-poor growth as the change in the Watts poverty index divided by the poverty headcount index from the base period.

Figure 11.2 shows good pro-poor performance in the three periods of 1993–1997, 2004–2006, and 2006–2009, especially in 2006–2009, whereas the other periods witnessed no pro-poor growth.

11.3.1.3 Kakwani, Khandker, and Son's PEGR Measurement Results

Figure 11.3 presents the (PEGR) measurement results as defined by Kakwani, Khandker, and Son. This result accorded with that measured by Kakwani and Pernia's PPGI, with the exception that the PEGR considered growth, inequality, and poverty. The results indicated that growth in 2006–2009 was pro-poor.

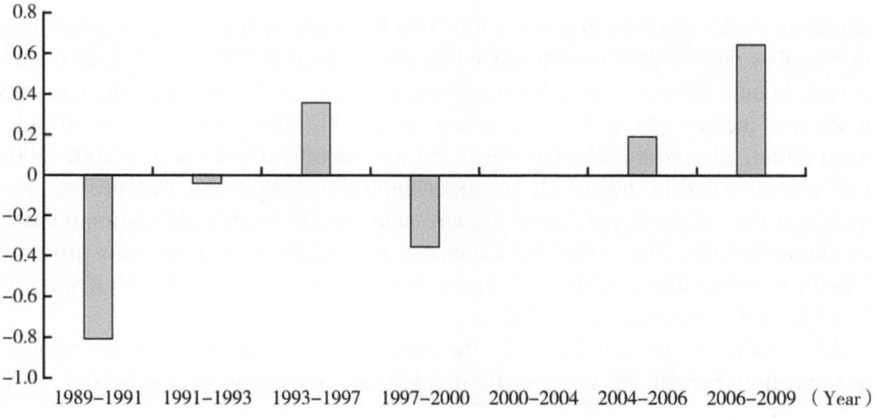

Fig. 11.2 Ravallion and Chen's PPGI measurement results

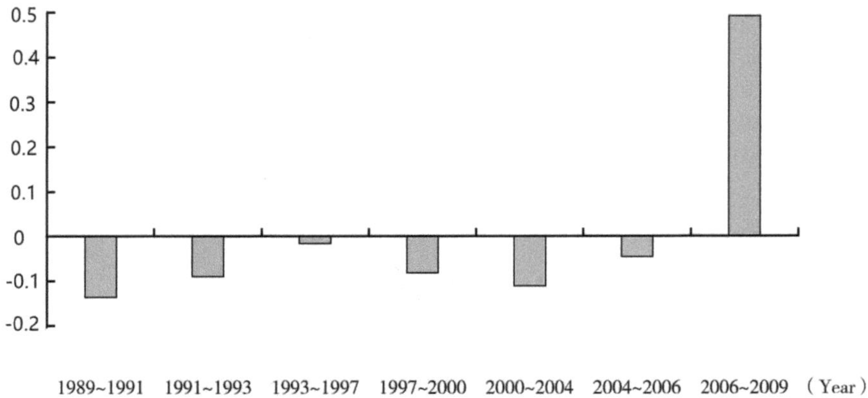

Fig. 11.3 Kakwani, Khandker, and Son's PEGR measurement results

11.3.2 Explanation of the Reasons for Pro-Poor Growth

All three approaches suggest that the growth in 2006–2009 was pro-poor. To investigate what factors led to strictly pro-poor economic growth in China in 2006–2009, the income composition of rural residents during this period (Table 11.1) was analyzed, revealing that the income structure of low-income farmers has undergone significant changes. First, wage income increased from 32.6% in 2006 to 36.3% in 2009; second, transfer income almost doubled from 6.6% in 2006 to 12.5% in 2009. Wage and transfer income increased by 9.6% points in total. In particular, the share of transfer income in the low-income group was much higher than that for other income groups. Income distribution policies introduced by the country in 2006 to strengthen agriculture, benefit farmers, and alleviate poverty have directly increased the earnings of the low-income group. Poverty reduction in 2004–2006 relied on the "trickle-down effect" of growth, whereas this effect and income distribution in 2006–2009 jointly contributed to the strictly pro-poor nature in this period. This proves once again that the "*Three Rural Issues*" policies and special poverty alleviation policies are unquestionably correct and that China's growth will become even more pro-poor with the implementation of the *Outline for Development-oriented Poverty Reduction for China's Rural Areas (2011–2020).*

After 2006, the policies issued by the central government to strengthen agriculture and thus benefit farmers can be divided into six categories: subsidies, agricultural production, rural public services, special poverty alleviation, infrastructure construction, and ecological environment construction. Three types of policies were chosen in this chapter to illustrate subsidies, rural public services, and special poverty alleviation. Since the standards of subsidies vary in different places, the policies implemented in Shanxi Province are used as an example.

(1) Subsidy policies. When China joined the WTO early in the 21st century, the central government implemented a policy of "giving more, taking less,

Table 11.1 Income structure of rural residents (% of per capita net income) (Unit: %)

	2006	2007	2008	2009
Low-income households				
Wage income	32.6	33.2	35.2	36.3
Family business income	59.1	57.1	52.1	49.5
Property income	1.7	2.2	2.1	1.7
Transfer income	6.6	7.5	10.6	12.5
Lower-middle-income households				
Wage income	36.6	37.6	37.3	38.6
Family business income	57.0	55.3	53.8	51.7
Property income	1.5	1.8	1.6	1.6
Transfer income	4.9	5.3	7.3	8.1
Middle-income households				
Wage income	39.1	39.6	40.1	41.4
Family business income	55.0	54.1	51.6	49.7
Property income	1.6	1.8	1.9	1.9
Transfer income	4.3	4.5	6.3	6.9
Middle-high-income households				
Wage income	40.6	41.8	42.1	43.4
Family business income	53.0	51.4	49.7	47.6
Property income	2.0	2.3	2.2	2.2
Transfer income	4.3	4.6	6.0	6.8
High-income households				
Wage income	41.2	40.1	40.1	40.5
Family business income	49.2	49.6	48.8	46.9
Property income	4.2	4.6	4.7	5.1
Transfer income	5.3	5.6	6.4	7.4

Source Calculations are based on data from the *China Statistical Yearbook (2000–2011)* of the National Bureau of Statistics

and letting go" for rural areas to cope with the impact of the international food market as well as safeguard farmers' enthusiasm, increase their income, promote rural development, and ensure national food security. After the complete abolition of agricultural tax on January 1, 2006, the subsidy policies and types of projects continued to increase, along with the intensity of subsidies. Currently, subsidies have become a major source of income for farmers. Table 11.2 summarizes the main types of subsidies currently in effect.

(2) Rural public services. In the 21st century, numerous studies have confirmed that the supply of public services in rural China is seriously lacking, supply and demand do not match, and the gap between urban and rural public services has

Table 11.2 Subsidy policies (A case study of Shanxi)

	Policy objectives	Implementation time	Subsidy standard
Subsidies for returning farmland to forests	To protect and improve the ecological environment, promote the restructuring of the agricultural industry, and increase farmers' income	2000	One-round subsidies: food subsidies RMB140/mu and living subsidies RMB20/mu. After the expiration of one-round subsidies (eight years for ecological forestry, five years for economic forestry), subsidy standards: RMB70/mu in cash for converted land per year and an annual subsidy of RMB20 for living expenses. Subsidy period: eight years for ecological forests and five years for economic forests
Feeding subsidies	To motivate farmers to grow grain to ensure national food security	2004	Wheat RMB10/mu, corn and other grains RMB5/mu, and reseeding RMB5/mu
Agricultural subsidies	To reduce the cost of growing food for farmers to ensure national food security	2007	Wheat RMB51/mu; corn and other grains RMB35/mu
Good seed subsidies	To motivate farmers to grow grain to ensure national food security	2008	Wheat and corn RMB10/mu
Farm machinery purchase subsidy	To improve the level of agricultural modernization to ensure national food security	2004	No more than 30% of the machinery price, the maximum subsidy for a single machine is no more than RMB50,000, and part of the agricultural machinery provinces and cities have cumulative subsidies, up to 15%

(continued)

Table 11.2 (continued)

	Policy objectives	Implementation time	Subsidy standard
Subsidy for breeding sows	Stabilize pig production	2008	Financial subsidy RMB50/pig
Cow subsidy	To protect the foundations of dairy development and steadily increase dairy production capacity	2008	In 2008, the central government subsidized RMB200/cow, while provincial government subsidized RMB100/cow
Subsidies for sow and dairy insurance and premium	To reduce the risk of farming and promote sound and sustainable development of the farming industry	2008	Breeding sow insurance: The central government subsidized 50% of the premiums, while local government subsidized 30% of the premiums. Dairy cattle insurance: 30% of premiums were subsidized by central government and local government each

widened (Wang, 2008).[4] Central government has therefore begun to introduce policies to promote the equalization of urban and rural public services. Table 11.3 summarizes the major rural public service policies currently in place.

(3) Special poverty alleviation policies. In accordance with the tasks and goals set forth in the *Outline for Development-oriented Poverty Reduction for China's Rural Areas (2011–2020)*, the 2010 development-oriented poverty reduction work has resulted in brilliant achievements. The special poverty alleviation policies that were implemented included promotion of the whole village, skills training, industrialized poverty alleviation, contiguous development, migration and relocation, and the linkage of development-oriented poverty alleviation with minimum subsistence needs. The implementation of these special poverty alleviation policies has improved the development capacity of both poor areas and poor people.

Advancing the development of entire villages is essential to alleviate poverty in poor villages, and by the end of 2010, the program had been implemented in 120,000 villages. Skills training is also necessary to improve the quality of the labor force. Since 2004, the government has allocated 3 billion yuan in financial resources for poverty alleviation, implemented the "Yulu Plan" which focuses on labor force transfer, and trained more than 4 million people, of whom more than 80% have moved to other jobs. Industrialized poverty alleviation along with the promotion of

[4] Fan (2011).

Table 11.3 Rural public service policies (A case study in Shanxi)

	Policy objectives	Implementation time	Implementation scope and method
Rural compulsory education	To popularize, consolidate, and improve the nine-year compulsory education and promote a sound and balanced development of basic education	Implemented the "Two Exemptions and One Subsidy" in 2005 and reformed the rural compulsory education funding guarantee mechanism in 2007	Eleven cities and 119 counties (cities and districts) in the province were exempt from education expenses
New rural cooperative health care	To solve the problem of limited access to health care and expensive health care for farmers	Pilot in 2003 and province-wide coverage in 2004	Eleven cities and 119 counties (cities and districts) in the province were exempt from medical expenses
Rural subsistence allowance	To protect the basic livelihood of the rural poor	Pilot in 1997 and province-wide coverage in 2005	Eleven cities and 119 counties (cities and districts) in the province were granted policy subsidies
New rural social pension insurance	To ensure the basic livelihood of rural residents, gradually narrow the gap between urban and rural areas, and maintain social stability in rural areas	Pilot in 2008	Forty-two (30 national and 12 provincial) counties (cities and districts) were included in the pilot project of new rural insurance, with the basic pension for the national pilot fully subsidized by central government and the provincial pilot fully subsidized by the provincial government

the whole village, contiguous development, and scientific and technological poverty alleviation helps to improve the income of poor farmers. Leading industries such as the farming of potatoes and non-wood forest fruits, grassland animal husbandry, and cotton farming have been fostered. Contiguous development enhances the overall development level. The pilot project of "county as a unit, resource integration, whole village promotion, and contiguous development" was carried out. Each pilot county invested a certain amount of financial funds for poverty alleviation as a guide to attract relevant departments to invest agricultural funds in industrial development and supporting projects. Comprehensive management of extremely poor areas explored ways to concentrate on tackling tough problems. For contiguous poverty-stricken areas, resources were integrated from all sides to focus on the fight against poverty. In Sichuan Aba Prefecture, the combination of development-oriented poverty alleviation along with the comprehensive prevention and treatment of osteoarthritis were conducted. The "two systems" of development-oriented poverty alleviation and minimum subsistence guarantee were linked to promote comprehensive implementation of these policies. Beginning in 2008, a multi-departmental pilot project was launched in 689 counties across the country to effectively link the rural minimum subsistence guarantee system and development-oriented poverty alleviation policies, laying a foundation for the full implementation of poverty alleviation policies for low-income people. Relocation for poverty alleviation has changed the conditions for survival and development. Some poor areas in the central and western regions fully seized the opportunity to promote industrialization and urbanization and combined relocation for poverty alleviation with the construction of counties, central towns, and industrial parks to promote farmers' employment transfer (Fan, 2011).[5]

References

Atkinson, A. B. (1987). On the measurement of poverty. *Econometric, 55.*

Fan, X. (2011, June 20). Ten years of achievements in rural development-oriented poverty alleviation. *Economic Daily.*

Foster, J., & Shorrocks, A. F. (1991). Subgroup consistent poverty indices. *Econometric, 59.*

Kakwani, N., & Pernia, E. M. (2000). What is pro-poor growth? *Asian Development Review, 18*(1).

Kakwani, N., & Son, H. (2004). Pro-poor growth: Concepts and measurement with country case studies. *The Pakistan Development Review, 42*(4)

Kwasi Fosu, A. (2011). *Growth, inequality and poverty reduction in developing countries* (Working Paper, January). UNU-WIDER.

Ravallion, M. & Chen, S. (2003). *Measuring pro-poor growth* (Policy Research Working Paper).

Sen, A. (1976). Poverty: An ordinal approach to measurement. *Econometric, 44.*

Sen, A. (1993). Capability and well-being. In M. Nussbaum, & A. Sen (Eds.), *The quality of life.* Clarendon Press.

Wang, X. (2008). *Rural public services and public finance policy in structural transformation.* China Development Press.

[5] Wang (2008).

Chapter 12
Inclusive Measurement of China's Economic Growth

Despite rapid economic growth in Asia over the past three decades that has resulted in a significant reduction in poor populations, there remain large numbers of poor people in developing countries in this region. In 2005, 27% of the population in developing countries in Asia lived below the international poverty line of USD1.25/person/day, while over 50% of the population lived below the international poverty line of USD2.00/person/day. Both income poverty and wealth disparity and non-income poverty and wealth disparity remain high, mainly due to the increasing inequality in access to compulsory education and basic health services as well as slow progress in eliminating non-income poverty. Although countries in Asia and the Pacific are able to meet the Millennium Development Goals (MDGs) for reducing income poverty, many are struggling to meet the targets for reducing non-income poverty (ESCAP, 2006).

In 2010, China's GDP per capita exceeded USD 4,000, entering the internationally recognized "middle-income" stage of development. However, China faces the challenge of a "middle-income trap" due to the consolidation of income mobility at all levels of society, lack of opportunities for upward mobility for the low-income class, and a widening capability gap (Yang, 2011). Inclusive growth can increase employment opportunities and improve equity in access to education, health care, and social security, thus achieving sustainable economic growth and avoiding the "middle-income trap" (World Bank, 2011). The concept of inclusive growth has been recognized by many governments including the Chinese government. India's 11th Five-Year Plan (2007–2012) set out a strategy to implement inclusive growth (India, 2006), which was the first Asian country to incorporate inclusive growth into its national development strategy.

This chapter was co-authored with Dr. Yu Min and originally published in the Economic Review, No. 3, 2012.

© Social Sciences Academic Press 2022

X. Wang, *Multidimensional Poverty Measurement*,
International Research on Poverty Reduction,
https://doi.org/10.1007/978-981-19-1189-7_12

12.1 Connotation of Inclusive Growth

12.1.1 Evolution of Poverty Reduction Strategies

Inclusive growth is based on a deepening understanding of poverty. Classical economists have argued that economic growth ultimately benefits the poor through a "trickle-down effect" and that economic growth is a major factor in poverty reduction (Bourguignon, 2003; Deininger & Squire, 1996; Dollar & Kraay, 2002; Ravallion, 2001; White & Anderson, 2001). However, empirical research shows that not all economic growth reduces poverty and that widespread poverty reduction can only be achieved when economic growth is sustained, when it benefits a broad range of workers and when labor income accounts for a high share of income growth. Bourguignon (2003) proposed a triangle of "poverty—economic growth—income distribution," arguing that along with the growth effect, the income distribution effect is also a factor that affects the poverty reduction effect of economic growth. Ravallion (2001) and Kakwani and Hyun (2004) suggested that "pro-poor growth" benefits from income redistribution. Sen (2001) analyzed poverty from the perspective of welfare economics and argued that poverty of rights is the root cause that limits people's access to all kinds of freedom and that the first way to eliminate poverty is for all people to obtain equal rights and freedom, the latter being the primary purpose of development and the means by which to promote it. He advocates improving social security capabilities by giving people economic freedom and social opportunities. Inspired by his vision of poverty of rights, the Asian Development Bank (ADB) recognized that unequal opportunity was a major cause of income inequality and, in 2007, revised its long-term strategic framework to develop an inclusive growth strategy.

The understanding of poverty has gone through three stages: income poverty, capability poverty, and poverty of rights. Accordingly, the understanding of the relationship between economic growth and poverty reduction has deepened. The concept of growth has evolved from a pure emphasis on speed to "pro-poor growth" and finally "inclusive growth" (Fig. 12.1).

12.1.2 Connotation of Inclusive Growth

In academic research, the definition of inclusive growth remains inconsistent, but the main ideas focus on the following aspects. Inclusive growth must reduce all inequality, both income (Rauniyar & Kanbur, 2010) and non-income inequality (Grosse et al., 2008; Klasen, 2008), and ensure the poor's income grows faster than that of the non-poor; where the poor includes those below the poverty line as well as the low- and middle-income populations. Ali and Son (2007) argue that inclusive growth requires increasing access to various social benefits such as health and education, and that structural changes in income distribution are used to test whether

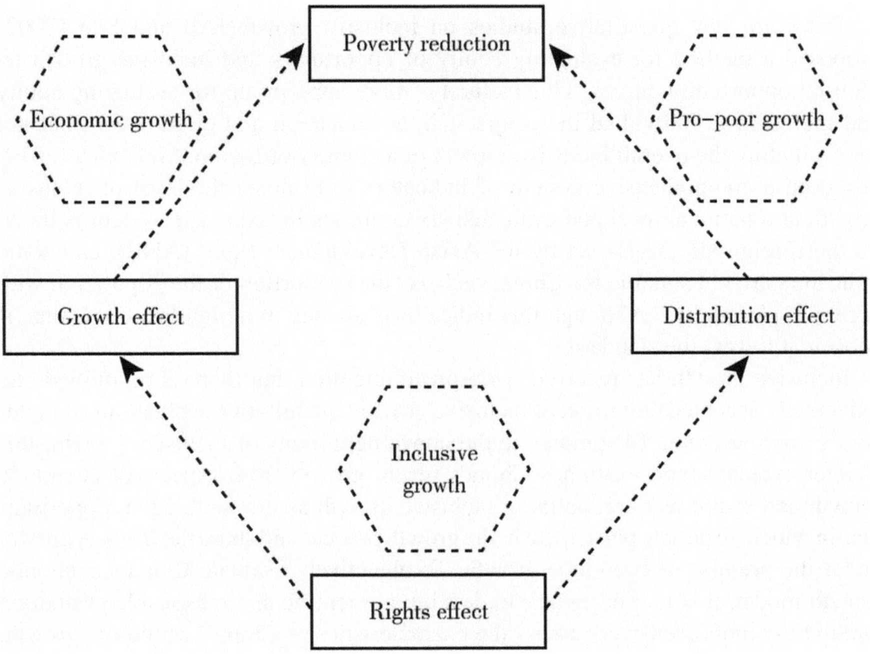

Fig. 12.1 Poverty reduction effects and strategies

the growth is inclusive. The core of inclusive growth is similar to Roemer's (1998) definition of equality of opportunity. Ali and Zhuang (2007) and Zhuang and Ali (2009) further argue that rapid and sustainable economic growth is a prerequisite for job creation and development.

The process of economic growth is more emphasized in inclusive growth than in pro-poor growth, highlights ex ante analysis, and considers the constraints to sustainable, high-speed growth. In addition to the poor, inclusive growth also considers how to utilize the labor force trapped in low productivity who are excluded from the growth process. The concept is based on a combination of market and non-market actions to eradicate poverty and social exclusion and to promote a high-speed and sustainable growth model with equal opportunities. Inclusive growth focuses on increasing development opportunities and improving the welfare of people (Du et al., 2010).

Inclusive growth is similar to multidimensional poverty in terms of objectives, taking health, education, and income as the goals for development rather than its means (Alkire et al., 2010). Zhuang (2008) argues that to achieve inclusive growth in developing countries, governments should take the following measures: first, increase investment in basic education and health care and other basic social services to improve the fundamental quality and capabilities of disadvantaged groups; second, strengthen the fairness of policies and institutions to eliminate social injustice, improve market mechanisms, and create conditions for equal competition; and third, establish social risk management systems to prevent and eradicate extreme poverty.

There are few quantitative studies on inclusive growth. Ali and Son (2007) proposed a method for evaluating equity of opportunity and inclusive growth by plotting opportunity curves. This method is more appropriate for evaluating equity and inclusion in individual indicators such as education and employment but not for evaluating the overall inclusive growth of a country or region. McKinley (2010) proposed a comprehensive system of indicators to evaluate the level of inclusive growth at a national level and evaluated six countries in Asia. The system is based on the foreign aid targets set by the Asian Development Bank (ADB), and some indicators are not suitable for China, such as "the proportion of the population with access to electricity." Although this indicator is already at a high level in China, if chosen, it lowers the standard.

Inclusive growth has received widespread attention, but there is no unified and universally accepted definition of inclusive growth; quantitative evaluations of inclusive growth are rare. To summarize the above definitions of inclusive growth, this chapter evaluates and examines China's recent growth from aspects of economic growth and social welfare, defining inclusive growth as that with equal opportunities, in which all people participate in the growth process and share the fruits of growth under the premise of economic growth. To objectively evaluate China's economic growth model, it is first necessary to develop a scientific and reasonable evaluation method to comprehensively assess the characteristics of China's economic growth, so as to provide a reference for the Chinese government to make relevant policies.

12.2 Measurement Methods of Inclusive Growth

Based on McKinley's (2010) research findings, this chapter constructs an inclusive growth index to measure the inclusiveness of economic growth, accounting for China's national conditions.

12.2.1 Construction of the Inclusive Growth Index

There are four steps in constructing the inclusive growth index.

Step 1: Select the dimensions and indicators.

Let the evaluation dimension set of the inclusive growth index be $U = \{u_1, u_2, \ldots, u_j\}$, the evaluation domain set $U = \{u_{j1}, u_{j2}, \ldots, u_{ji}\}$, and the evaluation indicator set $U = \{u_{j11}, u_{j21}, \ldots, u_{jim}\}$, where j is the evaluation dimension, i is the evaluation domain, and m is the evaluation indicator.

Step 2: Set indicator weights.

In this chapter, we used the expert panel method to determine the weights and set the weight as W, and $W = \{w_1, w_2, \ldots, w_i\}$.

Step 3: Single-factor standardization.

After constructing the evaluation indicators, the indicators were quantified one by one, that is, a single factor was used to evaluate the affiliation of the indicators to various levels of fuzzy subsets. After calculating the affiliation of all indicators, the matrix U_R is as follows:

$U_R = [r_{111}, r_{112}, \ldots, r_{11m}]'$

Step 4: Aggregate the weights to obtain the inclusive growth index (IGI).

$$\mathrm{IGI} = \sum_{j=1}^{n} U_R \times w_i \tag{12.1}$$

where, U_R is the standardized score of the individual indicators and w_i is the weight of the individual indicators at that level.

The IGI sets an overall target value of 100, and the closer the evaluation result is to 100, the more inclusive is the economic growth.

12.2.2 Selection of Dimensions and Indicators

Based on the concept of inclusive growth and its definition by the Asian Development Bank, this chapter uses McKinley's (2010) dimensions of inclusive growth to evaluate it in four dimensions: sustainability of economic growth, reductions in poverty and income inequality, fairness of participation in economic opportunities, and access to basic social security.

(1) Sustainability of economic growth. Sustained economic growth is a prerequisite for inclusive growth. Only high-speed and sustainable economic growth can increase wealth and create jobs for the whole society. Sustainable economic growth has two meanings: the rate and sustainability of economic growth and the most common indicator used to evaluate the former is the GDP per capita growth rate, which measures the rate of economic growth. However, the most commonly used indicator to measure the sustainability of economic growth is the share of the tertiary sector in GDP, which is used as a proxy for the sustainability of economic growth.

(2) Reductions in poverty and income inequality. Inclusive growth ensures fairness in the process and equality of opportunity, while the ultimate goal is to ensure fair results and benefit the poor. The proportion of poor people and the degree of inequality in society as a whole are direct indicators of whether social outcomes are shared. If economic growth addresses poverty by reducing inequality, it will also contribute to sustainable economic growth. This study chose the "resident Gini coefficient" as a proxy to measure national income inequality, the "urban–rural Gini coefficient" as an indicator to measure urban–rural inequality, and the

"proportion of the population below the national poverty line" and "proportion of population at USD2.5/person/day" as proxies for poverty measurement.

(3) Fairness of participation in economic opportunities. This is a condition for the inclusiveness of the economic growth process. The ability to participate in economic activities depends not only on the objective economic growth rate and employment opportunities but also on the ability of individuals to participate in economic opportunities; this, in turn, depends on individual capabilities and the availability of public services such as roads, drinking water, health, and education provided by the government to improve human quality. Therefore, to demonstrate the fairness of the process with indicators of expanded human capacity, the following were selected: "under-five mortality rate per 1,000 live births," "proportion of underweight children < 5 years of age," "transition rate of junior high school graduates," and "index of per capita education expenditure" as proxies to indicate fairness in people's access to health and education.

(4) Access to basic social security. Inclusive growth is concerned with opening up opportunities for all people, that is, making these opportunities equally accessible to all, and thus eliminating extreme poverty. The social security function of public action—guaranteeing the rights and capabilities of citizens—has an instrumental and technical meaning as well as a profound social meaning. Social security has the functions of "protection" and "promotion," that is, protecting against a decline in people's living standards and promoting them while expanding people's basic capabilities, and thus should be a goal of public action rather than a series of specific policies on a small scale. Therefore, the eradication of extreme poverty needs to emphasize basic social security or social safety nets (Ali & Zhuang, 2007). The level of social security demonstrates the basic status and is defined as the extent to which members of society in a country or region enjoy social security benefits over a certain period of time, revealing a share of social security in income distribution and the actual level of security. Internationally, it is common to measure the level of social security using the social security benefit rate, which is calculated by the following formula: social security benefit rate = total social security expenditure/GDP.

In this chapter, an IGI is constructed that includes 4 dimensions, 7 domains, and 13 indicators, factoring in China's national conditions, as shown in Table 12.1.

12.2.3 Weights, Standardization, and Indicator Thresholds

The weight setting of the IGI adopts the expert discussion method. Twenty-one experts from the International Poverty Reduction Center in China (IPRCC), Peking University, and Renmin University of China discussed the weighting of the IGI. They concluded that economic sustainability and fairness of opportunities are at the core of sustainable growth and basic social security is an inevitable requirement for

Table 12.1 Inclusive growth index and weights

Dimension indicator		Domain indicator		Indicator	
Indicator	Weight	Indicator	Weight	Indicator	Weight
Sustainability of economic growth (U_1)	0.30	Sustainable economic growth U_{11}	0.15	GDP per capita growth rate U_{111}	0.10
				Share of tertiary sector in GDP U_{112}	0.05
		Job opportunities U_{12}	0.15	Employment rate in secondary and tertiary sectors U_{121}	0.10
				Number of migrant workers in the year U_{122}	0.05
Reductions in poverty and income inequality (U_2)	0.30	Income inequality U_{21}	0.20	Resident Gini coefficient U_{211}	0.10
				Urban–rural Gini coefficient U_{212}	0.10
		Poverty incidence U_{22}	0.10	Proportion of the population below the national poverty line U_{221}	0.05
				Proportion of population at USD2.5/person/day U_{222}	0.05
Fairness of participation in economic opportunities (U_3)	0.30	Health and nutrition U_{31}	0.15	Under-five mortality rate per 1,000 live births U_{311}	0.075
				Proportion of underweight children < 5 years of age U_{312}	0.075
		Education U_{32}	0.15	Transition rate of junior high school graduates U_{321}	0.075
				Index of per capita education expenditure U_{322}	0.075
Access to basic social security (U_4)	0.10	Social security level U_{41}	0.10	Social security rate U_{411}	0.10
Total	1.00		1.00		1.00

Note The setting of indicator weights is described later in this section

inclusive growth. In the weight setting of the four dimensions of the IGI, the first three dimensions should be given equal and higher weights; hence, the weights set for the four dimensions were as follows: 30% weight for each of the first three dimensions and 10% for basic social security. The average results of the experts' weighting of the indicators are shown in Table 12.1.

The indicator system in this chapter contains both forward and reverse indicators, as well as interval indicators, which are standardized in different ways, as follows:

(1) Standardization method for forward indicators

$$V_{y,j} = X_{y,j} / Z_{y,j} \times 100 \tag{12.2}$$

where $V_{y,j}$ is the standardized score of indicator j in year y, $Z_{y,j}$ is the target value of indicator j in year y, and $X_{y,j}$ is the actual value of indicator j in year y.

(2) Standardization method for inverse indicators

$$V_{y,j} = \frac{\max_{y,j} - X_{y,j}}{Z_{y,j}} \times 100 \tag{12.3}$$

$V_{y,j}$ is the score of indicator j in year y, $max_{y,j}$ is the highest value of indicator j, and $Z_{y,j}$ and $X_{y,j}$ have the same meaning as those of forward indicators.

(3) Interval indicators

The score of each indicator is specified according to the upper and lower limits of the interval, as shown in the following section.

12.2.4 Score Range and Target Value for Individual Indicators

GDP per capita growth rate. This indicator reflects the average economic growth rate over a period of time. According to actual economic growth in China, the target value is 100 points at twice the world average growth rate, and the benchmark value is 60 points of the average growth rate.

Share of the tertiary sector in GDP. In developed countries, the share of the tertiary sector in GDP is generally 70%, which is thus the target value.

Employment rate in secondary and tertiary sectors. In 2007, the employment rate in these sectors in Japan and Korea was around 94%. The development model of China is close to that of Japan, Korea, and other developed Asian countries; thus, 94% is the target value.

Number of migrant workers in a year. Since the 1990s, China has gradually liberalized restrictions on the movement of people, but serious urban–rural barriers still exist. The upper limit of this indicator is 80 and the lower limit is 60, with three scoring levels of 60, 70, and 80 points.

Resident Gini coefficient. According to internationally accepted standards, the Gini coefficient of 0.2–0.3 = fair, 80–100 points; 0.3–0.4 = relatively reasonable, 60–80 points; 0.4–0.5 = a large income gap, 0–60 points; and more than 0.5 scores, 0 points.

Urban–rural Gini coefficient. The scoring method is the same as that indicated in the resident Gini coefficient.

Proportions of the population below the national poverty line and those at USD2.5/person/day. Both indicators are based on the target of eradicating absolute poverty, that is, taking poverty incidence of 0 as the target value, at 100 points.

Under-five mortality rate per 1,000 live births. With a target value of 0, the world's highest mortality rate for this indicator is the lowest value of 200.

Proportion of underweight children <5 years of age. This was considered with 0 as the target value and 100% the minimum value.

Transition rate of junior high school graduates. This was with 100% as the target value and 0 as the minimum value.

Index of per capita education expenditure. This index is the ratio of per capita education expenditure to GNP per capita and is a relative measure of how much is spent on education. According to the statistics of the more populous countries in the world, the index of per capita education expenditures for secondary school students is generally 0.15–0.22.[1] China has always attached importance to basic education, and human capital investment is needed to overcome the "middle-income trap." Therefore, the index of per capita education expenditure of 0.20 for secondary school students was used as the target value.

Proportion of social security expenditure in GNP. With reference to the standard calculation method in Mu's *Study on the adequate level of social security* (1997), the appropriate upper limits in 1992, 2000, and 2009 were 11.31%, 10.76%, and 13.73%, respectively, and the appropriate lower limits were 9.45%, 8.89%, and 11.86%, respectively. Since the current social security level in China is low, the lower limit was adopted as the target value.

In summary, the score ranges and target values for individual indicators are shown in Table 12.2.

12.2.5 Robustness Test of Indicator Results

The weights for the indicators in this chapter were derived from expert panels that were highly controversial. To test the robustness of the weighting results, this chapter draws on the Human Development Index (HDI) and the multidimensional poverty weighting method developed by the University of Oxford, both of which used the average weighting method (Alkire & Foster, 2011). The other three weighting methods were used here, and the results were calculated separately. These three

[1] Hu Angang and Wang Lei, "Social Investment in Education: The Core Indicator of Educational Development," Tsinghua University Education Research, No. 3, 2010.

Table 12.2 Target values of individual indicators

Indicator	Unit	Target Value
GDP per capita growth rate U_{111}	%	Twice the world average growth rate
Share of the tertiary sector in GDP U_{112}	%	70%
Employment rate in the secondary and tertiary sectors U_{121}	%	94%
Number of migrant workers in the year U_{122}	In 10,000 s	Relative indicator
Resident Gini coefficient U_{211}	–	Gini coefficient
Urban–rural Gini coefficient U_{212}	–	Gini coefficient
Proportion of the population below the national poverty line U_{221}	%	0
Proportion of population at USD2.5/person/day U_{222}	%	0
Under-five mortality rate per 1,000 live births U_{311}	%	0
Proportion of underweight children <5 years of age U_{312}	%	0
Transition rate of junior high school graduates U_{321}	%	100%
Index of per capita education expenditure U_{322}	–	0.20
Social security rate U_{411}	%	The target values in 1992, 2000, and 2009 were 9.45%, 8.89%, and 11.86%, respectively

methods are as follows: (1) the average weighting of the indicators in four dimensions, that is, each dimension has a weight of 1/4 (that is, 0.25), and the weights of indicators are averaged according to the weight of each dimension; (2) the average weighting of the indicators in seven domains, that is, each domain indicator has a weight of 1/7 (that is, appr. 0.143), and each indicator is divided into specific indicators on average; and (3) the average weighting of the 13 evaluation indicators, that is, 1/13 (appr. 0.077).

12.3 Data and Results

Since 1978, China's economy has undergone several institutional changes. Effective economic organization is the key to economic growth (North & Thomas, 1973) and the process of institutional change in China's economic system implies the vital role of institutions in economic development. The year 1978 was an important turning point in the history of economic development in New China, which witnessed the innovation of China's rural production system. In the 1980s, farmers' income increased rapidly. In the 1990s, with urban economic reform as the priority, the reforms of state-owned enterprises and the fiscal and financial systems were put into operation. The first decade of the twenty-first century saw the pursuit of harmonious social development: the Chinese government implemented rural tax reform and successively issued nine "No. 1" policies for the development of agriculture and the rural economy. A series of policies to promote economic development in central and western China were also introduced to reduce regional disparities. Therefore, this chapter examines the trends and characteristics of China's inclusive economic growth in the 1980s, 1990s, and the first decade of the twenty-first century, using 1990, 2000, and 2009 as the cutoff years.[2]

12.3.1 Indicator Values and Data Sources

According to the statistical yearbook and scholars' calculations, the value of each indicator is summarized and listed in Table 12.3.

The standardized IGI was calculated according to the method of standardizing the IGI (Eqs. 12.2 and 12.3) and the target values for individual indicators (Table 12.3). The results are shown in Table 12.4.

12.3.2 Robustness Test of Evaluation Results and Indicator Results

Based on the above methods, the individual indicator scores and composite index scores for the inclusive growth indicators were calculated, as shown in Tables 12.5 and 12.6.

The other three weighting methods were used here to test the robustness of the results. The results of the three weighting methods agreed with each other, but the weights assigned varied and the progress of inclusive growth differed at each stage (Table 12.7). Overall, China's IGI showed an upward trend from 1990 to 2009: From 1990 to 2000, the progress of inclusive growth was fast, but from 2000 to 2009, the progress declined. Therefore, the results obtained using the expert evaluation method are reliable.

12.3.3 Analysis of Evaluation Results

(1) From 1990 to 2009, the index of inclusive growth made great progress, which shows that China's economic growth has become increasingly inclusive over

[2] Due to data source limitations, some data were replaced with data from other closer years.

Table 12.3 Indicator values of inclusive growth in China (1990–2009)

Indicator	Indicator value			Data source
	1990	2000	2009	
GDP per capita growth rate U_{111}	7.8	9.3	9.8	*China Statistical Yearbook*
Share of the tertiary sector in GDP U_{112}	31.6	39	43[a]	*China Statistical Yearbook*
Employment rate in the secondary and tertiary sectors U_{121}	39.9	50	61.9	*The Glorious Thirty Years from 1978 to 2007*; *China's Regional Economic Statistical Yearbook*
Number of migrant workers in the year U_{122}	0.216	0.8	1.5	*China Statistical Yearbook; China Population Statistical Yearbook*; *China Population Census Data*
Resident Gini coefficient U_{211}	0.3485	0.4382	>0.45	Chen and Ravallion (2007); *International Statistical Yearbook (2002–2010)*
Urban–rural Gini coefficient U_{212}	0.36[b]	0.4[c]	0.44[d]	World Bank
Proportion of the population below the national poverty line U_{221}	9.4	3.4	3.6	*China Poverty Monitoring Report*; *China Rural Household Survey Yearbook*
Proportion of population at USD2.5/person/day U_{222}	91.6	71.7[c]	49.5[e]	Chen and Ravallion (2010)
Under-five mortality rate per 1,000 live births U_{311}	45.5	36	19.1	UN Millennium Development Goals Indicators website
Proportion of underweight children <5 years of age U_{312}	19.1	11.2	6.9	UN Millennium Development Goals Indicators website
Transition rate of junior high school graduates U_{321}	40.6	51.2	83.4	*China Statistical Yearbook*
Index of per capita education expenditure U_{322}	0.09[f]	0.1	0.12[g]	Calculated by the author according to the *China Statistical Yearbook* and *China Education Expenditure Statistical Yearbook*
Social security rate U_{411}	4.2[h]	6.4	6.1[g]	Calculated by the author according to the *China Statistical Yearbook*

Note a—2008 data; b—1988 data; c—1999 data; d—2007 data; e—2005; f—1995 data; g—2006 data; h—1992 data

the past 30 years. In terms of stages, from 1990 to 2000, the progress of the IGI was fast (rising from 61.12 to 65.06) but slow from 2000 to 2009 (rising from 65.06 to 66.21; Table 12.5).

(2) The overall level of China's IGI was low. The indicators of sustainable economic growth, the proportion of the population below the national poverty line, and health and nutrition achieved high scores (standardized scores: above

Table 12.4 Standardized values of inclusive growth indicators

Indicator	Standardized value		
	1990	2000	2009
GDP per capita growth rate U_{111}	100	100	100
Share of the tertiary sector in GDP U_{112}	45	56	61
Employment rate in the secondary and tertiary sectors U_{121}	42	53	66
Number of migrant workers in the year U_{122}	60	70	80
Resident Gini coefficient U_{211}	70	40	20
Urban–rural Gini coefficient U_{212}	70	60	30
Proportion of the population below the national poverty line U_{221}	91	97	96
Proportion of population at USD2.5/person/day U_{222}	8	28	50
Under-five mortality rate per 1,000 live births U_{311}	77	82	90
Proportion of underweight children <5 years of age U_{312}	81	89	93
Transition rate of junior high school graduates U_{321}	41	51	83
Index of per capita education expenditure U_{322}	45	50	60
Social security rate U_{411}	44	68	58

80), whereas other indicators achieved low scores, especially employment rate in the secondary and tertiary sectors, the proportion of population at USD2.5/person/day, index of per capita education expenditure, and social security rate (Table 12.5).

(3) From 1990 to 2009, the scores for all indicators at the domain level showed an upward trend, except for the income inequality indicator, which showed a downward trend. The significant decrease in the score of the income inequality indicator offset the progress of the other indicators. From 1990 to 2009, the score for the income inequality indicator, a composite of the resident Gini coefficient and the urban–rural Gini coefficient, decreased from 14 to 5, the largest change of any indicator (Table 12.6). The resident Gini coefficient rose from 0.3485 in 1990 to over 0.45 in 2009, and the urban–rural Gini coefficient rose from 0.36 to 0.44 (Table 12.3).

12.4 Conclusion and Recommendations

Based on the basic concept and meaning of inclusive growth and the characteristics of China's economic growth, a set of indicators was designed to evaluate the inclusiveness of China's economic growth; in the period 1990 to 2009, evaluation was based on this system of indicators.

The evaluation results showed that, since the 1990s, China's economic growth has demonstrated a general trend of inclusiveness, with rapid economic growth, widespread employment, and improvements in basic human capabilities and basic

Table 12.5 Indicator scores of inclusive growth

Dimension indicator	Weight	Domain indicator	Weight	Indicator	Weight	1990		2000		2009	
						Score	Weighted score	Score	Weighted score	Score	Weighted score
Sustainability of economic growth (U_1)	0.30	Sustainable economic growth U_{11}	0.15	GDP per capita growth rate U_{111}	0.10	100	10	100	10	100	10
				Share of tertiary sector in GDP U_{112}	0.05	45	2.25	56	2.80	61	3.05
		Job opportunities U_{12}	0.15	Employment rate in secondary and tertiary sectors U_{121}	0.10	42	4.20	53	5.30	66	6.60
				Number of migrant workers in the year U_{122}	0.05	603	3	70	3.50	80	4
Reductions in poverty and income inequality (U_2)	0.30	Income inequality U_{21}	0.20	Resident Gini coefficient U_{211}	0.10	70	7	40	4	20	2
				Urban–rural Gini coefficient U_{212}	0.10	70	7	60	6	30	3
		Poverty incidence U_{22}	0.10	Proportion of the population below the national poverty line U_{221}	0.05	91	4.55	97	4.85	96	4.80
				Proportion of population at USD2.5/person/day U_{222}	0.05	8	0.40	28	1.40	50	2.50

(continued)

Table 12.5 (continued)

Dimension indicator	Weight	Domain indicator	Weight	Indicator	Weight	1990		2000		2009	
						Score	Weighted score	Score	Weighted score	Score	Weighted score
Fairness of participation in economic opportunities (U_3)	0.30	Health and nutrition U_{31}	0.15	Under-five mortality rate per 1,000 live births U_{311}	0.075	77	5.78	82	6.15	90	6.75
				Proportion of underweight children <5 years of age U_{312}	0.075	81	6.08	89	6.68	93	6.98
		Education U_{32}	0.15	Transition rate of junior high school graduates U_{321}	0.075	41	3.08	51	3.83	83	6.23
				Index of per capita education expenditure U_{322}	0.075	45	3.38	50	3.75	60	4.50
Access to basic social security (U_4)	0.10	Social security level U_{41}	0.10	Social security rate U_{411}	0.10	44	4.40	68	6.80	58	5.80
Total	1.00	-	1.00	-	1.00	-	61.12	-	65.06	-	66.21

Table 12.6 Indicator scores of the inclusive growth index at the dimension and domain levels

Dimension indicator	Weight	Weighted score			Domain indicator	Weight	Weighted score		
		1990	2000	2009			1990	2000	2009
Sustainability of economic growth (U_1)	0.30	19.70	21.60	23.65	Sustainable economic growth U_{11}	0.15	12.25	12.80	13.05
					Job opportunities U_{12}	0.15	7.20	8.80	10.60
Reductions in poverty and income inequality (U_2)	0.30	18.95	16.25	12.30	Income inequality U_{21}	0.20	14	10	5
					Poverty incidence U_{22}	0.10	4.95	6.25	7.30
Fairness of participation in economic opportunities (U_3)	0.30	17.60	20.05	23.50	Health and nutrition U_{31}	0.15	11.86	12.83	13.73
					Education U_{32}	0.15	6.46	7.58	10.73
Access to basic social security (U_4)	0.10	4.40	6.80	5.80	Social security level U_{41}	0.10	4.40	6.80	5.80
Total	1.00	-	-	-	-	1.00	61.12	65.06	66.21

Table 12.7 Robustness tests of evaluation results

Dimension indicator & weight	Indicator weight	1990	2000	2009	Domain indicator & weight	Indicator weight	1990	2000	2009	Indicator weight	1990	2000	2009
U_1 (0.25)	0.0625	6.25	6.25	6.25	U_{11} (0.143)	0.0715	3.20	3.98	4.33	U_{111} (0.077)	7.69	7.69	27.69
	0.0625	2.81	3.50	3.81		0.0715	2.98	3.76	4.69	U_{112} (0.077)	3.46	4.31	4.69
	0.0625	2.63	3.31	4.13	U_{12} (0.143)	0.0715	4.26	4.97	5.68	U_{121} (0.077)	3.23	4.08	5.08
	0.0625	3.75	4.38	5.00		0.0715	4.97	2.84	1.42	U_{122} (0.077)	4.62	5.38	6.15
U_2 (0.25)	0.0625	4.38	2.50	1.25	U_{21} (0.143)	0.0715	4.97	4.26	2.13	U_{211} (0.077)	5.38	3.08	1.54
	0.0625	4.38	3.75	1.88		0.0715	6.46	6.89	6.82	U_{212} (0.077)	5.38	4.62	2.31
	0.0625	5.69	6.06	6.00	U_{22} (0.143)	0.0715	0.57	1.99	3.55	U_{221} (0.077)	7.00	7.46	7.38
	0.0625	0.50	1.75	3.13		0.0715	5.47	5.82	6.39	U_{222} (0.077)	0.62	2.15	3.85
U_3 (0.25)	0.0625	4.81	5.13	5.63	U_{31} (0.143)	0.0715	5.75	6.32	6.60	U_{311} (0.077)	5.92	6.31	6.92
	0.0625	5.06	5.56	5.81		0.0715	2.91	3.62	5.89	U_{312} (0.077)	6.23	6.85	7.15
	0.0625	2.56	3.19	5.19	U_{32} (0.143)	0.0715	3.20	3.55	4.26	U_{321} (0.077)	3.15	3.92	6.38
	0.0625	2.81	3.13	3.75		0.0715	6.25	9.66	8.24	U_{322} (0.077)	3.46	3.85	4.62
U_4 (0.25)	0.25	11.00	17.00	14.50	U_{41} (0.143)	0.143	3.20	3.98	4.33	U_{411} (0.077)	3.38	5.23	4.46
Total	1.00	56.63	65.51	66.33	-	1.00	54.19	61.64	64.33	1.00	59.52	64.93	68.22

social security. However, the overall level of inclusive growth in China has been low and has developed slowly, and income inequality has been increasing, both of which have become an enormous obstacle to achieving inclusive economic growth. To realize this, the following four areas of improvements are recommended.

First, increase employment opportunities and improve fairness in employment opportunities.

China's rapid economic growth has been disproportionate to the employment growth rate, and until 2009, the employment rate in the secondary and tertiary sectors was only 61.9%. Thus, it is essential to improve the industrial structure, increase the proportion of tertiary sector, and create more job opportunities, thereby allowing more people to participate in the economic growth process.

Second, raise the income of low-income groups and improve the fairness of income outcomes.

Rising income inequality in China has reduced the poverty reduction effect of economic growth. To achieve inclusive growth in China, it is necessary to not only maintain the economic growth rate but to formulate effective policies to raise per capita income in western and rural areas; adjust the flow of resources between regions and between urban and rural areas; and mobilize governmental, corporate, and non-governmental resources to promote the flow of production factors from developed areas to less developed and rural areas in the central and western regions, so as to narrow the income gap and reduce poverty.

Third, increase investment in human capital and improve fairness of participation in economic opportunities.

Evaluation indicators on access to education scored low, especially per capita education expenditure. It is therefore vital to provide more complete basic services to backward regions and disadvantaged populations in order to provide the human capital base for economic participation and break the intergenerational transmission of poverty.

Fourth, improve basic social security and enhance the fairness of security.

Although social security in China has made progress, it is slow compared with that of GNP and remains low for rural residents. Hence, in the future, China should increase investment in basic social security in rural areas; improve health care, old-age pensions, and other basic guarantees; and explore mechanisms to effectively link the two systems of subsistence allowances and poverty alleviation in poor areas, thus improving rural social security.

References

Ali, I., & Son, H.H. (2007). Measuring inclusive growth. *Asian Development Review, 10*(24).

Ali, I., & Zhuang, J. (2007). *Inclusive growth toward a prosperous Asia: Policy implications.* (ERD Working Paper, No. 97). Manila: Economic and Research Department, Asian Development Bank.

Alkire, S., & Foster, J. (2011). Counting and multidimensional poverty measurement. *Journal of Public Economics, 95*(7–8).

Alkire, S. et al., (2010). The missing dimensions of poverty data. Liu Minquan & Han Hua (Trans.) Science Press.

Bourguignon, F. (2003). *The growth flexibility of poverty reduction: Explaining heterogeneity across countries and time periods. Inequality and Growth: Theory and Policy Implications*. MIT Press.

Chen, S., & Ravallion, M. (2007). Absolute poverty measures for the developing world, 1981–2004. *Proceedings of the National Academy of Sciences, 104*(43).

Chen, S., & Ravallion, M. (2010). The developing world is poorer than we thought, but no less successful in the fight against poverty. *The Quarterly Journal of Economics, 125*(4).

Deininger, K., & Squire, L. (1996). A new data set measuring income inequality. *World Bank Economic Review, 10*(3).

Dollar, D., & Kraay, A. (2002). Growth is good for the poor. *Journal of Economic Growth, 7*(3).

Du, Z, Weidong, X., & Lin, Z. (2010). The context, essentials and policy connotation of inclusive growth theory. *Chinese Rural Economy*, No. 11.

ESCAP, UNDP, & ADB. (2006). *The Millennium Development Goals: Progress in Asia and the Pacific 2006*. ADB.

Grosse, M., Harttgen, K., & Klasen, S. (2008). Measuring pro-poor growth in non-income dimensions. *World Development Report, 36*(6).

India. Planning Commission. (2006). *Towards faster and more inclusive growth: An approach to the 11th five year plan*. New Delhi.

Kakwani, N., & Hyun., H. (2004). Pro-poor growth: Concepts and measurement with country case studies. *The Pakistan Development Review, 42*(4).

Klasen, S. (2008). Economic growth and poverty reduction: Measurement issues in income and non-income dimensions. *World Development, 36*(3).

McKinley, T. (2010). *Inclusive growth criteria and indicators: An inclusive growth index for diagnosis of country progress* (Working Paper). Asian Development Bank.

Mu, H. (1997). Study on the adequate level of social security. *Economic Research Journal*, No. 2.

North, D., & Thomas, R. (1973). *The rise of the Western world: A new economic history*. Cambridge: Cambridge University Press.

Rauniyar, G., & Kanbur, R. (2010). Inclusive development: Two papers on conceptualization, application and the ADB perspective (Revised, January, 2010). *Journal of the Asia Pacific Economy, 15*(4).

Ravallion, M. (2001). Growth, inequality and poverty: Looking beyond averages. *World Development, 29*(11).

Roemer, J. (1998). *Equality of opportunity*. Harvard University Press.

Sen, A. (2001). *Poverty and famines: An essay on entitlement and deprivation*. Y. Wang & W. Wang (Trans.) The Commercial Press.

White, H., & Anderson, E. (2001). Growth vs. redistribution: Does the pattern of growth matter? *Development Policy Review, 19*(3).

World Bank. (2011). Bridging the gap and promoting equality: Realizing the shared growth of Guangdong's economy. Guangdong People's Publishing House.

Yang, Y. (2011, April 26). Avoiding the middle-income trap with reforms. *Netease Finance*,

Zhuang, J., & Ali, I. (2009). *Inequality and inclusive growth in developing Asia: Introduction to a book publication* (Working Paper). ADB.

Zhuang, J. (2008). *Promoting social harmony with shared growth*. China Planning Press.

Postscript

China has done its utmost to win a new round of poverty alleviation, aiming to lift the poor out of poverty by 2020. The human, material, and financial resources invested in this round of poverty alleviation are unprecedented. I firmly believe that by 2020, China would be able to achieve its development-oriented poverty alleviation goals. At various national and international lectures and discussions and also while updating and revising this book, I have often been asked several questions: Will there still be poverty in China after 2020? How will China's poverty criterion be set after 2020? Will it still be necessary to establish a poverty alleviation office after 2020? These are the questions I want to answer briefly in the Afterword. These questions are answered in the forthcoming book *Towards 2030: Poverty reduction in China and global poverty governance* (Social Sciences Academic Press), and I would like to discuss it briefly here.

First, Chapter 1, "The Evolution of Thinking About the Concept of Poverty," and Chapter 2, "The Poverty Principle and World Poverty," clearly address several ideas and facts. Poverty is ever present, but the meaning of poverty is constantly being expanded with economic and social development. Developed countries such as the USA and the UK define poverty in monetary terms (absolute poverty in the former and relative and absolute poverty in the UK), whereas Latin American countries and a growing number of other developing countries define it in terms of multidimensional poverty. In any event, we can see that the meaning of poverty continues to expand with economic and social development. By 2020, the poor would be lifted out of poverty under the current standard. However, even if China has built a moderately well-off society by 2020, GNP per capita would be among that of the high-income countries, the HDI would be among the countries with high human development, and the poverty criterion would be raised to a level appropriate to China's economic and social development. In other words, even if, under the current principle, the poor population has been eliminated by 2020, a new poverty criterion would have to be developed. In accordance with the new poverty criterion, the poor will continue to be targeted and supported. Some people in society question why "the more poverty

© Social Sciences Academic Press 2022

X. Wang, *Multidimensional Poverty Measurement*,
International Research on Poverty Reduction,
https://doi.org/10.1007/978-981-19-1189-7

we eradicate, the more poor people we have." The fact is that after each round of poverty alleviation, we set new poverty criteria based on the level of economic and social development.

Second, how will China's poverty criterion be set after 2020? This book devotes a great deal of space to explaining the Chinese word "*pinkun*" (literally "poverty") and providing a multidimensional poverty analysis of the poverty in China. "*pinkun*" includes both "*pin*" (literally "insufficiency") caused by insufficient income and "*kun*" (literally "hardship") due to a lack of access to education, health, social security, and housing security. China's poverty criterion should cover "*pin*" that measures insufficient income and "*kun*" that measures the natural and social environment. The poverty alleviation principle in this new round is that the per capita net income steadily exceeds the national poverty alleviation principle; there are no concerns about food and clothing; and compulsory education, basic health care, and housing security are guaranteed. This is the multidimensional poverty criterion that involves not only "income" but also "two no worries, three guarantees." The poverty measurement theories and methods that have been developed, as well as the practice of defining poverty worldwide, have all verified the rationality and validity of defining poverty from a multidimensional perspective. The definition of poverty in the future should and will be multidimensional as indicated in the definition of "poverty" in Chinese culture, the establishment of an interdepartmental poverty alleviation agency under the State Council Leading Group of Development-oriented Poverty Reduction, the successful practice of multi-departmental policy "combinations," the "all-round development" of a moderately prosperous society, and the requirement to "eradicate all forms of poverty" as stated in the UN 2030 Sustainable Development Goals. With economic and social development, China needs to raise the monetary poverty criterion defined in terms of income/consumption and increase the level of protection against poverty in education, health, social security, housing, life basics (drinking water, fuel, toilets, and other living environments), and employment.

Third, is it necessary for China to continue to have a poverty alleviation office after 2020? Many people believe that since those who have not been lifted out of poverty by 2020 through development-oriented poverty alleviation would be covered by a social security system, poverty alleviation and civil affairs should be merged and poverty alleviation should be carried out through the subsistence security system. To answer this question, I have conducted an in-depth study on the setup of poverty alleviation organizations around the world. The conclusion is that most countries have set up poverty alleviation organizations such as the Social Welfare Coordination Department and the Civil Affairs Department, which seem to make sense on the surface. However, if we simply draw on international experience and abolish the poverty alleviation office, we are essentially going in the wrong direction. What we need to reflect on is why the majority of developing countries have not achieved the same level of poverty reduction as China and what developing countries could learn from China's experience in this regard. Through international comparative studies and a review of historical data on poverty alleviation in China, it was found that the path of development-oriented poverty alleviation with Chinese characteristics has three major weapons: a multidimensional definition of poverty, an interdepartmental leading group for development-oriented poverty alleviation, and multi-departmental policy "combinations," a combination that is arguably unique in the world. The World Bank helped China establish an income/consumption poverty line in the 1980s. However, under China's interdepartmental poverty alleviation organizations and multi-departmental policy combinations, rather than implementing a single "income support" policy to alleviate poverty, a "development-oriented poverty alleviation" policy was created and improved and ultimately integrated with "guaranteed poverty alleviation." At this point, the experience of foreign or developed countries is not necessarily helpful; we need institutional and cultural self-confidence. There is no doubt that China needs to retain and improve the institutional setup of the interdepartmental leading group on development-oriented poverty alleviation and assign more interdepartmental responsibilities for the comprehensive coordination of poverty alleviation, so as to raise the living standards and capabilities of the poor in a multidimensional way and advance toward the goal of common prosperity.

As China's economic and political role in the world grows, it needs to play its due role in global governance. Poverty eradication is a global challenge, and poverty reduction is China's soft power. China's philosophy and methods of poverty reduction will be a crucial force in promoting global poverty reduction and sustainable development; thus, China's experience will provide wisdom and solutions to enrich global poverty governance.

With the realization of China's first centennial goal, we look forward to the emergence of a more equitable and common prosperous society!

Beijing

September 25, 2016

MIX
Papier aus verantwortungsvollen Quellen
Paper from responsible sources
FSC® C105338

If you have any concerns about our products,
you can contact us on
ProductSafety@springernature.com

In case Publisher is established outside the EU,
the EU authorized representative is:
Springer Nature Customer Service Center GmbH
Europaplatz 3, 69115 Heidelberg, Germany

Printed by Libri Plureos GmbH
in Hamburg, Germany